# A Guide to Ezra Pound's
## *Selected Poems*

D0583750

# A Guide to Ezra Pound's
## *Selected Poems*

Christine Froula

A NEW DIRECTIONS BOOK

ACKNOWLEDGMENTS

All copyrighted material by Ezra Pound is quoted by permission of New Directions Publishing Corporation and the Trustees of the Ezra Pound Literary Property Trust. All cited works of Pound are listed in the Abbreviations. The books of poetry referred to most often are: *The Cantos of Ezra Pound* (Copyright 1934, 1937, 1940, 1948 by Ezra Pound; Copyright © 1956, 1959, 1962, 1963, 1966, 1968 by Ezra Pound; Copyright © 1972 by the Estate of Ezra Pound); *Personae* (Copyright 1926 by Ezra Pound); *The Selected Poems of Ezra Pound* (Copyright 1926, 1934, 1940, 1948, 1949 by Ezra Pound; Copyright © 1956, 1957 by Ezra Pound).

Grateful acknowledgment is also made for permission to quote sections of the following: K. K. Ruthven, *A Guide to Ezra Pound's Personae* (Copyright © 1969, University of California Press), used by permission of University of California Press; Homer, *The Odyssey*, translated by Robert Fitzgerald (Copyright © 1961 by Robert Fitzgerald), by permission of Doubleday & Co., Inc.; "On the Fly-Leaf of Pound's Cantos," from Basil Bunting, *Collected Poems* (Copyright © 1978 by Basil Bunting), by permission of Oxford University Press.

Portions of the "Introduction to *The Pisan Cantos*" were previously published in *The Yale Review*.

Manufactured in the United States of America
First published clothbound and as New Directions Paperbook 548 in 1983
Published simultaneously in Canada by George McLeod, Ltd., Toronto

Library of Congress Cataloging in Publication Data

Froula, Christine
    A guide to Ezra Pound's selected poems.
    (A New Directions Book)
    Bibliography: p. 254
    Includes index.
    1.  Pound, Ezra, 1885–1972—Criticism and
interpretation.    I.  Title
PS3531.O82Z632        1983        811'.52        82-18776
ISBN 0-8112-0856-7
ISBN 0-8112-0857-5 (pbk.)

New Directions Books are published for James Laughlin
by New Directions Publishing Corporation

*For James and Helen Froula*
*my "Grecian voices"*

# *Contents*

# ACKNOWLEDGMENTS

My thanks are due, first, to the community of Pound scholars and critics who have created the foundation on which this guide depends, and whose members are many more than my "Works Cited" list can show. So wide-ranging and variously stimulating is the body of Pound studies that it is impossible to list all my debts to individual contributors. But it is a pleasure to acknowledge here those whose work has been of special value in the preparation of this *Guide*. Donald Gallup's *A Bibliography of Ezra Pound* is the cornerstone of Pound studies. The five previously published guides to Pound's poetry have immeasurably lightened the task of preparing this one: K. K. Ruthven's *A Guide to Ezra Pound's Personae*, John Edwards and William Vasse's *Annotated Index to The Cantos of Ezra Pound*, Carroll F. Terrell's *Companion to The Cantos of Ezra Pound*, George Kearns's *Guide to Ezra Pound's Selected Cantos*, and Peter Brooker's *A Student's Guide to the Selected Poems of Ezra Pound*. In matters of critical perspective and interpretation, I have learned from many, but I owe most to Donald Davie and Hugh Kenner, who in their different ways make for "study with the white wings of time passing."

I have also been fortunate in having a closer community with whom to share talk of Pound and poetry. I particularly wish to thank James Laughlin, who requested this guide, waited patiently for me to produce it, and made many improving suggestions; Mary de Rachewiltz, whose generosity, humor, and incomparable knowledge of Pound's poetry have become for me part of the pleasure of studying her father's work, and whose careful reading of the manuscript resulted in numerous refinements; Robert Fitzgerald, who kindly scrutinized the manuscript with a classicist's eye, a poet's ear, and an elephant's memory, and saved me from many errors; Penelope Laurans, for her sustaining friendship as well as her fine criticism of the manuscript; and Peter Glassgold, for his perceptive and meticulous editing. The errors that remain are my own. I am also grateful to Jerome J. McGann, Robert von Hallberg, and James E. Miller, Jr., with whom I first began to study Pound's poetry, and to Donald Gallup and Louis L. Martz for help and encouragement over many years. Finally, I wish to thank Michael Groden, Alice Levine, Jeffrey Merrick, Adrienne Munich, Fred C. Robinson, and Paul Wallich, for help with special points; and the students with whom I've read and discussed Pound and poetry, especially Elisabeth Albritton, Robert Crooks, David Frackelton, Jocelyn Lieu, Seth Magalaner, Heather Muir, Dennis Philbin, Donna Richman, and Doug Tifft, for having taught me so much, and for having been my imaginary readers.

# ABBREVIATIONS FOR
# EZRA POUND'S WORKS

The following works by Ezra Pound are cited by abbreviations within the text. Unless otherwise stated, the publisher is New Directions. When two dates are given, they are those of the first publication and the edition used. For full information concerning the publishing history of Pound's works, see Donald Gallup's *A Bibliography of Ezra Pound* (London: Rupert Hart-Davis, 1969; revised edition: Charlottesville, Va.: St. Paul's Bibliographies by University Press of Virginia, 1983).

ABCR  *ABC of Reading* (1934, 1960)

C  *The Cantos of Ezra Pound* (1975)

CEP  *Collected Early Poems*, edited by Michael John King, introduced by Louis L. Martz (1977)

CWC  *The Chinese Written Character as a Medium for Poetry* (1936; San Francisco: City Lights, 1968)

Conf  *Confucius: The Unwobbling Pivot, The Great Digest, The Analects* (1969)

EPS  *Ezra Pound Speaking*, ed. Leonard W. Doob (Westport, Conn.: Greenwood, 1978)

GB  *Gaudier-Brzeska: A Memoir* (1916; 1960)

GK  *Guide to Kulchur* (1938; 1970)

HSM  *Hugh Selwyn Mauberley* (in *Selected Poems*)

HSP  "Homage to Sextus Propertius" (in *Personae*)

I  *Impact: Essays on Ignorance and the Decline of American Civilization* (Chicago: Henry Regnery, 1960)

JM  *Jefferson and/or Mussolini* (1935; New York: Norton, Liveright, 1970)

LE  *Literary Essays of Ezra Pound*, edited by T. S. Eliot (1954)

P  *Personae* (1926; 1949)

PD  *Pavannes and Divagations* (1958)

PE  *Polite Essays* (1937; 1940)

PJ  *Pound/Joyce*, edited by Forrest Read (1965)

PVA  *Ezra Pound and the Visual Arts*, edited by Harriet Zinnes (1980)

SL   *Selected Letters of Ezra Pound, 1907–1941*, edited by D. D. Paige (1950; 1971)

SP   *Selected Poems of Ezra Pound* (1957)

SPF  *Selected Poems of Ezra Pound*, edited by T. S. Eliot (London: Faber and Faber, 1928, 1959)

SPr  *Selected Prose of Ezra Pound (1909–1965)*, edited by William Cookson (1973)

SR   *The Spirit of Romance* (1910; 1953)

Tr   *The Translations of Ezra Pound*, edited by Hugh Kenner (1953)

U    *Umbra* (London: Elkin Mathews, 1920)

## Manuscript Collections

L    Letters of Ezra Pound transcribed by D. D. Paige, Yale Collection of American Literature, Beinecke Rare Book and Manuscript Library, Yale University

Chicago MSS  Poetry Magazine Papers 1912–1936, University of Chicago Library

Yale MSS  Papers of Ezra Pound, Yale Collection of American Literature, Beinecke Rare Book and Manuscript Library, Yale University

# Introduction

Anyone who has had even a casual brush with twentieth-century literature is probably aware of Ezra Pound's important place in modern literary history. He was, in T. S. Eliot's words, "more responsible for the XXth Century revolution in poetry than any other individual." No poet did more than he to renew the poetic line and to expand the possibilities of open form. No one recognized more quickly or promoted more generously the work of other modern artists, among them James Joyce, H. D., William Carlos Williams, Robert Frost, Marianne Moore, and Eliot himself. No one, according to Eliot, Williams, and many other poets, had a finer ear for the music of language. And none was engaged more strenuously with the social issues of our century, or more deeply committed to the social importance of the arts.

But despite all this, Pound's poetry is still better known by reputation, and by its evidence in the work of other poets (for example, Eliot's *The Waste Land,* which he helped to shape) than by firsthand encounter. The reason for this is simple: on the face of it, Pound's poetry appears to the new reader formidably difficult. The general reader, who finds modern literature as a whole obscure enough, is likely to decide at a glance that Pound in particular is impossible. In his poems, images half-form and dissolve; uncongenial words and ideas are disconcertingly juxtaposed. Almost every page seems mined with allusions, and words in every language from Greek and Egyptian hieroglyph to Italian dialect are strung like barbed wire along the lines. In the later poetry, the very page seems esoteric and forbidding: in place of the regular, manageable strophes of traditional verse, we find lines suspended in space, floating in uncanny disconnection like so many typographical tightropes. It is not surprising, then, that

1

many readers conclude that Pound was an elitist who wrote poetry meant to be read only by those few people who know world literature just the way he did—and put it aside.

Surprising, no; but unfortunate, and for many reasons. First, Pound's elitism is something of a misunderstanding. It is true that much of the poetry contains unfamiliar allusions, and that it is difficult to read in the ways we have been taught to read. But it is also true that Pound could say even of *The Cantos* that "there is no *intentional* obscurity," and that they could, furthermore, be read as he intended without the reader's grasping all the allusions. In the very midst of composing them, he wrote, "I don't care about 'minority culture.' I have never cared a damn about snobbisms or for writing *ultimately* for the few." (SPr, 231) He was writing, he said, "the tale of the tribe"—an epic, a public poem, which he meant to belong to the modern "tribe" as Homer's *Iliad* belonged to the ancient Greeks. The discrepancy between Pound's expressed aims and his perceived elitism raises two questions: first, what we expect from poetry, and how we read it; and second, how the relationship between poet and audience has changed in modern times.

To take the second first, the perceived difficulty of Pound's work dramatizes the breakdown of the "contract" between the modern author and modern readers, the loss of a sense of common ground and shared values which itself only mirrors the fragmentation and isolation in our culture at large. In his *ABC of Reading*, Pound could write of Chaucer that "His mind is the mind of Europe, not the mind of an annex or outlying province," and that "Chaucer wrote while England was still a part of Europe. There was one culture from Ferrara to Paris, and it extended to England." (100–01) The medieval world view was underpinned by the Catholicism which then embraced all of Europe. But in our time, there is no comparable unifying vision to bring people together despite our differences. In the West, it is modern capitalism which has taken to itself the power formerly exercised by the common religion to determine the forms of our social structures, creating conditions in which competition and individualism hold sway above the common good and isolate the individual from other human beings, from nature, even from the real value of the work that he or she does. Chaucer could speak widely and easily to his audience, who shared with him the common "mind of Europe." They laughed at his jokes, and understood his character-drawing according to shared social norms. We, more than they, live in a world full of different voices, speaking from different perspectives for different values, with a far more abstract sense of community. It is hard to understand each other at all, let alone to share a joke.

Modern poets have responded to this crisis in many different ways. Poets like William Butler Yeats and Wallace Stevens accepted the condition of the solitary self and, in their different ways, extended the Romantic tradition, writing poetry about the creation of the world by the imagination—Yeats by inventing a personal symbology, Stevens by exploring ideas of order, "supreme fictions." William Carlos Williams, wishing to remain among other people and seeing the futility of generalities for describing a world of differences, coined the maxim "No ideas but in things," and set himself to recording the look and taste, the smell and the speech of its unique unfoldings. Marianne Moore, with a similarly acute eye for the distinctions of things, declared that she disliked "poetry" and invented verses conceived as "imaginary gardens with real toads in them." Gertrude Stein explored the representational limits of language and, inspired by Cubist painting, experimented more radically than other modern writers with the pure pleasures of sound and syntax: "Nothing aiming," as she put it, "is a flower." Robert Frost, rooted in New England, extended the American Puritan tradition into the twentieth century. H. D., Langston Hughes, Stevie Smith, and many more invented resonant individual voices for which the "great tradition" of English poetry offered no models. Eliot, and later W. H. Auden, lamenting the fragmentation and alienation of modern life, came to advocate the recovery of the communal force and conscience of Christianity.

And Pound? As Pound is our main subject, and many kinds of poetry are included in the *Selected Poems*, we will consider his response in more detail. In his early career, from about 1908 to 1920, Pound pursued several directions at once. He was learning the craft of poetry by imitating the forms and voices of earlier poets, and his curiosity ranged widely from classical authors to modern, from symbolist poetics to dramatic monologue, from Sapphics and epigram to villanelle and modern free verse, from lyricism to antibourgeois "blasts," as he searched for a distinctive voice of his own. The work of this first period includes many excellent poems, but it is characterized by experimentation rather than an achieved "voice." Pound, who was trained in Romance philology at Hamilton College and the University of Pennsylvania, began his poetic career in the "spirit of romance," as we see from his many imitations and translations of the troubadour poets, Cavalcanti, and Villon. He was strongly attracted to the "trobar clus"—an intentionally difficult style—both because of its musical beauty and intricacy and because of its affinities to the riddle: to break through the barrier of language and discover an unstated meaning is to overcome the distance between one mind and another. Pound understood troubadour poetics as a secular ritual creating and affirming common ground, and his own modern poetics in many ways recreates this ritual form.

In 1908, when he moved to London, Pound looked up Yeats, whom he considered the greatest living poet, and began an apprenticeship during which he composed many imitations of the Pre-Raphaelites and the "decadent" poets of the nineties. This phase taught him some things about technique, but it ultimately proved, for him, a sterile vein. The English Romantic tradition had, as far as he was concerned, exhausted itself in the aestheticism of the nineties, and he had little desire to revive it. (He would later dismiss his first published poems, *A Lume Spento*, as "stale creampuffs.") Another early interest, the dramatic monologue form developed by Robert Browning, proved more enduring. In the dramatic monologue, a character (or "persona") is revealed through a speech which is "overheard" by the reader, who must read between the lines to grasp what is not spoken by means of what is. Reading a dramatic monologue is, again, a little like playing with a riddle; it is an exercise in imagination which proves the common ground of different minds. Pound's Imagist experiments similarly reflect this interest in saying-by-not-saying, and in conveying by language what is not *literally* said.

A fourth important strain in Pound's early poetry is translation. A classic training ground for poets, translation becomes, in Pound's hands, considerably more. Many of his translations surpass the aim of bringing Chinese or Latin or French over into English to become vital English poems in their own right. And translation itself as Pound uses it is a response to the diversity of modern culture. His "The Seafarer," for example, seeks to recall to the modern English-speaking reader the remote origins of English poetry and language, and in so doing, remembers a common history. And his *Cathay*, which Eliot said "invented Chinese poetry for our time," begins Pound's lifelong interest in bringing not only the poetry but the social values of China into dialogue with the West. Pound's use of translation, like the linguistic polyphony of his poetry, reflects his awareness that we live in a world of different voices, in which making sense of each other's words requires special efforts.

One more aspect of Pound's early work appears in poems which express an antagonism between the modern author and the rest of society, exemplified in such poems as "The Garret," "The Garden," "Salutation," "Salvationists," and "Amities." This theme is endemic to modern literature. Pound's treatment of it in such poems as these appears simpler than it is, for their rebellion is not against any literal "audience," but against the social conditions which have eroded the communal function of art in modern society. Inveighing against "the thoroughly smug / and thoroughly uncomfortable," they take arms against the materialism that has removed the "useless" pleasures of poetry and the arts to the farthest peripheries of modern life. Pound pictures the scene in "The Rest," addressing

> Artists broken against her [America],
> A-stray, lost in the villages,
> Mistrusted, spoken-against,
>
> Lovers of beauty, starved,
> Thwarted with systems,
> Helpless against the control.

It is nothing so simple as an "audience" that such poems complain of. Underlying their bravado is a deep frustration with the curtailed possibilities for poetry in the modern world. Pound had no wish to retreat to the inner vision. His poetry, from beginning to end, reflects the tension between his conviction of art's importance to society and his awareness of how minor a role art plays in the common life of our time.

Pound's career reaches a watershed about 1918–20, following World War I, embodied in the two sequences "Homage to Sextus Propertius" (1918/1919) and *Hugh Selwyn Mauberley* (1920). With these poems, Pound breaks with his early career; he would never write poems like "Apparuit," "Near Perigord," or "The Return" again. Both poems take stock of and comment upon the early career. In the "Homage," Pound dons the mask of Propertius in order to reflect ironically on the vicissitudes of the artist in an age of imperialism. Propertius' inclination for writing love songs instead of paeans to the glory of the Roman Empire is made to express the discord between the values of the mercenary, imperial, warmaking state and those of human beings; Pound intends an analogy between Propertius' Rome and the modern British Empire in which he himself writes. As the parallel suggests, "modernity" has nothing to do with chronological relativity but is rather a state of mind, a stance of critical, dissenting irony. In *Mauberley*, Pound abandons historical allegory and lets the mask half slip, writing about the fate of two artists in modern England—"E. P." and Mauberley, who is, as John Espey says, not Pound himself but the poet Pound feared to become if he stayed in England. Pound's representation of the conflict between art and the modern age in this poem is complex: while he satirizes citizens of literary London, he also criticizes the aestheticist productions of both "E. P." and Mauberley, which are at once inappropriate to and symptomatic of the decadent culture from which they emerge.

Both poems mark the transition between the early career and Pound's major work, *The Cantos*, which he began working on about 1915. The early poetry, while much of it stands on its own, prepares the approach to Pound's epic—"a poem including history," or, "the tale of the tribe." The open spaces of the canto reflect his changed ideas about form. In place of the comfortably self-enclosed and self-limiting stanzas (or "rooms") of traditional verse, we find in *The Cantos* what Donald Davie aptly describes as "a sea where we must be on the lookout for waterspouts." The poem exists no longer as a beautiful object but as a field in which things happen, in which energies arise and take shape as moving, changing forms—the "vortices," or "waterspouts," which Davie describes. In contrast to the timeless urns of traditional verse, the canto is a fragmentary form which erases the boundary between itself and the world, and which becomes intelligible only as the reader's energies become engaged with it. It is a form which refuses to impose meaning as literary language conventionally does, and this refusal has a political significance which lies at the very core of the poem. We can begin to understand this by considering the compositional principle of *The Cantos*, which Pound called the "ideogrammic method," inspired by the workings of a certain kind of Chinese ideogram. In his favorite example, the ideogram for "red," images of a cherry, iron rust, a flamingo, and sunset are juxtaposed to get the idea of redness across. The theory of this kind of sign is that its meaning is not "imposed" on the reader but deduced from sense perceptions common to everyone. In a time when no system of belief exists to give authority to the poet's words, the ideogrammic method lays out "the components of thought" by which readers can, in theory at least, arrive at meaning by the authority of their own perceptions. "Authority," then, resides not in the author alone, but in author and readers together. In this way, the common ground on which an epic poem must rest would be simultaneously created and affirmed.

I have said "in theory" and "would be" because in fact Pound's attempt to create common ground by means of ideogrammic presentation in *The Cantos* does not always work. His ideogrammic method expresses the dream of a common language, but the progress from "the components of thought" to the idea is rarely simple. And here the paradox of the poem's difficulty begins to become comprehensible. *The Cantos* aspires to be the "tale of the tribe," in a time when there is no shared mythology on which to ground the tale, by creating a way of reading that affirms the common ground of different minds. This, however, is an impossible dream, for there is no question of the modern "tribe's" being able to understand *The Cantos* in the way that Homer's listeners could understand the *Iliad*, or Chaucer's listeners *The Canterbury Tales*. The poem does not "cohere" in the way Pound dreamed that it would. Yet this is not to say that the poem is a failure in any simple way, for *The Cantos*, in its inclusion of fragments of many cultures and many languages, its multiple historical lines, its anthropological perspectives, remains a powerfully and often movingly expressive image of the modern world. It marks the end of the old idea of the tribe as a group who participate in and share a single, closed culture, and redefines it as the human community in all its complex diversity. It holds the mirror of art up to what Marshall McLuhan, who visited Pound in St. Elizabeths during the fifties, would later name "the global village": many different cultures, with different historical roots and points of view, all impinging more and more inevitably upon one another as they share a world that seems to grow smaller each day.

In this light, the allusiveness of *The Cantos*, its inclusive openness, appear not as elitism, nostalgia, or culture-mongering but as a merely necessary feature of any modern attempt to tell "the tale of the tribe." Confronting its particular difficulties, we tend to forget that all epic is allusive; that the tale of the tribe, in its very nature, alludes to the historical and philosophical bases of the culture which the epic celebrates. Homer has his myths, his genealogies, his catalogue of ships; Dante has his Florentine characters and Thomas Aquinas' systematic formulation of medieval theology; and Milton has the Genesis myth read through Puritan theology, on which to build their poems. The importance of these substructures explains in part why Eliot laments the loss of the Christian world view which gave Dante, Chaucer, Spenser, and Milton their epic frameworks.

Pound, too, missed having an "Aquinas-map," but he could not embrace modern Christianity. Indeed, he poked fun at "the Reverend Eliot" for his religious conservatism. Neither is his poem merely a reflection of the complexity of modern culture. It is rather a very serious—indeed, passionately serious—attempt to imagine a new and vital culture to supersede the failing Western tradition, to find what he called "a new paideuma," by which he meant the "entanglement of root ideas" that gives a period its character or "mind." *The Cantos* can be described as an epic ven-

ALLUSIVE
PAIDEUMA

ture which seeks a viable means of uniting diverse peoples, a working sense of the human community. Christianity had earlier served this need, and Eliot thought that it could continue to do so. Pound, however, objected to the asceticism of late Christianity, its mystification of authority, its promise of an otherworldly paradise. Further, he, like Marx and Weber, judged the late Christian "paideuma" to be perniciously bound up with modern materialism and the corrupt economic systems that allow for the manipulation of the masses according to the financial interests of the few. "I think," he wrote, "that 'Christ,' as presented in the New Testament . . . is a most profound philosophic genius, [but also] an intuitive, inexperienced man, dying before middle age. The things unthought of in his philosophy are precisely the things that would be unthought in the philosophy of a provincial genius. . . . The whole sense of social order is absent." (SPr, 193) Against the Christian denial of the body and the senses, he advocated a return to pagany, to a celebration of bodily harmony with nature in its cycles of birth, death, and rebirth. Against its idea of divine authority, he posed the this-worldly, *social* ground of Confucian ethics; and against its "painted paradise," he imagined an earthly paradise which would come into being with the drastic reform of modern economic institutions, the mutually respectful social relations valued in Confucian ethics, and a "natural" religion. *The Cantos,* he said, take form "between KUNG [Confucius] and ELEUSIS" (C, 258)—that is, between an ethics which had proved itself by underwriting thousands of years of Chinese civilization and the Eleusinian mysteries, the yearly rites of the ancient Greeks which, according to one ancient historian, "bound the whole human race together" in the celebration of birth, death, and regeneration.

Compared with the idea of Christianity to which Eliot committed himself, the new common ground toward which Pound's epic strives reflects a wider curiosity about the world, a broader inquiry into problems, causes, and possibilities for change, and a less conservative sensibility. To say this, however, is to raise the issue of his attraction to fascism, which seems to contradict the attitude toward political authority reflected in both the methods and the themes of *The Cantos.* How could Pound, the range of whose work manifests the depth and passion of his belief in "the right of difference to exist" and the value of "interest in finding things different" (LE, 298), have embraced totalitarianism? This question has not been resolved satisfactorily by anyone yet, but a few observations might cast some light on it. The first point is that Pound's epic is *literally* "a poem including history," not only past history but the actualities of the present. He was not simply writing *about* a *paradiso terrestre;* rather the very act and form of his writing constituted an attempt to bring about social change. His poem is not a "beautiful object" but a verbal war against economic corruption, against literal wars, against materialism, against the habits of mind that permit the perpetuation of political domination. It advocates economic reform as the basis of social and cultural reform, and it could not have held aloof from political reality.

Pound lived, as a poet and as a human being, in the world, and he made the real political choices that he thought would bring his vision into being. Residing in Italy, and reading mainly government-controlled newspapers, he was taken in by Mussolini, as were other insufficiently wary intellectuals. There is no question that Pound's faith in Mussolini was naïve and misplaced. But we would be mistaken to equate Pound's politics with Mussolini's, as some commentators have done. "Fundamentally, I do not care 'politically,'" Pound wrote, "I care for civilisation"—defined as "the enrichment of life and the abolition of violence." (SPr, 199) Like most twentieth-century social thinkers, he considered that "civilisation" required radical reform of the economic system; and his politics issued from his sense of what those reforms should be, and of how they should be implemented. His writings make clear that his politics was not antidemocratic in spirit, but rather, against the degeneration of democracy into what he called "the usurocracy"—political control by moneyed interests. In *Jefferson and/or Mussolini*, he states explicitly that he does not " 'advocate' fascism in and for America. . . . I think the American system *de jure* is probably quite good enough, if there were only 500 men with guts and the sense to USE it, or even with a capacity for answering letters or printing a paper." (98) Taken in by propaganda about Mussolini's economic reforms, he likened Mussolini to Jefferson on the basis of their economic policies. He saw both as antithetical to modern capitalism, which, he wrote, "has shown itself as little else than the idea that unprincipled thieves and anti-social groups should be allowed to gnaw into . . . the right to share out the fruits of a common co-operative labour." (SPr, 298) He was interested in any political program which set itself against the "usurocracy." Referring to Lenin's "Imperialism, the Highest Stage of Capitalism," he noted, rightly, that "you could quote the same substance from Hitler, who is a Nazi, . . . from Mussolini, a fascist, from C. H. Douglas, who calls himself a democrat . . . , from McNair Wilson, who is a Christian Monarchy man. You could quote it from a dozen camps that have no suspicion that they are quoting Lenin." (SPr, 298–99) Similarly, his remark that "Gents who make guns like to sell 'em; such is the present state of the world, in the bourgeois demo-liberal anti-Marxian anti-fascist anti-Leninist system" (JM, 72) reflects the fact that his broad concern is to oppose the evils of the capitalist system rather than to embrace a particular party. "No party programme ever contains enough of [the artist's] programme to give him the least satisfaction," he once remarked. (SPr, 215) But he hoped—however misguidedly—that the economic reforms advertised by Mussolini's fascism would rectify some of the more egregious economic injustices of modern industrial society.

The society which Pound erringly took Mussolini to be engineering was ultimately not a dictatorship but a restoration of democracy. "A good state," he wrote, "is one which impinges least upon the peripheries of its citizens." (SPr, 213) He saw Major C. H. Douglas, whose economics informed his own, as "a Don Quixote desiring to *Make democracy safe for the individual,*" opposing "the 'demand to subordinate the individuality to the need of some external organization, the exaltation of the State into an authority from which there is no appeal' " which made socialism suspect. (SPr, 210–11) Yet "we must have something at least as good as socialism" (SPr, 194), and he considered that Douglas's reforms would effect "economic democracy" while providing "an alternative to bloody and violent revolutions." (SPr, 212) Pound did not advocate a repressive and uniforming state; on the contrary, he inveighed against such an idea:

"The desire to coerce the acts of another is evil. . . . Provincialism I have defined as an ignorance of the nature and customs of foreign peoples, a desire to coerce others, a desire for uniformity." (SPr, 195–97) "Totalitarianism," as he used the word, signified not enforced conformity but a society whose structure and workings recognized and maintained the human relations of mutual respect which an exploitative economic system denies. Thus he could hypothesize that "Kung [Confucius] is superior to Aristotle by totalitarian instinct. His thought is never something scaled off the surface of facts. It is root volition branching out, the ethical weight is present in every phrase." (GK, 279)

The fact remains that Mussolini was not the just ruler Pound believed him to be, and the best way to understand Pound's disastrous backing of him is, perhaps, as the naïve and desperate "act of faith" which he himself described: "Any thorough judgment of Mussolini will be in a measure an act of faith, it will depend on what you *believe* the man means, what you believe that he wants to accomplish." (JM, 33) Unhappy as this leap of faith was, it testifies to human error, to a commitment not to evil but to a social vision whose risks Pound either could not see or did not judge to be worse than those of the existing system. I do not mean, in pointing this out, to approve or justify Pound's politics, but rather to suggest some of the ways in which, even in its errors—or even *because of* errors—his politics must interest anyone who recognizes the power of words. Pound's social views are neither idiosyncratic nor easily dismissed. Moreover, his errors—including the antisemitism which he later repudiated as his "worst mistake"—are the errors of his time, and we still have much to learn from their record in his "poem including history." To dismiss Pound's work because of his mistaken political judgments is, in a sense, to recapitulate his error of dividing people and actions into "good" and "evil" instead of learning from the false division in Pound's thinking that good and evil are bound up together in all of us.

It is not hard to see how the tension between poetry and history, between imagining the "earthly paradise" and condemning the social abuses that, as Pound thought, prevent its existence, made Pound's epic what he called "a record of struggle"—a poem which must create its own ground as it goes along, and which cannot have, therefore, the finish and ease of a poem that continues and celebrates established cultural norms. But it is equally true that its engagement with history is the source of the poem's greatest successes. *The Pisan Cantos*, one of the great poems of the century, would not have existed had Pound not thirty years earlier broken with the "well-wrought urn" poetics of his early days; nor is the lyric brilliance of *The Cantos* as a whole imaginable apart from the poem's didactic stretches and obscure cul-de-sacs, its irritating and sometimes appalling errors, its sometimes rawly expressed pain and fury. Despite its failure to create "a new paideuma," and despite its disrupted and unpolished form, Pound's epic remains one of the most important and rewarding poems of our time. As Davie compares it to a sea with waterspouts, Basil Bunting compares it to high mountains in his poem "On the Fly-Leaf of Pound's Cantos":

These are the Alps. What is there to say about them?
They don't make sense. Fatal glaciers, crags cranks climb,
jumbled boulder and weed, pasture and boulder, scree,
*et l'on entend,* maybe, *le refrain joyeux et léger.*
Who knows what the ice will have scraped on the rock it is
    smoothing?

The natural metaphors suggest, besides a certain sublimity, something which is not exactly a "poem" in the conventional sense at all; something which is more like a piece of the rock of the world. For those curious about the modern world and its images, it is true that, as Bunting says, "you will have to go a long way round / if you want to avoid them."

*The Cantos* do not so much conclude as break off into sudden silence. Out of that silence, Pound spoke a few words which gave it the meaning of a penance. It eloquently expressed the loss of his faith in his own words and in the power of his poetry to bring different voices into harmony. Pound ends where he began, without a language that he felt could communicate anything, vastly saddened by his own work and by his inability to "make it cohere." To us, however, as readers of modern poetry, in which we seek images of ourselves and our world, this last silence may seem an appropriate ending for *The Cantos*. In its very failure, its very inconclusiveness, Pound's poem has more to tell us than many more "successful" poems which venture less. The wreckage of its intentions calls to mind a warning Pound offers in *Guide to Kulchur* in speaking of the relation between art and life: "the one thing you shd. not do is to suppose that when something is wrong with the arts, it is wrong with the arts ONLY." (60) He saw the arts as an index to the health of a culture as a whole. While, thematically, a poem may express nothing more than a lover's pleasure or misery, in its form and craft it represents the state of thought, language, sensibility, in the culture from which it emerges:

> It appears to me quite tenable that the function of literature . . . is precisely that it does incite humanity to continue living; that it eases the mind of strain, and feeds it, I mean definitely as *nutrition of impulse*. . . . It has to do with the clarity and vigour of "any and every" thought and opinion. . . . the individual cannot think and communicate his thought, the governor and legislator cannot act effectively or frame his laws, without words, and the solidity and validity of those words is in the care of the damned and despised *litterati*. When their work goes rotten—by that I do not mean when they express indecorous thoughts—but when their very medium, the very essence of their work, the application of word to thing goes rotten, i.e., becomes slushy and inexact, or excessive or bloated, the whole machinery of social and of individual thought and order goes to pot. This is a lesson of history, and a lesson not half learned.
>
> (LE, 20–21)

What I want to suggest is that there is something quite "exact" in Pound's failure to conclude, in the failure of his poem to create the illusion that we are engaged with something final and absolute. And most of the time, there is, further, extreme care and exactness in the words, both with respect to their local meaning and with respect to their sounds and shapes. As they proceed to their unforeseen end, the words of *The Cantos* everywhere live along the line, as Williams put it. If the poem's most honest and

instructive dimension is bound up with its lack of finish and con-
clusion, its most pleasurable aspect is its verbal music. Consider,
for example, this passage from Canto LXXXII:

> "Fvy! in Tdaenmarck efen dh'beasantz gnow him,"
>> meaning Whitman, exotic, still suspect
>> four miles from Camden
>> "O troubled reflection
>> "O throat, O throbbing heart"
>> How drawn, O GEA TERRA [O earth earth]
>>> what draws as thou drawest
>>> till one sink into thee by an arm's width
>> embracing thee. Drawest,
>>> truly thou drawest.
>> Wisdom lies next thee,
>>> simply, past metaphor.
> Where I lie let the thyme rise
>>> and basilicum
>>> let the herbs rise in April abundant

This is Pound in Pisa, at death's edge, held back only by words—
by the remembered words of the old German professor alluding
indignantly to the neglect of Walt Whitman in America, by
words remembered from Whitman's death song "Out of the
Cradle," and by his own words which have reached "past meta-
phor" to a purity, a lightness and transparency that is almost
closer to music than poetry. The themes of the passage embrace
Pound's feeling for the life of the poetic tradition, his sense of
the gulf that separates modern poets and their audience (it was
Whitman who said, "To have great poets there must be great
audiences too"), his instinctive feeling for the sacredness of na-
ture, his intensely physical and sensual perception, and the ve-
hement energies, partly right and partly wrong in their judg-
ments, that have brought him to the prison camp where the
shadow of death falls on him. But how easily, and how musically,
all these things compose in the passage. It is the language of a
great master, one who, as many poets have said, has not been sur-
passed in our time, and, Davie adds, "seldom in any time." Its
music is felt even before we know what the passage is "about,"

and makes up in large measure for the certitudes which the poem and its readers must do without.

Such music draws us to *The Cantos* long before we can begin to understand them, and keeps us coming back despite the frustrations we encounter in trying to make sense of them. And this brings us back to the challenges *The Cantos* pose to our usual ways of reading. The power of this music is, in the context of Pound's work as a whole, an interpretable thing. Many distinguished readers of *The Cantos* have complained that they offer no ideas, that they are incoherent and scattered as well as obscure, that they don't make sense. On one level, there is truth in all this. But it is a limited kind of truth, which judges the poem by values which cannot measure it very well, and which may themselves belong to a bygone time—for these same values condemn modern painting, sculpture, music, and dance. It "makes sense," after all, that the abstract music of words should be the force which has power to bring differences into harmony. And it makes sense that Pound's pages should create, instead of a complete and perfectly poised structure, the illusion of registering in minute detail the things and relations of the world as they impinge upon the senses, and through the senses, the mind.

This is, again, McLuhan's idea that the "endless sentence" of Pound's poetry anticipates the changes in the structure of perception and the modes of knowing which our modern technological media have created. In the pages of *The Cantos*, the printed words seem to break with a past that has concluded, and to reach toward a future "beyond literature," in which the old myths give way to abstract, open compositions whose asymmetrical rhythms seem more truly expressive of our perpetually unfolding perceptions and experience. Pound's poetics, one might conclude, has more in common with the perceptual and expressive structures of cinema and modern music, and with the Dionysian tendencies in modern culture, than with the kind of literature which encloses experience into conventional structures of language (the kind Verlaine had in mind when he tossed it away in the line, "And all the rest is literature"). And this is appropriate for the modern epic, the tale of the diverse and all-inclusive human tribe whose language is a Babel of tongues, and whose common culture we move closer to creating with every resistance to war, every breaking of the artificial barriers of race, sex, and class, every effort we make toward understanding what is "difficult" because it is not ourselves. In this light, Pound's work indeed appears, for all its failures, most interestingly full of successes, and most valuable in helping us to understand, as Stevens says great poetry does, "how to live, what to do."

I have aimed in composing this *Guide* to ease the difficulties a new reader encounters with Pound's poetry. My experience of this problem is that the reader needs help at first not only with the allusions and other points of difficulty but also with making sense of the poems in a more general way in the context of Pound's career and times. To that end, I have written a brief introduction for each poem, along with a general introduction to the Pisan sequence. In addition to the facts of publication, these headnotes often contain speculative and impressionistic readings; they are intended as a starting point for the reader's own engagement with the poems, not at all as a last word. Any guide to Pound is a product of choices made at every point, and both the introductions and the glosses in this one inevitably reflect my own judgments about what is most important. But if it begins a dialogue in the reader's mind with all that I have omitted, it will have served its purpose. I hope not to have "covered" the subject of Pound's poetry but to help open it up to new eyes and new minds, for much thinking remains to be done before we will know how to value its achievement.

# Early Poems (1908-12)

## CINO (1908)                                    [SP, 1]

Cino da Pistoia (1270–1337) was an Italian poet, a friend of Dante. He was exiled from the Tuscan city of Pistoia in 1303, and in "Cino" Pound imagines his wanderer's song. Pound reprinted "Cino" in *Personae* in 1926, though he had earlier told William Carlos Williams that he thought it "banal; he might be anyone. Besides he is catalogued in his epitaph." (SL, 6) It exemplifies Pound's early interest in the dramatic monologue as a means of recreating the atmosphere of a past world through the speech of a single character. His tough, exotic, amorous Cino is a "spirit of romance" whose obsession with love and song evokes the passionate and articulate troubadour culture for which the young Pound—whose academic training was in Romance philology—had a passion of his own.

*Campagna:* Italian: countryside.

Them, they: the women Cino has known (except in line 29, where "they" refers to vagabonds like Cino).

Eyes, dreams . . . : Pound gives this line as a prosodic example in "I Gather the Limbs of Osiris" (SPr, 38).

Polnesi: dialect, "Bolognese." Cino studied at the University of Bologna, where he met Dante.

Peste!: Italian: A plague!

And all I knew: archaic: "If all I knew."

18

Sinistro: Italian: left. In heraldry, the "bend sinister" signals illegitimacy. By this address, Cino implies that the "Lord" who has succeeded him in the women's affections is a bastard, a "lackland" who cannot inherit.

grey eyes: in medieval literature, grey eyes indicate beauty.

'Pollo Phoibee: i.e., Phoebus Apollo, the sun-god.

aegis: shield of armor. boss: the nub or point projecting from the center of the shield. "Zeus' aegis-day" thus pictures the sky as a great shield with the sun shining from its center, as befits the constantly feuding lords of Provence.

wander-lied: German: a song of the open road.

'fulgence: i.e., refulgence, radiance.

cloud and . . . : i.e., "May cloud and rain pass swiftly!"

rast-way: "rastel-way," a road or path leading to a portcullis.

# NA AUDIART  (1908)                                           [SP, 3]

As the epigraph explains, "Na Audiart" is a take-off on the Provençal troubadour Bertran de Born's "Dompna, pois de me no'us cal" ("Lady, though you care not for me"), which Pound translated in 1911 (See P, 105). In that poem, Bertran has been rebuffed by the Lady Maent, and he composes a "borrowed lady" of features of various women to console himself. Of the Lady Audiart who "wishes him ill," he asks "her form that's laced / So cunningly." (P, 106) In "Na Audiart," the young Pound dons Bertran's mask and elaborates a retaliatory song from this stanza. His idea is not unworthy of Bertran (see also "Near Perigord")— Dante places him in the circle of hell reserved for "makers of discord." The poem's last lines pun on the idea of reincarnation: for Bertran's imaginary Audiart, "reincarnation," the taking of a new body after death, will be her own old age after the "death" of her youth, in a form bent and wrinkled by the years. Then,

Pound's wounded persona pretends, her pride will relent as she remembers her former beauty.

Na: Lady, from the Provençal *dompna* or *domna.*

*Que be·m vols mal:* Provençal: Though thou well dost wish me ill.

read it set / in rose and gold: Bertran goads Audiart with the prospect of his song appearing in an illuminated manuscript book.

lays: medieval songs.

Aultaforte: Hautefort, the name of Bertran's castle.

limning: line, outline.

casement: i.e., her aged body.

young and wry'd: i.e., a young soul in an old body.

# VILLONAUD FOR THIS YULE  (1908)      [SP, 5]

"Villonaud" is Pound's coinage for the two poems he wrote in homage to the French poet François Villon (1431–63), a colorful low-life figure whose checkered career included gang membership and a sentence of hanging, commuted to an exile from which he never returned. The hard realism of Villon's poetry preserves the tone of his life, employing underworld slang and daring rhymes. Pound thought Villon the "hardest, the most authentic, the most absolute poet of France," and found him difficult to translate "because he rhymes on the exact word, on a word meaning sausages, for example." (ABCR, 104) He resorted to setting Villon's "Testament" to music instead, composing the opera *The Testament of François Villon* in 1920–21.

In this "Villonaud," Pound aimed at "an expression akin to, if not of, the spirit breathed in Villon's own poeting" (SL, 3). He constructs this seasonal, elegiac drinking song upon several motifs in Villon's poems. From "Le Lais" ("The Legacy") he takes his setting:

> Sur le Noel, morte saison
> Que les loups se vivent du vent

("Near Christmastime, that dead season / when wolves live on the wind"). One ballad in the "Testament" inspires his refrain, "Wining the ghosts of yesteryear," with its "Où sont les neiges d'antan?" ("Where are the snows of yesteryear?" in Rossetti's translation). And another, sung by an aged, formerly beautiful "heaulmière" or helmet-seller, gives Pound the theme of a toast to the speaker's old, lost loves. His tone is a poignant, naïve nostalgia as he remakes his Yuletide cheer by toasting the ghosts of Christmases past. The poem is also a technical experiment: Pound uses Villon's ballad form, but takes only two rhyme sounds—a difficult exercise which he does not entirely bring off, as we see in a few strained phrases (such as "memories that me cheer").

morte saison: dead season.

everychone: Middle English: everyone. Pound uses archaic diction—"gueredon," "foison," and "feat"—throughout the poem to create a sense of the distance in time of his original.

gueredon: guerdon, reward.

Skoal!: Health! (drinking toast).

magians: the Three Wise Men of the Nativity story.

foison: plenteous.

(*Saturn . . . near!*): This "*Signum Nativitatis*" (Latin: "Sign of the Nativity") skeptically reduces the Star of Bethlehem to a rare conjunction of planets.

feat: Middle English, Old French: fitting, neat, elegant.

mere: sea. Grey eyes are a medieval literary convention signifying beauty.

Prince . . . yester-year: Compare Dante Gabriel Rossetti's rendering of Villon's "Ballad of Dead Ladies":
> Nay, never ask this week, fair lord,
> Where they are gone, nor yet this year,

Save with thus much for an overword,—
But where are the snows of yester-year?
(*Poems and Translations*, 102)

## THE TREE  (1908)                                    [SP, 6]

Pound held the view that Greek myth originated "when some-
one having passed through delightful psychic experience, tried to
communicate it to others and found it necessary to screen himself
from persecution" (SR, 92):

> The first myths arose when a man walked sheer into "nonsense,"
> that is to say, when some very vivid and undeniable adventure
> befell him, and he told someone else who called him a liar. There-
> upon, after bitter experience, perceiving that no one could
> understand what he meant when he said that he "turned into a tree"
> he made a myth—a work of art that is,—an impersonal or objective
> story woven out of his own emotion, as the nearest equation that
> he was capable of putting into words.
>
> (LE, 431)

"The Tree" embodies this theory of myth: the speaker "walks
sheer into nonsense" and suddenly understands myth, remem-
bering Daphne who, fleeing from Apollo, was turned into a laurel
tree, and Baucis and Philemon, an old couple whom Zeus re-
warded for their kindness by changing them into two inter-
twining trees upon their death (Ovid, *Metamorphoses*, I, VIII).
Myths and metamorphoses occur often in Pound's poetry. Com-
pare "La Fraisne," "Masks," "Peire Vidal Old," "A Girl," "Dance
Figure," "Constellations of Heaven," HSM, Part I, XII, Cantos II,
IV, XVII, LXXVI, and XC.

wold: wood.

Nathless: Nonetheless.

# THE WHITE STAG  (1909)                    [SP, 7]

Poets, like everyone else, learn by imitation. The young Pound
sought out the Irish poet W. B. Yeats, whom he judged "the
greatest living master of the art of poetry," when he moved to
London in 1908 and began his apprenticeship, serving intermit-
tently as Yeats's companion and secretary at Stone Cottage in
Sussex between 1913 and 1916. "The White Stag" is a perfect
example of the disciple's exercise. Its ethereal imagery and its
structure of verse and refrain recall such early Yeats poems as
"Who Goes with Fergus," "The Stolen Child," and "The Mad-
ness of King Goll." These, along with the faint echo of Robert
Burns, suggest that Pound was following Yeats's exposition of
symbolist poetry in an essay of 1900:

> There are no lines with more melancholy beauty than these by
> Burns—
>> The white moon is setting behind the white wave,
>> And Time is setting with me, O!
> . . . Take from them the whiteness of the moon and of the wave,
> whose relation to the setting of Time is too subtle for the intellect,
> and you take from them their beauty. But, when all are together,
> moon and wave and whiteness and setting Time and the last
> melancholy cry, they evoke an emotion which cannot be evoked
> by any other arrangement of colours and sounds and forms.
>
>                                                    (155–56)

Pound's white stag, white hart, and white wind appear to make
a program of this example. The poem's imagery may have an-
other source in Malory's *Tale of King Arthur* (III, 5), in which
wedding guests see "a whyght herte . . . and a whyght brachet"
pursued by sixty hounds. This, too, is a fitting provenance, as the
Pre-Raphaelite poets and painters frequently returned to medi-
eval romance for their subjects and imagery.

Pound soon gained ground on the white stag Fame; a few days
after the volume which included this poem appeared, the twenty-
three-year-old Ezra wrote to his friend William Carlos Williams,

"I have been praised by the greatest living poet"—his master, W. B. Yeats. (SL, 41)

## SESTINA: ALTAFORTE (1909)                    [SP, 7]

In this poem, Pound again conjoins his efforts to revive the troubadours with metrical experimentation, this time in the sestina form. "Sestina: Altaforte," like "Na Audiart" and "Near Perigord," is not a translation of but an extrapolation from Bertran de Born's poems and persona. Pound explains how he came to write it in "How I Began" (1913):

> I had had De Born in my mind. I had found him untranslatable. Then it occurred to me that I might present him in this manner. I wanted the curious involution and recurrence of the Sestina. I knew more of less of the arrangement. I wrote the first strophe and then went to the [British] Museum to make sure of the right order of the permutations. . . . I did the rest of the poem at a sitting. Technically, it is one of my best, though a poem on such a theme could never be very important.
>
> (*T. P.'s Weekly*, 6 June 1913, 707)

The sestina form, which the troubadours invented, consists of six stanzas of six lines each, followed by an envoy of three lines. Instead of a rhyme pattern, the sestina creates its pattern by repeating, in a different order, the end-words of the first stanza as the end-words of each subsequent stanza; thus:

| stanza | 1 | ABCDEF |
|---|---|---|
| | 2 | FAEBDC |
| | 3 | CFDABE |
| | 4 | ECBFAD |
| | 5 | DEACFB |
| | 6 | BDFECA |
| envoy | | ECA or ACE |

Pound follows this pattern with a slight deviation in stanza 4. He found "the curious involution and recurrence of the sestina" appropriate for his presentation of Bertran because the returning end-words emphasize this troublemaker's obsessive passion for battle. The repetitions of the end-words show Bertran's mind revolving tightly about his war theme, seeing thunderstorm and sunrise alike as emblems of the strife he desires.

Pound declaimed this poem with much gusto at a meeting of the Poets' Club, whose members included T. E. Hulme, F. S. Flint, and Richard Aldington, and immediately established a place for himself. He later read it to the young French sculptor Gaudier-Brzeska, and remarked, "I think it was the 'Altaforte' that convinced him that I would do to be sculpted." (GB, 45; Pound refers to the marble bust Gaudier sculpted of him.) As it turned out, however, Gaudier had been most impressed by a nonexistent feature of the poem. Betrayed by his Latin ear, he comically mistook "peace" for "piss" and praised Pound enthusiastically to a friend for having had the nerve to use it. "When I told this to Ezra," John Cournos wrote, "he was delighted." (*Autobiography*, 260)

Epigraph: LOQUITUR: Latin: he speaks. *En:* Provençal: Sir, Lord. See Dante's *Inferno*, XXVIII. Eccovi!: Italian: Look you! jongleur: French: singer.

But . . . purple: Cf. Bertran's "Quan vei pels vergiers desplejar / Los sendatz grocs, indis e blaus" which Pound translated, "When I see the standards spread through the gardens / Yellow and indigo and blue" (SR, 46). vair: of variegated color.

destriers: war horses.

stour: fierce contest.

# BALLAD OF THE GOODLY FERE (1909)  [SP, 9]

Pound's vestigial Presbyterian sensibilities were offended at some point by what he described as "a certain sort of cheap irreverence which was new to me" (*T. P.'s Weekly*, 6 June 1913, 707), and the result was this poem, which, he modestly informed his father upon completing it, he thought "probably the strongest [ballad] in English since 'Reading Gaol' " (by Oscar Wilde). (L, April 1909) It met with immediate success, but Pound eventually grew irritated when it continued to be praised at the expense of his more "serious" and "modern" work. For this reason, he declined to allow Edward Marsh to reprint it in his anthology, *Georgian Poetry, 1911–12:* "Isn't there anything in the earlier books that you like? (not *The Goodly Fere*, as it doesn't illustrate any modern tendency.)" (Ruthven, 42) There was not, and Marsh's unventuresome taste helped stir Pound's contempt for British culture. "Having written this ballad about Christ," he complained to Malcolm Cowley, "I had only to write similar ballads about James, Matthew, Mark, Luke, and John and my fortune was made." (121) Eliot agreed, and omitted the ballad from his 1928 selection of Pound's poems "because it has a much greater popularity than it deserves" (SPF, 21), but Yeats thought it had "permanent value"—which it does, as much as a monument to popular literary taste around 1910 as for its own sake.

The four-line ballad stanza alternates four- and three-stress lines which rhyme abcb. Typically, its effect is of homely sincerity. Pound alludes to Robert Burns, a master of the ballad form, in the dropped consonants throughout the poem, and in such dialect words as "fere," "twey," and "suddently." He uses only one rhyme sound throughout the ballad, and its recurrence underlines the tenacity of Simon Zelotes' faith in his "goodly fere." The two-line cadenza makes a strong ending, as Simon briefly and cryptically, with the reluctance of the initiate speaking to the uninitiated, alludes to Christ's resurrection: "I ha' seen him eat o' the honeycomb / Sin' they nailed him to the tree."

fere: companion.

Simon Zelotes: one of the twelve apostles (Luke 6:15), whose name (Greek: "zealot") bespeaks his fervent faith.

gallows tree: Simon, whose speech contains medieval archaisms, refers to the gallows rather than the cross because hanging was a more familiar punishment than crucifixion in medieval times.

"First let these go!": Cf. the Gospel of John, 18:8: "I have told you that I am *he:* if therefore ye seek me, let these go their way."

"Why took . . . town?": Cf. the Gospel of Luke, 22:52–53: "Be ye come out, as against a thief, with swords and staves? When I was daily with you in the temple, ye stretched forth no hands against me: but this is your hour, and the power of darkness."

Oh we drank . . . company: Cf. Matthew's account of the Last Supper, 26:27–28: "And he took the cup, and gave thanks, and gave it to them, saying, Drink ye all of it; for this is my blood of the new testament, which is shed for the remission of sins."

I ha' seen . . . treasury: Pound here elaborates the account of Christ's driving out the moneychangers from the temple in Matthew 21:12–13: "And Jesus went into the temple of God, and cast out all them that sold and bought in the temple, and overthrew the tables of the money-changers, and the seats of them that sold doves. And said unto them, It is written, My house shall be called the house of prayer; but ye have made it a den of thieves."

stanzas 11–12: Cf. Mark's account of Christ's walking upon the water and calming the rough seas that hindered the apostles' rowing, 6:47–53. The "thousand men" are Pound's addition, remainders of the "five thousand" whom Christ had just fed with the five loaves and two fishes. Cf. also "Partenza di Venezia" (CEP, 65–66).

Genseret: Gennesaret, where Christ calmed the waves.

twey words: two words, i.e., "Fear not."

I ha' seen . . . tree: Cf. Luke 24:37–43, in which Christ proves to the terror-stricken disciples that he is not a spirit by letting them touch his flesh and by asking for food: "And they gave him a piece of a broiled fish, and of an honeycomb. And he took it, and did eat before them."

# PLANH FOR THE
# YOUNG ENGLISH KING  (1909)          [SP, 12]

This poem freely translates an elegy by Bertran de Born for his close friend Prince Henry, son of Henry II, called "the young king" because he was crowned in 1170, long before his father's death in 1189. When Prince Henry died of fever in 1183, Bertran was grief-stricken and remorseful—for political reasons as well as for friendship's sake, since their friendship had enabled him to enlist Henry's aid in fighting against Henry II and Richard the Lion-hearted, after Richard attempted to take Bertran's castle, Altaforte. Although Prince Henry died before the fighting began, Bertran may have been partly responsible for his death: his stirring up of strife between father and son is the reason why Dante places him in the Ninth Circle of Hell, for "Makers of Discord" (*Inferno*, XXVIII). Bertran paces Hell as a headless trunk swinging his head like a lantern, and says to Dante, "know me, Bertrans de Born; who never gave comfort to the young king. I made the father and the son rebels between them. . . . Because I have sundered persons so joined (in kinship), I bear my brain parted, *Lasso!* from its beginning, which is this torse." (SR, 45)

Bertran's dirge provided Pound with another exercise in prosodic imitation, though he does not construct his English sounds as tightly as Bertran's Provençal. The original poem consists of five eight-line stanzas, each with these line endings:

> Si tuit li dol e·lh plor e·lh *marrimen*
> E las dolors e·lh dans e·lh chaitiv*ier*
> Que om anc auzis en est segle dol*en*
> Fossen ensems, sembleran tuit leug*ier*
> Contra la mort de·l *jove rei engles*,
> Don rema pretz e jovens dolor*os*
> E·l mons osurs e teintz e tenebr*os*
> Sems de tot joi, ples de tristor ea d'*ira*.

Pound's first, fifth, and last lines in each stanza preserve something of this regularity, always ending with the words "bitterness," "the young English king," and "sadness." The other lines range freely instead of following Bertran's rhyme scheme, but Pound uses alliteration and assonance extensively to recreate in English the musical effect of the Provençal.

planh: Provençal: lament, elegy.

If all . . . bitterness: Pound remembers Bertran's original Provençal for this line in Cantos LXXX and LXXXIV (C, 516, 537).

teen: trouble, suffering.

## "BLANDULA, TENELLA, VAGULA" (1911) [SP, 13]

The title of this little paean to the paradisal beauty of Lake Garda in northern Italy was inspired by a verse addressed by the dying Hadrian to his soul:

> Animula vagula blandula
> hospes comesque corporis
> quae nunc abibis in loca
> pallidula rigida nudula?
>
> (*Scriptores Historiae Augustae*, I, Loeb, 78)

("O blithe little soul, thou, flitting away, / Guest and comrade of this my clay, / Whither now goest thou, to what place, / Bare and ghastly and without grace?" [Loeb]) The word "tenella," "tender," comes from a poem by Marcus Aurelius Flaminius, "Ut flos tennelles" ("As a delicate flower") which Pound quotes and translates in *The Spirit of Romance:*

> As a fragile and lovely flower unfolds its gleaming foliage on the breast-fold of the fostering earth, if the dew and rain draw it forth; thus doth my tender mind flourish if it be fed with the sweet dew of the Fostering Spirit.
> Lacking this, it straightway beginneth to languish even as a flower born upon dry earth, if the dew and rain tend it not.
>
> (228)

Pound's title folds together these two descriptions of the soul/mind, and translates "Blithe one, delicate one, ephemeral one." It is a phrase that he repeated (misquoting "tenella" as "tenulla" and "tenula") in speaking of Remy de Gourmont's death in *Poetry,*

January 1916: "M. de Gourmont has gone—Blandula, tenulla, vagula—almost with a jest on his lips"; and it recurs in Canto CV: "Barocco, anima: stuff left from the 5 & 10 / vagula, tenula / and with splendours" (C, 747), where it describes a stone cupid stored in the sacristy of an Italian church (cf. JM 50–51).

Sirmio: Latin for Sirmione, a town on a peninsula in Lake Garda in northern Italy where the Latin poet Catullus had a villa. Catullus praised it thus:

> Paene insularum, Sirmio, insularumque
> ocelle, quascumque in liquentibus stagnis
> marique vasto fert uterque Neptunus.

(Poem XXXI, Catullus, Loeb, 36)

("Sirmio, bright eye of peninsulas and islands, all that in liquid lakes or vast oceans either Neptune bears.") Pound revered both Catullus and Sirmio; he wrote to his parents when he first saw it in 1910, "I know paradise when I see it," and described it as "the same old Sirmio that Catullus raved over a few years back, or Marcus Aurelius Flaminius more recently." (Stock, 107) For Pound, the spirit of the poetry inhered in the natural beauty of the place. He once wrote that he would "rather lie on what is left of Catullus' parlour floor and speculate the azure beneath it and the hills off to Salò and Riva with their forgotten gods moving unhindered amongst them than discuss any processes or theories of poetry whatsoever." (LE, 9) He also speaks of the gods of Lago di Garda in "The Flame" (in which he uses Garda's Latin name, Benacus), and the place figures in "The Study in Aesthetics" (P, 50, 96) and in Cantos LXXIV, LXXVI, and LXXVIII (C, 427, 456, 478).

Title: Cf. Pound's quotation of Fontenelle's French translation of Hadrian's words in PD, 142.

terrene: earthly.

cyanine: a blue dye.

triune: three-in-one. Compare the ritual three cups of honey and three cups of milk that Flaminius offers to the Muse of Sirmio (SR, 230).

if She met us there: i.e., the earthly paradise that Pound imagines at Sirmio will be perfected if "She" is also there—"She" being indeterminate enough to imply both a beloved woman and, as Ronald E. Thomas suggests, the Muse of Catullus' haunt.

Riva: town on the northern end of Lake Garda, with the Alps rising behind it.

## ERAT HORA (1911) [SP, 14]

The Latin title of this sentimental little piece means "It was the hour."

## THE HOUSE OF SPLENDOUR (1911) [SP, 14]

This poem is Pre-Raphaelite pastiche. Compare, for example, Pound's other-worldly Lady with her exotic invented name to Rossetti's "Blessed Damozel," with her "gold," "three lilies," "seven stars," "robe," abundant hair, exotic "house," "aureoles," and idealized "Love."

émail: enameling.

## THE TOMB AT AKR ÇAAR (1912) [SP, 15]

This poem reflects the early interest of Pound and other Imagist and Vorticist artists (H. D., T. E. Hulme, Gaudier-Brzeska) in the ancient Egyptian artifacts that archaeologists were unearthing in the early years of the century. (Pound remarks that Gaudier drew a design for this poem in his copy of *Ripostes* [GB, 45].) It is a fantasy of the complaint of an immortal soul to the body to which it is tied, a dramatic monologue in which the soul addresses the unmoving mummy in the tomb, which it calls Nikoptis. The soul expresses an understandable boredom after its 5,000 years in the tomb, but also a curious attachment to the body and a longing for its reawakening. Instead of following the normal course of the soul in Egyptian mythology, reincarnation, this spirit has remained with its beloved body. The poem pays romantic homage to the Egyptian belief in immortality, even as the tomb's sacred seal is about to be broken by modern archaeologists. The poem reflects Pound's reading of E. A. Wallis Budge's *The Book of the Dead* and *Egyptian Magic*, though no particular source has been found for the names Akr Çaar and Nikoptis. Pound would much later collaborate with the Egyptologist Boris de Rachewiltz on some Egyptian translations; and hieroglyphs occasionally appear in the later cantos (C, 612, 623, 626–27).

any saffron thing: an image of the soul as a pale-yellow substance, like light.

the signs: ancient Egyptian tombs were inscribed with hieroglyphs.

I have been kind. . . . smooth on thee: The body was laid in the tomb with food, clothing, and useful objects for its new life in the hereafter.

—Even the river . . . : The soul reminisces about the river of life that bore this body upon it, and of its own triumph over three other souls for possession of it.

And I flowed in . . . : The soul's words confuse the divisibility of body and soul by addressing the body as though it had a life and being of its own, even as it states that the soul itself is its only life and being: "Was I not thee and Thee?" Similarly, the soul has its own means of sensory knowledge: it reads, longs for the light, listens for the body's word.

despite the marks: The hieroglyphs on the door of the tomb were supposed to have the magic power of preventing any crossing of the threshold.

The title recalls Henry James's *Portrait of a Lady* (1881), much admired by Pound. Pound later spoke of *Mauberley* (1920) as "an attempt to condense the James novel," and this poem is an early exercise in that vein, a character sketch recalling the descriptive vignettes of the Jamesian novel of manners. Pound first met "the Master" in a London drawing room in February 1912, and after James's death he composed a lengthy essay honoring him for "book after early book against oppression, against all the sordid petty personal crushing oppression, the domination of modern life." (LE, 296)

Pound uses a prosaic and flexible blank verse and portrays the "lady" by means of the extended metaphor of the "Sargasso Sea," a relatively static area of the North Atlantic stretching between the West Indies and the Azores, where the currents deposit masses of seaweed (or "sargasso"). As the Sargasso collects seaweed, so this woman has, after twenty years of backwash from London's social currents, accumulated the flotsam and jetsam which makes her, paradoxically, both a "richly paying" institution in the eyes of the young and an impoverished self whose only interest is as repository of this "sea-hoard."

Pound sent "Portrait d'une Femme" to an American periodical, and its rejection inspired him to a cynical demonstration of the backward prudery and pedantry of American taste in the early essay *Patria Mia* (1912–13): "I sent them a real poem, a modern poem, containing the word 'uxorious,' and they wrote back that I had used the letter 'r' three times in the first line, and that it was very difficult to pronounce, and that I might not remember that Tennyson had once condemned the use of four 's's' in a certain line of a different meter. . . . Never once does the editor ask himself the only question which the critic has a right to ask himself in weighing a work of art, to wit: Is this man a serious artist?" (SPr, 113–14). Tennyson, whose taste ran to the mellifluous, thought Pope's opening line in "The Rape of the Lock"—"What dire Offense from am'rous Causes springs"—"horrible"; Pound's snarl of r's seems an onomatopoeic imitation of the weed-choked sea.

33

# AN OBJECT  (1912)                                    [SP, 18]

A character sketch condensed into the scope of an epigram, a
Greek form which makes a satiric, complimentary, or aphoristic
observation in a few brief, biting phrases.


# THE SEAFARER  (1911)                                 [SP, 18]

Pound's version of the thousand-year-old Anglo-Saxon poem
"The Seafarer" is a triumph of creative translation. Its rugged
language, with its disrupted syntax and its diction crabbed with
archaisms and homemade compound words, embodies in an im-
mediate, sensual way the harsh, lonely world of its speaker. The
seafarer, the "wretched outcast," is at once the solitary wanderer
whose song has endured from the beginnings of English poetry
and the modern exile drawn irresistibly to "seek out a foreign
fastness." He is, as Pound puts it, a "major persona" (U, 128), a
figure for the exiled poet and the homeless self that is as old as the
oldest songs.
    Pound's "The Seafarer," like his other translations, has met with
a good deal of incomprehension, and consequently has been much
maligned. Some Anglo-Saxon specialists have scoffed at what they
take to be howlers, and have objected to the obscurity of its lan-
guage. Pound's assertion that his version was "as nearly literal, I
think, as any translation can be" (SPr, 39) could hardly be ex-
pected to pacify them. Even sympathetic Anglo-Saxon scholars,
such as Michael Alexander, have defended Pound's translation on
the grounds of its poetic qualities rather than its philological
accuracy. Recently, however, Fred C. Robinson has shown, by
recreating the historical context of Pound's translation, that
"Pound's version is the product of a serious engagement with the
Anglo-Saxon text, not of casual guessing at Anglo-Saxon words
and of passing off personal prejudice as Anglo-Saxon poetry."
(220) Indeed, he judges that some of Pound's unconventional
readings may be superior to those established by scholars in the
field. Pound's interest in "The Seafarer" was certainly more than

philological, but his unusual readings cannot be dismissed as the blunders of someone too impatient to consider carefully the text he was translating. He was, to paraphrase W. P. Ker, translating like a free human being instead of "word for word, like the illiterate in all ages" (Alexander, 71)—but he *was* translating, and not merely imitating, guessing, or rewriting his original.

He was, further, translating like a great poet. With all the fuss about its literal accuracy or inaccuracy, the broader interests of Pound's "The Seafarer" have been slighted. Its strange language, to a new reader, might itself seem to need translation, and any attempt to understand what Pound was doing must ask what its motives are. They originate in the fact that Pound's version is "literal" not only with respect to the meanings of words but also with respect to their sounds: Pound holds as closely as possible not only to the syntax, diction, and prosody of the original but to its very consonants and vowels. Take, for example, the following line:

Mæg ic be me sylfum      soþgied wrecan

May I for my own self // song's truth reckon

Pound adapts the standard four-stress line of Old English poetry, divided by a pause into two half-lines with strong alliterative patterning. He preserves, however, not merely the syntactic and prosodic *structures* of the original but, as much as possible, its actual *sounds*.

This curious purpose helps to account for what seems at first an incomprehensibly distorted language. Pound's fidelity to the sound of the original "Seafarer" explains his deviations from conventional syntax and diction, as well as the motives for some of his editorial decisions. The extraordinary musical strength of Pound's poem is unmistakable (he can be heard reading it on a Harvard recording), and would in itself be enough to justify its peculiarily wrought language. Yet the poem would be something of a *tour de force* were it not for a special resonance in the phonetic fidelity by which it stresses the continuity between Anglo-Saxon and modern English. When Pound first presented the poem in an article titled, "I Gather the Limbs of Osiris," he explained that he was seeking an elemental English "chemical." Being a poem in the earliest indigenous English prosody, "The Seafarer" exemplified for Pound the pure essence of English speech, "a certain element which has transmuted the various qualities of poetry which have drifted up from the south, which has sometimes enriched and made them English, sometimes rejected them and refused combination." (SPr, 24) The language of Pound's "The Seafarer," comprehensible and yet resistant and remote, is an homage in modern English to its ancient source. In its sound as well as its sense, it recovers a symbolic moment of origin, the shape of the first indigenous cry. It is a myth of beginnings, of a "home" for the wandering exile in the earliest native words.

The one extant manuscript of the Anglo-Saxon "Seafarer," like most manuscripts of the period, has a number of scribal errors and uncertain readings. For this reason, there is a long tradition of controversy over the poem's text and meaning. The question of greatest moment among scholars at the time Pound was studying the poem was whether the manuscript text is close to that of the "original" poem, or whether the true original was in fact a pagan poem upon which scribes later superimposed an occasional Christian image and a spurious Christian ending. Pound made his own editorial position clear in a "Philological Note" which accompanied his translation in its first publication:

> The text of this poem is rather confused. I have rejected half of line 76, read "Angles" for angels in line 78, and stopped translating before the passage about the soul and the longer lines beginning "Mickle is the fear of the almighty," and ending in a dignified but platitudinous address to the Deity: "World's elder, eminent creator, in all ages, amen." There are many conjectures as to how the text came into its present form. It seems most likely that a fragment of the original poem, clear through about the first thirty lines and thereafter increasingly illegible, fell into the hands of a monk with literary ambitions, who filled in the gaps with his own guesses and "improvements." The groundwork may have been a longer narrative poem, but the "lyric," as I have accepted it, divides fairly well into "The Trials of the Sea," its Lure, and the Lament for Age.

> (*The New Age*, 30 November 1911, 107)

In other words, Pound saw the Christian themes in "The Seafarer" as inauthentic late additions, and, consistent with his interest in recovering the Anglo-Saxon essence in its original, pre-Christian purity, excluded them from his translation. Several critics have interpreted this move as a "modernizing" tendency on Pound's part, but Robinson shows that Pound—whatever his affinities to a paganized "Seafarer"—was also in accord with the best scholarly opinion of his day. Alexander writes that this "Analytic" approach to the text is "less in favour today, partly because there are no criteria for determining what is original and what corrupt, . . . and partly because modern critics find a holistic approach both safer and more convenient"; but even today, "the orthodox editorial position on 'The Seafarer' is that the moralizing fourth section is an addition." (72–73) In his textual judgments too, then, Pound was seeking, necessarily speculatively, the original poem.

This is not to say that Pound's interest in "The Seafarer" is antiquarian. He intended his work on the poem not merely to resurrect the past but to serve "the living art. For it is certain that we have had no 'greatest poet' and no 'great period' save at, or after, a time when many people were busy examining the media and the tradition of the art." (SPr, 24) Pound's approach to the translation of Anglo-Saxon has indeed inspired later translators, for example, W. H. Auden and Michael Alexander; and its influence, as Goodwin shows, is perceptible in poets as diverse as T. S. Eliot, Robert Lowell, C. Day Lewis, and W. S. Merwin (206–08). And his groundwork for "the living art" fulfilled itself in a way he could not have foreseen in 1911, in his own first canto, in which he translates a part of the *Odyssey* into a freer version of his "Seafarer" line. This line enabled him to "break the back of the pentameter," as he later put it, renewing the poetic line both for *The Cantos* and for the tradition it inaugurated. The beginning which Pound reimagined in "The Seafarer," then, qualifies as one of the great rebeginnings of modern literature.

A good text for comparison with Pound's "The Seafarer" is found in Michael Alexander's *The Earliest English Poems*, which gives the Anglo-Saxon text along with Alexander's translation.

sea-surge: Compare the onomatopoeic line in HSM: "the imaginary / Audition of the phantasmal sea-surge" (SP, 75).

Mere-weary: sea-weary.

hail-scur: a half-modernization of the Old English poetic compound *hægl-scur*, "hail shower," which was suggested to Pound by the words *hægl scurum fleag*, "hail flew in showers," in line 17 of the Old English "Seafarer." Old English *scur* (pronounced "shoor") is the earlier form of "shower." Cf. "snow scur" in Canto XLIX (C, 244).

Did . . . clamour: i.e., the gannet's clamour was his only diversion.

mews': gulls'.

burghers: Brooker (69–70) notes Pound's "flagrant" modernization in the "extrapolated class envy" here and at line 56; but Robinson shows that "burgher" is the word suggested by the Old English dictionaries Pound would have been using for the terms he was translating here.

Corn of the coldest: from the Old English *corna caldast*, coldest grain, a metaphor for hail. Nathless: Nonetheless.

He hath not . . . winsomeness to wife: that is, he "hath not heart" to marry "winsomeness," or a charming woman; or alternatively, he "hath not heart" for sweetness to a wife. Pound's version departs from the Old English *ne to wife wynn*, "nor for pleasure with a woman."

Bosque: variant of the early Middle English *bosk(e)* or *busk*, meaning "bush."

mere-flood: sea-flood.

English: Old English *englum*, the angels that Pound thought must have been English folk before the speculated "monk with literary ambitions" improved the text. *Englum* can mean either "angels" or "English."

gone companions: i.e., friends now dead.

Lordly men . . . : In Canto LXXIV, this line becomes an elegy for Pound's old friends who have died, Ford Madox Ford, William Butler Yeats, James Joyce, and Henry James.

Nor . . . flesh-cover: i.e., nor may he then have flesh, a body to "cover" his spirit.

ΔΏΡΙΑ (DORIA) (1912)


The Dorians were one of the ancient Greek peoples centered in Sparta and Crete whose dialect gave rise to the choral lyric and whose culture valued discipline, simplicity, and strength. Pound knew Victor Plarr's *In the Dorian Mood,* and was also familiar with T. E. Hulme's theory of abstract art (see Hulme's essays "Romanticism and Classicism" and "Modern Art and Its Philosophy") which links it with a longing for immortality and a desire to transcend the flux of nature. In his "Vorticism" essay, discussing a poetics which would be analogous to abstract art, Pound wrote, "By the 'image' I mean . . . not an equation of mathematics, not something about *a, b,* and *c* having something to do with form, but about *sea, cliffs, night,* having something to do with mood." (GB, 92) The imagery of bleak winds, sunless cliffs, grey sea, and the shadowy flowers of the underworld in "Doria" evokes this affinity for "eternal things," as against the transient gaiety of earthly beauty.

The poem seems to address a beloved in ceremonial invocation of this eternal bond (it has been suggested that Pound wrote the poem for his bride-to-be, Dorothy Shakespear). Still, its chiselled starkness and the indeterminacy of its speaker and occasion make it a highly abstract form, an experiment in the "equation" of imagery and emotion.

The shadowy . . . thee: that is, "Let . . . the shadowy flowers of Orcus remember thee," a poetic association of the beloved with the eternal flowers of the underworld, as opposed to the "transient . . . gaiety" of earthly flowers.

Orcus: Hades, the underworld.


# APPARUIT (1912)


This poem, another of Pound's verse exercises, experiments with English Sapphics, an adaptation of a Greek quantitative verse form

named for its inventor, Sappho. The Latin title, which translates
"She appeared," comes from the words Dante's soul utters when
he first sees Beatrice in the *Vita Nuova:* "Apparuit iam beatitudo
vestra" (translated by Rossetti as "Your blessedness hath now been
made manifest unto you"). Pound's imagery of ethereal light, wind,
and movement gives this figure too an otherworldly glamor (com-
pare the more concrete iconography of "The House of Splen-
dour"). Pound saw the *Vita Nuova* as "the idealization of a real
woman" (SR, 126), and his own poem may be an imitation in this
respect also.

   The Sapphic stanza, associated with passion and elegiac solem-
nity, consists of three eleven-syllable lines (hendecasyllabics) fol-
lowed by one five-syllable line. In English, accented and unaccented
syllables substitute for Greek long and short syllables in the fol-
lowing pattern: — ◡ — ◡̆ — ◡◡ — ◡ — —/◡̆◡◡— ◡̆. The
difficulty of the form lies in its relative inflexibility, for the poet
must follow this pattern as closely as possible, and in doing so,
forego the powerful effects of rhythmic variation. (In fact, the
principles of this experiment directly contradict Pound's ideal of
"absolute rhythm," or at least demand a poetic theme for which
this rhythm *is* "absolute.") In "Apparuit," Pound follows this pat-
tern meticulously with a few variations, and achieves a marvelously
fluid and delicate movement despite the metrical artifice—a diffi-
cult feat. (Contrast, for example, Swinburne's stiffer "Sapphics.")
Pound wrote some time after composing "Apparuit," "I think prog-
ress lies rather in an attempt to approximate classical quantitative
metres (NOT to copy them) than in a carelessness regarding such
things." (LE, 13)

   The paragon of Georgian verse, Edward Marsh, recounts his
horrified response to "Apparuit" when Pound showed it to him in
manuscript:

> In the middle of dinner he asked me if I was up in the new system
> of quantitative verse; . . . I admitted that I was. Whereupon he
> produced a version of Sappho's ode to Aphrodite [which "Ap-
> paruit" is not], and begged me to tell him if he had made any
> mistakes. He had; and when I pointed them out to him, he put the
> paper back in his pocket, blushing murkily, and muttering that

it was only a first attempt. "Judge of my surprise" when some weeks later the piece appeared in the *Poetry Review* without a single amendment.

Marsh was thenceforth afflicted with "a lasting suspicion" of Pound's "artistic seriousness." (328–29)

roses bend: the image occurs in Pound's 1910 translation of Cavalcanti's Sonnet VII: "Who is she coming, that the roses bend / Their shameless heads to do her passing honour?" (CEP, 143)

cast-/ing, loveli-/est: This is a permissible move in quantitative verse, exemplified in Sappho LXXXVI. Cf. also Marianne Moore's syllabic verse.

thine oriel: the radiance that emanates from her.

# A VIRGINAL  (1912)                              [SP, 23]

A virginal is a small rectangular harpsichord. The instrument was popular in the sixteenth and seventeenth centuries, and Pound had acquired a modern copy made by Arnold Dolmetsch while living in London. Here, the word comes to mean also a "song of a virgin." Pound experiments with the sonnet form, using fourteen lines of iambic pentameter. The poem shares the subject and imagery of "Apparuit," and the contrast in the two poems illustrates how important the choice of meter can be in the creation of tone.

Another poem Pound published in 1912, "L'Invitation," employs the same rhetorical situation, beginning rather melodramatically, "Go from me. I am one of those who spoil / And leave fair souls less fair for knowing them." (CEP, 208) In both, he echoes Lionel Johnson's "Mystic and Cavalier" ("Go from me: I am one of those who fall"), which appears in Pound's 1915 edition of *The Collected Poems of Lionel Johnson.*

# OF JACOPO DEL SELLAIO (1912)

Jacopo del Sellaio was an Italian renaissance painter (1442–93). His "Venus Reclining" in London's National Gallery is the subject of this poem, and of another, "The Picture," which also begins and ends with the line, "The eyes of this dead lady speak to me." (CEP, 197) Venus is called "The Cyprian" because it was upon the isle of Cyprus that she landed upon rising from the sea-foam, and she is especially honored there. Islands like Cyprus and Lesbos were known as the "isles of love"; "The Isles" here alludes to the British Isles, and to the Englishwoman Dorothy Shakespear, who married Pound in 1914.

secret ways of love: Pound echoes Swinburne's description of Venus in "A Ballad of Death": "Upon her raiment of dyed sendaline / Were painted all the secret ways of love."

The eyes . . . : Cf. "Dans un Omnibus de Londres" (1916): "Les yeux d'une morte / M'ont salué." (P, 160)

# THE RETURN (1912)

Yeats praised "The Return" as "the most beautiful poem that has been written in the free form, one of the few in which I find real organic rhythm" (Ruthven, 204). He aptly registered its delicate, indefinite mood in remarking that it seemed to have been "translated at sight from an unknown Greek masterpiece" (*Oxford Book of Modern Verse*, xxvi). Pound himself, who composed the poem before he knew the work of the sculptor Gaudier-Brzeska, later described it as "an objective reality [which] has a complicated sort of significance, like Mr. Epstein's 'Sun God' or Mr. Brzeska's 'Boy with a Coney' " (GB, 85)—two works which he described as combining "organic with inorganic forms." The comparison illustrates the correspondences between the aims of the visual and verbal arts of the Vorticist movement. Just as Gaudier's small statue (two photographs of which appear in GB, plate XXIII) abstracts the natural forms of the kneeling boy and the rabbit he holds to a "harmony of planes in relation," Pound's poem abstracts a narrative of the revenants into a harmony of carved verbal rhythms. It is these rhythms, and not narrative events, which embody "the return"—the recurring patterns which compose its nonrepresentational harmonies. There is perhaps no better illustration of Pound's theory of "absolute rhythm"—"form cut into TIME" (ABCR, 198), as the Gaudier harmonies are cut into space.

"Wing'd-with-Awe": Pound here imitates (or abstracts) the Homeric epithet, the formulaic descriptive phrase attached to the names of mortals and immortals, and used repeatedly as a metrical unit; e.g., "many-minded Odysseus," "grey-eyed Athena," "Helen shaped by heaven," and so on. His use of quotation marks measures the conscious distance of his own poem from the ancient poetry to which the phrase alludes. "The Return" is thus the return of a past which survives only as fragments of an ancient statue survive, and which is transfigured by the modern poetic landscape which contains it.

Haie!: Robert Fitzgerald explains: "Ai! Greek for Ha! English—he put 'em together."

# Lustra (1916/1917)

## TENZONE (1913)                                          [sp, 24]

This was one of twelve poems published in *Poetry* in April 1913 as "Contemporania," which included "The Garret," "Salutation," "A Pact," "Dance Figure," and "In a Station of the Metro." A "tenzone" is a Provençal form, a dialogue or debate in verse which may either be interiorized, as here, or take place between two rivals. Pound uses it to treat the antagonism between the modern poet and society. He affects an aloof insouciance about his lack of an audience, which he pictures fleeing from his poems and their "verisimilitudes"; he wrote to Harriet Monroe, editor of *Poetry*, "I don't know that America is ready to be diverted by the ultra-modern, ultra-effete tenuity of Contemporania." (SL, 11) However, when the American critic Floyd Dell praised the series as having "brought back into the world a grace which (probably) never existed, but which we discover by an imaginative process in Horatius and Catullus" (Homberger, 98–99), Pound found his praise "very consoling" and astute in detecting "the Latin tone." (SL, 19)

centaur: This mythological creature, half man, half horse, was Pound's image for poetry, which required the union of Apollonian clarity and order with Dionysian instinct and sensuality. In "The Serious Artist," also published in 1913, Pound wrote, "Poetry is a centaur. The thinking word-arranging, clarifying faculty must move and leap with the energizing, sentient, musical faculties" (LE, 52).

44

# THE GARRET (1913)

Pound considered this scenario of the consolations of the bohemian life "about the best" of his "Contemporania" (Chicago MSS).

Dawn . . . Pavlova: Cf. the "golden-slippered Dawn" of Sappho's Poem XIX and the "slim gilded feet" of Beauty in Oscar Wilde's "The Critic as Artist" (Ruthven, 77). The Russian ballerina Anna Pavlova (1885–1931) danced in London in 1910 with Diaghilev's Ballet Russe. Pound wrote that "it was her own delicate and very personal comment of emotion upon the choreographic lines of Fokine which won her the myriad hearts." (*Athenaeum*, 32 April 1920, 553)


# THE GARDEN (1913)

The "garden" of title, epigraph, and opening line quickly turns to a satiric scenario of a bourgeois sensibility delicately decaying amid the robust avatars of the future. The epigraph comes from Albert Samain's *Au Jardin de l'Infante*, which begins, "Mon âme est une infante en robe de parade" ("My soul is a child in promenade dress"). Pound praised this poem in *The Little Review* in 1918, but later criticized Samain as " 'soft,' there is just a suggestion of muzziness." (LE, 285) His friend Richard Aldington parodied "The Garden" and other poems in *The Egoist* in 1914:

> Like an armful of greasy engineer's-cotton
> Flung by a typhoon against a broken crate of ducks' eggs
> She stands by the rail of the old Bailey dock.
> Her intoxication is exquisite and excessive,
> And delicate her delicate sterility.
> Her delicacy is so delicate that she would feel affronted
> If I remarked nonchalantly, "Saay, stranger, ain't you dandy."
> (Ruthven, 76)

Pound enjoyed the parodies, and remarked, "Good art thrives in an atmosphere of parody. Parody is, I suppose, the best criticism—it sifts the durable from the apparent." (SL, 13)

They shall inherit . . . :  Matthew 5:5: "Blessed are the meek: for they shall inherit the earth."

# SALUTATION  (1913)                              [SP, 26]

Another strike at the soul-less propriety of the bourgeoisie.

# THE SPRING  (1915)                              [SP, 27]

"The Spring" is a freehand translation of the poem from which its epigraph is taken. Pound admired Ibycus, a Greek lyric poet of the sixth century B.C., because he "presented 'the Image' " (GB, 83) in a clear, pure style which opposed itself to "pretentious and decorated verse." (LE, 216) Pound adapts his original (which contrasts the springtime awakening of the earth with the year-long surging of desire in the speaker) by ending with three new lines which transform it into elegy, a mood characteristic of Pound's Imagist poems.

Epigraph (Eri men ai te kydoniai): "Though in spring the Kydonian quinces." Cf. Canto XXXIX (C, 195).

Cydonian: of Cydonia (or Kydonia), a town in Crete for which the quince (kydon) is named.

maelids: meliads, the nymphs of the fruit trees; cf. Canto III (C, 11).

boisterous wind from Thrace: i.e., a northeast wind.

# A PACT (1913)

The ambivalence of Pound's response to his poetic forefather Walt Whitman reflects his complex sense of his American literary heritage. As he was well aware, whatever he might say in explanation of Whitman would also in some measure define himself. While Pound recognized the authentic American eloquence of Whitman's "barbaric yawp," the self-conscious craftsman in him winced at the "exceeding great stench" of Whitman's "crudity," "an exceedingly nauseating pill" (LE, 145) which he parodically exemplified as "Lo! Behold, I eat watermelons."

In his 1909 essay "What I Feel about Walt Whitman," his distaste for Whitman's expansive self-singing struggles with an even more powerful conviction that Whitman "*is* America. . . . He *does* 'chant the crucial stage' and he is the 'voice triumphant.'" (LE, 145) In the end, Pound subordinates the superficial quarrel with Whitman's poetic means to the profound bond of their common origin and message. Whitman is to America "what Dante is to Italy"; "the vital part of my message, taken from the sap and fibre of America, is the same as his"; "It is a great thing, reading a man to know, not 'His Tricks are not as yet my Tricks, but I can easily make them mine' but 'His message is my message. We will see that men hear it.'" (LE, 146)

Pound's "pact" is movingly recalled in Canto LXXXII, one of *The Pisan Cantos*, in which Whitman's "Out of the Cradle Endlessly Rocking" helps to keep Pound "from the gates of death." (C, 525–27)

pact: The word was "truce" in the first publication of the poem in *Poetry*, 1913.


# DANCE FIGURE (1913)

"Dance Figure" was one of Pound's "Contemporania" of 1913. Rather less contemporary in theme than the others in that group, its true subject is the free verse patterns of its lines. Pound wrote to Harriet Monroe, editor of *Poetry*, that the poem had "little but its rhythm to recommend it." In those early days, when the modernists' free verse was just being invented, that was recommendation enough. In some remarks on free verse of about the same time, Pound used "Dance Figure" as an example of "vers libre with accent heavily marked" in contrast to free verse tending toward a quantitative measure. (LE, 12) In manuscript, "Dance Figure" had a subtitle, "A Thoroughly Sensuous Image," which points to his interest in the pure shaping of its sound.

Epigraph: Cf. John 2:1: "And the third day there was a marriage in Cana of Galilee." Biblical verse apparently served Pound as model for rhythmic variation within a structure of repetition: e.g., the anaphoric "I have not found thee in the tents, / In the broken darkness. / I have not found thee at the well-head."

Nathat-Ikanaie: Pound apparently invents an exotic name for the dancer, then "translates" its appropriate literal meaning.

# APRIL  (1912)  .  [SP, 29]

"April" exemplifies a structure typical of Imagist poems: a concrete description followed by a succinct line of metaphysical interpretation (cf. "In a Station of the Metro"). Richard Aldington, Pound's Imagist colleague, parodied it in his "Elevators" of 1914:

> Let us soar up higher than the eighteenth floor
> And consider the delicate delectable monocles
> Of the musical virgins of Parnassus:
> Pale slaughter beneath purple skies.

> (Ruthven, 40)

Epigraph: "the nymphs' scattered limbs," adapted from Pentheus' scattered limbs ("deiectis . . . membris") in Ovid's *Metamorphoses*, III.724.

# THE REST (1913) [SP, 29]

In this poem Pound addresses his fellow American artists who have remained at home to be broken by an indifferent public, offering them the example of his own successful exile. He invites them to follow the path taken by the painter James McNeill Whistler, Henry James, T. S. Eliot, and himself, the tradition of American expatriate artists. Soon after he published this poem, Pound praised the American poet John Gould Fletcher for having elected exile, "imperative for any American who has serious intentions toward poetry" (*Poetry*, December 1913). Two years later, however, he foresaw the possibility of an American renaissance to be created by the "fighting minority . . . that has been until now gradually forced out of the country. We have looked to the wrong powers. We have not sufficiently looked to ourselves. We have not defined the hostility or inertia that is against us. We have not recognized with any Voltairian clearness the nature of this opposition, and we have not realized to what an extent a renaissance is a thing made— a thing made by conscious propaganda." (LE, 219–20)

Rhetorically and stylistically, "The Rest" could be described as expansive Whitmanesque lines that have been "carved" (see "A Pact") into *vers libre*, as if Pound required for this communion with his fellows the authoritative voice of the American poetic tradition. This is not the contradiction it seems: Pound's 1909 essay on Whitman begins with the words, "From this side of the Atlantic I am for the first time able to read Whitman, and from the vantage of . . . my world citizenship: I see him America's poet." (SPr, 145) Compare "The Rest" with *Patria Mia* (1912), "To Whistler, American" (1912), and "L'Homme Moyen Sensual" (1917).

# LES MILLWIN (1913) [SP, 30]

Pound here follows Henry James in the role of American expatriate as social observer, a role which turns a detached point of view and unaccustomed eye to advantage. The poem portrays the spiritless

incomprehension of the Millwins, scions of the bourgeoisie, against the art students' exhilaration at a performance of the Ballet Russe. "Les Millwin" relates to a passing remark on the social relativity of value in *Patria Mia:* "The Russian dancers present their splendid luxurious paganism, and everyone with a pre-Raphaelite or Swinburnian education is in raptures. What 'morality' will be two hundred years hence is beyond all prediction. Our present standards may seem as distasteful to that age as does mediaeval asceticism to the present." (SPr, 103)

Ballet Russe: Sergei Diaghilev's famous avant-garde Ballet Russe, whose flamboyant productions employed the genius of Stravinsky, Pavlova, Nijinsky, and Picasso. Cf. "The Garret."

mauve and greenish: i.e., effete and diluted, as against the "primary colors" of the art students' response.

boas: long, narrow wraps of dyed fur or feathers.

"Slade": the Slade School of Fine Art in London.

futuristic X's: The Italian Futurist movement hit London in 1912 with the Sackville Gallery's Futurist Exhibition and lectures by F. T. Marinetti, its leader. The Futurist aesthetic exalted speed, motion, the abstract qualities of life in the machine age. Pound considered it a "surface art," and defined Vorticism as its "intensive" antithesis. (GB, 90)

*Cleopatra:* a one-act ballet first performed by the Ballet Russe in 1909.


A SONG OF THE DEGREES (1913)                    [SP, 31]


This poem began as sections III–V of the seven-part "Xenia" (Greek: "gifts," used ironically by Martial for his scathing epigrams) which Pound published in *Poetry* in November 1913. The uncertainty of its presentation seems to reflect a certain obscurity in its intention. The title alludes to Psalms 120–34, each of which is subtitled "A Song of Degrees" (that is, a gradual), and suggests that the psalms are a model for the incantatory repetition of simple syntactic structures which Pound uses in this poem. Compare, for example, Psalm 124:1–5:

1 If it had not been the Lord who was on our side, now may Israel say;
2 If it had not been the Lord who was on our side, when men rose up against us:
3 Then they had swallowed us up quick, when their wrath was kindled against us;
4 Then the waters had overwhelmed us, the stream had gone over our soul:
5 Then the proud waters had gone over our soul.

The imagery of this poem, as Hans-Joachim Zimmermann shows, has affinities with that of "The Alchemist."

Rest me: Cf. the rhetorical structure of the Song of Solomon, 2:5: "Stay me with flagons, comfort me with apples: for I am sick of love." (Zimmermann, 227)

Chinese colours: Cf. "Further Instructions," also in the November 1913 issue of *Poetry:* "I will get you a green coat out of China / With dragons worked upon it, / I will get you the scarlet silk trousers / From the statue of the infant Christ in Santa Maria Novella" (P, 94).

the glass: perhaps a mirror.

The wind . . . metal: Cf. "The Alchemist": " 'Mid the silver rustling of wheat" (P, 75).

O glass . . . iridescence!: Contrast this imagery with its use in "The Alchemist" (P, 75–76), in which art is the valuable gold, or light, into which all other elements, or colors, fuse.


# ITÉ (1913) [SP, 31]


"Ité" (Latin: "Go") was originally section six of "Xenia" (see note to "A Song of the Degrees"). It is an envoy, the author's parting words to a book or poem as it enters the world, and its directives express something of Pound's aesthetic aims and of the audience he hopes to reach.

perfection: Cf. Pound's complaint to Harriet Monroe, editor of *Poetry*, in 1913: ". . . whom do you know who takes the Art of poetry seriously? As seriously that is as a painter takes painting? . . . Who in America believes in perfection and that nothing short of it is worth while?" (SL, 15)

hard Sophoclean light: the austere style of the Greek dramatist Sophocles (fifth century B.C.). Pound wrote in 1914, "we have had so many . . . pseudoglamours and glamourlets and mists and fogs since the nineties that one is about ready for hard light" (*Poetry*, May 1914, 67); he hoped for "a bit more Sophoclean severity in the ambitions of mes amis et confrères. The general weakness of the writers of the new school is looseness, lack of rhythmical construction and intensity." (SL, 50)

# SALVATIONISTS (1914)                              [SP, 32]

Pound's title, though ironic, reflects his strong belief in the social value of "serious" art. As he wrote in 1913, "the arts bear witness and define for us the inner nature and condition" of humanity. Good art is marked by its precision; "Bad art is inaccurate art." He considered satire, "the delineation of ugliness," as a valuable "art of diagnosis" or "surgery": it "reminds one that certain things are not worth while." (LE, 43–45)

perfection: See note to "Ité," above, and Pound's complaint in a review of Ford's *Collected Poems:* "it is impossible to talk about perfection without getting yourself very much disliked" (*Poetry*, June 1914, 112).

*Rusticus:* Latin: countrified, boorish.

Let us take arms . . . : Cf. *Hamlet*, III.i.59–60: "to take arms against a sea of troubles, / And by opposing end them."

Mumpodorus, Nimmim, Bulmenian literati: fictional names for the offending writers. Pound later thought that "one should name names in satire" (SL, 116), since circumlocution hampers the effectiveness of its "surgery."

# ARIDES  (1913)                                    [SP, 33]

This little poem satirizes the abuse of the marriage institution as a refuge for the crestfallen. It first appeared as the eighth of eleven poems entitled "Zenia" (*sic;* Greek: gifts) in *Smart Set,* December 1913. "Arides" probably disguises the name of an actual acquaintance of Pound's.

# AMITIES  (1914)                                    [SP, 33]

The full text of "Amities" consists of four epigrams (IV is in Latin). The epigraph comes from Yeats's "The Lover Pleads with His Friend for Old Friends" (1899): "But I think about old friends the most."

*Te Voilà, mon Bourrienne:* French: "There you are, my Bourrienne," a phrase which also appears in Canto XCIII. L. A. F. de Bourrienne was Napoleon's private secretary. Napoleon is said to have continued, *"Tu aussi seras immortel"* ("You also shall be immortal").

*bos amic:* Provençal: good friend; Aldington suggests that this is Harold Monro (1879–1932).

chop-house: Aldington identifies this as Bellotti's Ristorante Italiano, 12 Old Compton Street, London, recommended by Pound as the "cheapest clean restaurant with a real cook." (SL, 97)

# MEDITATIO (1914)

"Meditatio" (Latin: "Meditation") was one of nine poems which Elkin Mathews, Pound's London publisher, excluded from the trade edition of *Lustra* (1916) on grounds of their obscenity. (They were included in a "private" edition which he sold to any customer who asked for it specifically.) "The story of getting *Lustra* into print," Pound later wrote, "belongs to stage comedy, not even to memoirs." (SPr, 227–28) It thus stands as a minor document of the struggle of modern literature for freedom of expression in the early part of the century, along with the more famous example of Joyce's *Ulysses*. Pound wrote a prose note on censorship, published in the *Egoist* on 1 March 1916, which he also titled "Meditatio."

# CODA (1915)

"Coda" originally ended a series of five poems in *Others*, November 1915. A coda is an independent passage attached in conclusion to a musical composition. The lines reflect their own renovation of the classical epigram, in which contemporary subjects of satire replace the "lost dead" of the classical poems.

# THE COMING OF WAR: ACTAEON (1915)

Pound wrote this highly romantic evocation of war near the beginning of World War I. It is difficult to remember now that virtually all of England at that time cherished a similarly idealized expectation of a noble conflict, quickly decided, whose heroes would cover themselves with glory. But Pound's own stance toward the war was soon to change: in July 1915, his friend Gaudier-

Brzeska, the brilliant young sculptor, was killed in the war. In *Gaudier-Brzeska: A Memoir* (1916) and in *Hugh Selwyn Mauberley* (1920), Pound treats the war with bitter irony, and in 1918 he began, he says in the "Biography" of the *Selected Poems*, "investigation of causes of war, to oppose same."

Lethe: in Greek mythology, the river of forgetfulness which the dead must cross to reach Hades.

Actaeon: in Greek mythology, a youth who, while hunting, accidentally came upon Artemis (Diana) bathing and was torn to pieces by his own dogs in punishment. (Ovid, *Metamorphoses*, III) Pound uses him here as a type of the Greek hero rather than with specific reference to his story. Cf. Canto IV.

greaves: armor for the shins. "Of golden greaves" imitates the Homeric epithet, a descriptive phrase attached to a name to make a metrical unit which fits conveniently into a hexameter line and is used formulaically throughout the poem whenever its sense and metrical shape are required.

# IN A STATION OF THE METRO (1913)   [SP, 35]

This little poem looks to be a modern adaptation of the Japanese haiku. Pound wrote an account of its composition, however, which claims that the poem's form was determined by the experience which inspired it, evolving organically rather than being chosen arbitrarily. Whether truth or myth, the piece has become a famous document in the history of Imagism. Pound's story of how the "sudden emotion" which inspired the poem led first to "an equation in color" and only later to a precise verbal "equivalent" has much in common with certain contemporary developments in the visual arts. (He compares it in particular to Wassily Kandinsky's *On the Spiritual in Art*.) He wrote,

> Three years ago in Paris I got out of a "metro" train at La Concorde, and saw suddenly a beautiful face, and then another and another, and then a beautiful child's face, and then another beauti-

ful woman, and I tried all that day to find words for what this had meant to me, and I could not find any words that seemed to me worthy, or as lovely as that sudden emotion. And that evening, as I went home along the Rue Raynouard, I was still trying, and I found, suddenly, the expression. I do not mean that I found words, but there came an equation . . . not in speech, but in little splotches of colour. It was just that—a "pattern," or hardly a pattern, if by "pattern" you mean something with a "repeat" in it. But it was a word, the beginning, for me, of a language in colour.

. . . . Colour was, in that instance, the "primary pigment"; I mean that it was the first adequate equation that came into con-sciousness.

. . .

The "one image poem" is a form of super-position, that is to say, it is one idea set on top of another. I found it useful in getting out of the impasse in which I had been left by my metro emotion. I wrote a thirty-line poem, and destroyed it. . . . Six months later I made a poem half that length; a year later I made [one] *hokku*-like sentence. . . . In a poem of this sort one is trying to record the precise instant when a thing outward and objective trans-forms itself . . . into a thing inward and subjective.

(GB, 86–89)

In its original publication, the poem had extra spacing between phrases for emphasis.


## ALBA  (1913)                                      [SP, 36]


This poem began as poem II of "Zenia" (see note to "Arides"). An alba is a dawn song; this Imagist alba adapts the haiku form. Cf. "Alba: from 'Langue d'Oc.'"

# COITUS (1914) [SP, 36]

Elkin Mathews, the publisher of *Lustra* (1916), censored the title of this poem, whereupon Pound temporarily changed it to "Pervigilium." The new title alluded to the Latin poem "Pervigilium Veneris" ("Vigil of Venus"), an ancient celebration of spring and eros which Pound discusses in *The Spirit of Romance* (16–21). See also the note to "Meditatio."

phaloi: Greek: helmet ridges. Pound and Mathews had an interesting exchange on this word. "I judge [the printer of the volume] is not a hellenist," Pound wrote; "he seems to confuse the Greek PHALOS, plu. PHALOI (meaning the point of the helmet spike) with the latin Phallus." (PJ, 286) Robert Fitzgerald points out that Pound was perfectly right about "phalos," but Mathews' ears rang with the homonym, and he replied unsmilingly: "the Gk word Phallos means penis—*simply* and the Latin word Phallus is merely derived from it." (Homberger, 124)

Giulio Romano: (1499–1546), Italian artist, a pupil of Raphael, who painted the erotic frescoes of the gods in the Palazzo del Te in Mantua.

Dione: Greek earth goddess, mother of Venus, who brings the spring in the "Pervigilium Veneris" and figures in the sacred mysteries of Eleusis.

# THE ENCOUNTER (1913) [SP, 36]

This was originally poem IX of "Zenia" (see note to "Arides"). Ruthven suggests that "the new morality" may refer to Freud's writings; if so, the speaker in this poem typifies Pound's lack of interest in Freud. For Pound, "the last romantic," love was eros, divinity, and poetry. See his "Psychology and Troubadours," in which he explains "chivalric love" as "an art, that is to say, a religion." (SR, 87)

Pound takes his title (imerro, "I desire") from a fragmentary
text of a poem by the Greek poet Sappho (sixth century B.C.).
Discovered in 1896, the Greek text appeared, restored by J. M.
Edmonds, in the *Classical Review* in 1909. Richard Aldington
made a translation of it, which Pound printed in *Des Imagistes*
(1914). Another version of the Greek was published in *The Egoist*
in 1915. Pound's poem is not a translation but a design worked
from a few details in some lines of the Greek text which Edmonds
translates: "And oftentimes, when our beloved, wandering abroad,
calls to mind her gentle Atthis, the heart devours her tender breast
with the pain of longing." By contrast, the austere language and
fragmented syntax of Pound's poem creates a lyric voice which
seems as remote as Sappho's Greek, a mood in which the exotic,
half-erased text is not reconstructed but preserved as the fragment
it is. See Kenner's *Pound Era* (54f.) for a fascinating account of
Pound's work on Greek fragments; and cf. Canto V, where Pound
again draws on Sappho's poem for Atthis. The fastidious Elkin
Mathews (see note to "Meditatio") found the poem offensive—
"anything but *delicate*"—and excluded it from the trade edition
of *Lustra*.

Thy soul . . . satieties: Cf. Aldington's version: "I yearn to behold thy
delicate soul / To satiate my desire."

restless, ungathered: Cf. "wandering abroad" in Edmonds' translation.


TAME CAT  (1913)                                    [SP, 37]


Originally XI of "Zenia" (see note to "Arides"), "Tame Cat" is
a rather prosaic exercise in "perfectly plain statement," modeled
on a poem by the twelfth-century troubadour Arnaut Daniel.
"Daniel has moments of simplicity," Pound observed in 1912.
" 'Pensar de lieis m'es repaus'—'It rests me to think of her.' You

cannot get statement simpler than that, or clearer, or less rhetorical." (SPr, 43) Cf. Canto XCI.

## THE TEA SHOP  (1915)                          [SP, 37]

In this poem, Pound told the editors of *Poetry*, he had attempted to catch that "peculiar combination of sensuality and sentimentality to which we grossly apply the term 'post-Victorian' "; he thought it might be subtitled " 'A poem still touched with Victorian Sentimentality.' " (Chicago MSS) Indeed, in the original text of the poem, the present lines 5 and 9 were replaced by nine lines each, which Pound canceled before its first publication. See Ruthven for the full manuscript text.

## ANCIENT MUSIC  (1915)                          [SP, 38]

This poem, originally printed in *Blast*, parodies the Middle English lyric, "Sumer is icumen in, / Lhude sing cuccu!" Its decorum contrasts with that of another parody of 1915 by Frank Sidgwick, which begins "Wynter ys i-cumen in; / Lhoudly syng *tish-u*!" (Ruthven, 36).

## THE LAKE ISLE  (1916)                          [SP, 38]

This bathetic parody of Yeats's romantic idyl, "The Lake Isle of Innisfree" (1893), plays on the difficulty of "modernization," of learning to make poetry out of common things and common words. It "reads" Yeats's poem as a version of its own trivialized escapism. Elkin Mathews and his printers (see note to "Meditatio") excluded it from *Lustra*.

## EPITAPHS   (1914)                                        [SP, 39]

Fu I: a Chinese poet (555–639) who composed this strikingly "modern" epitaph for himself.

Li Po: a Chinese poet (701–62) whom Pound translates in *Cathay*. H. A. Giles writes that Li Po met his death by drowning "from leaning one night too far over the edge of a boat in a drunken effort to embrace the moon" (153).

## VILLANELLE: THE PSYCHOLOGICAL HOUR   (1915)        [SP, 39]

This poem appeared a month after Pound's thirtieth birthday. The unfulfilled "event" in the poem appears to be based on the early stage of his friendship with Henri Gaudier (1891–1915) and his "sister," Sophie Brzeska. Pound's account of their acquaintance in *Gaudier-Brzeska* says that he first met the young sculptor briefly at an art show in 1913. Later, he invited Gaudier to dinner, but "he did not arrive. His sister tells me that she prevailed with him to intend to come, but that there was a row at the last moment and that by the time he had got himself ready it was too late." When they did meet again, Pound feared that Gaudier, six years younger than himself, would be bored with "my rather middle-aged point of view, my intellectual tiredness, my general skepticism and quietness," so he read him some of his more fiery poems, "written when about his own age." Hearing them, Gaudier "tried to persuade me that I was not becoming middle-aged, but any man whose youth has been worth anything, any man who has lived his life at all in the sun, knows that he has seen the last of it when he finds thirty approaching; knows that he is entering a quieter realm, a place with a different psychology." (GB, 45–46) This "Villanelle" has something in common with T. S. Eliot's "The Love Song of J. Alfred Prufrock."

The villanelle form consists of five tercets (ABA) and a quatrain (ABAA); the first and third lines of the first tercet recur alternately as the last lines of the other four, and together end the quatrain. Pound's poem is obviously a metaphorical villanelle, in which the obsessive repetitions of the form are abstracted into thematic obsession with middle age, the absent friends, the things he wants to share with them. As he wrote elsewhere of the villanelle form, "the refrains are an emotional fact, which the intellect, in the various gyrations of the poem, tries in vain and in vain to escape." (LE, 369n) Pound was dissatisfied with the poem, and explained to his father, "I wanted the effect of a recurrence of a theme and meant 'Villanelle' to mean generally the feel of the villanelle form in a modern subject. . . . I wanted to convey the sense—the "feel" that something critical is happening to someone else at a distance. . . . I have however only succeeded in giving the impression that *I* was disappointed by their absence." (L, 18 December 1915)

Compare Pound's use of the sestina form in "Sestina: Altaforte."

*"Between the night . . ."*: A line from Yeats's then-unpublished poem "The People." The fact of quotation is itself an element of repetition.


# PAGANI'S, NOVEMBER 8  (1916)                    [SP, 41]


Pagani's was a favorite restaurant of Pound's in Great Portland Place, London. Cf. Canto LXXIV: "her eyes as in 'La Nascita' / whereas the child's face / is at Capoquadri" (C, 446).

British Museum assistant: possibly Laurence Binyon (1869–1934), poet, translator of Dante, and Deputy Keeper of the Prints and Drawings at the British Museum where Pound used to go to read and write in his London days.

# ALBA FROM "LANGUE D'OC" (1918)    [SP, 42]

The alba, or dawn song, is a twelfth-century Provençal form which originates in the medieval watchman's cry announcing the return of day. It usually proclaims the lovers' regret that day has come so soon to separate them. This alba, a translation of the anonymous "Quan lo rossinhols escria," began as one of six poems in a series entitled "Homage à la Langue d'Oc"; the "langue d'oc" is the Provençal dialect (in which "yes" is "oc") as opposed to the medieval dialect of northern France, the "langue d'oïl" (in which "yes" is "oïl"). Pound translated this poem into prose in *The Spirit of Romance:* "When the nightingale cries to his mate, night and day, I am with my fair mistress amidst the flowers, until the watchman from the tower cries 'Lover, arise, for I see the white light of the dawn, and the clear day.' " (40–41) The versified form stylizes the syntax and heightens the design of rhyme and alliteration already audible in the prose to imitate in English the music of Provençal.

# NEAR PERIGORD (1915)    [SP, 42]

"Near Perigord" first appeared in *Poetry* in December 1915 with Pound's translation of Bertran de Born's "The Borrowed Lady" (P, 105), the poem upon which "Near Perigord" muses. Bertran (1140–1215) is the war-mongering troubadour in whose poems "Sestina: Altaforte," "Na Audiart," and "Planh for the Young English King" have their beginnings. In his "The Borrowed Lady," Bertran fashions an imaginary ideal lady from attributes of various real women of the land (see "Na Audiart") in order to console himself after Lady Maent has rejected him. It thus appears to be a love poem for the Lady Maent. But part of Pound's fascination with troubadour poetry lay in its difficulty and indirectness, which, he theorized, served to conceal its real intentions from all but the initiated hearers. "No student of the period can doubt that the involved forms, and the veiled meanings in the 'trobar clus,' grew out of living conditions, and that these songs played a very real part in love intrigue and in the intrigue preceding warfare." (LE, 94)

The problem with which "Near Perigord" concerns itself is just what "veiled meanings" Bertran's "The Borrowed Lady" may have had in its original historical context. Pound, in his walking tours of Provence in 1908 and 1912, had noticed the strategic locations of the castles of the various troubadour lords; he wrote that by walking "the hill roads and river roads from Limoges and Charente to Dordogne and Narbonne," one might "learn a little, or more than a little, of what the country meant to the wandering singers, [and] why so many canzos open with speech of the weather; or why such a man made war on such and such castles." (LE, 95) He, for his part, had seen that the various castles mentioned in "The Borrowed Lady" surrounded Bertran's enemy, the Count of Perigord, and that Maent's castle, Montaignac, held a crucial position in this constellation. From this he conjectures that "The Borrowed Lady" may have been no simple love poem but a politic move to gain Lady Maent's favor, and thereby her alliance, as well as the support of the other castles he mentions in the song. "Near Perigord," then, revolves around this question of hidden motives, for which, as Pound wrote, "we have no evidence save . . . my geographical observations." (*Poetry*, December 1915, 146)

Pound wrote "Near Perigord" in 1915 when he was deeply engaged with the poetry of Robert Browning, who presides over the earliest drafts of *The Cantos*, begun about the same time. Browning's use of the dramatic monologue form in *The Ring and the Book* and in his shorter poems gave Pound a model for "reading between the lines" of historical documents and deciphering the hidden motives of a text from their subtle expression on its surface. "Near Perigord" shows Pound's increasing preoccupation with the relationship of poetry to history, and his interest in probing the social and psychological motives underlying particular poetic forms.

Title: Perigord: Périgueux, the capital of the old French province Perigord.

Epigraph: The first lines of a poem by Bertran which Pound translates, "At Perigord near to the wall, / Aye, within a mace throw of it . . ." (SR, 45).

Messire Cino . . . : Pound challenges his persona, "Cino," to tell the tale of Bertran. "Roundel for Arms" and "Roundel: After Joachim du Bellay" were both signed "Cino" (CEP, 234).

Uc St. Circ: Uc de Saint Circ, troubadour and author of some of the troubadour *vidas* or biographies..

En: Provençal: Sir, Lord.

a fine canzone: Born's "Dompna pois de me no'us cal," "The Borrowed Lady," translated by Pound in 1914 (P, 105) and the basis of the 1908 "Na Audiart."

The voice at Montfort . . . worthy of you: summary of "The Borrowed Lady."

Maent: the Lady Maent of Montaignac to whom Born addresses his poem.

Montfort: Lady Elis of Montfort, Maent's sister.

Agnes: Lady of Rochecouart.

Bel Miral: "Fair Mirror," an unidentified lady.

viscountess: of Chalais, Tibors of Montausier.

Montaignac: Maent's castle southeast of Périgueux.

One: the Viscountess of Chalais; another: Audiart of Malemort; cf. "Na Audiart."

Brive: place east of Périgueux.

Tairiran: Guillem Tairilan or Talairan, Maent's husband; modern "Talleyrand."

brother-in-law: Helias Talairan, count of Perigord, Maent's brother-in-law.

Altaforte: Hautefort, Bertran's castle, east of Périgueux, more or less at the center or "hub" of the castles named.

What could he do . . . : Dante places Bertran in the Ninth Circle of Hell as a "Maker of Discord" because he set Prince Henry against his brother Richard and his father Henry II. (*Inferno*, XXVIII)

had his way: Pound implies that Bertran staged the grief he showed at Prince Henry's death, which appeared so great that, ironically, Henry II forgave him, despite all the trouble he had caused. See 11. 40–46, and "Planh for the Young English King."

counterpass: Dante's Bertran, carrying his severed head in his hand, says "Cosi s'osserva in me lo contrapasso"; "thus do I show forth divine retribution"—meaning that his punishment of being divided from himself fits his sin of stirring up strife between kinsmen.

Poictiers: Poitiers, north of Périgueux.

Foix: south of Périgueux, near Montségur.

four brothers: possibly the brothers Talairan (Helias, Guillem, Olivier de Mauriac, and Ramnulf); or the sons of Henry II (Prince Henry, Richard Coeur de Lion, Geoffrey of Brittany, and John of England).

"Pawn . . . pay": free rendering of lines in a war song by Bertran which Pound elsewhere translates "Barons! put in pawn castles, and towns and cities before anyone makes war on us" (SR, 48). In "Troubadours: Their Sorts and Conditions," he explains, "De Born advises the barons to pawn their castles before making war, thus if they won they could redeem them, if they lost the loss fell on the holder of the mortgage." (LE, 94)

And the great scene . . . : When Bertran was captured by Richard in 1183 and brought before Henry II, the King supposedly pardoned his treason because of his great grief at Prince Henry's death (cf. "Planh for the Young English King"). Pound wondered about the authenticity of this story, and observed that the scene was "well recounted in Smith's *Troubadours at Home*. It is vouched for by many old manuscripts and seems as well authenticated as most Provençal history, though naturally there are found the usual perpetrators of 'historic doubt.'" (*Poetry*, December 1915, 146) the Talleyrand: the modern name of the Talairan family.

Chalais is high . . . : A geographical analysis suggests that Maent's indispensability has political as well as (or rather than) emotional grounds.

"Papiol, / Go forthright . . . : Bertran's speech is a ragbag of allusions to his poems, beginning with the envoy of "Dompna, pois de me no'us cal." It signifies Pound's revolving of Bertran's words in his mind as he seeks the historical motive of the poems. Papiol was the "jongleur" who sang the verses Bertran composed.

Anhes: Agnès, Lady of Rochecouart. Cembelins: the lady from whom Bertran borrows "the expression of her eyes" (SR, 47).

Born of a jongleur's tongue: The pun illustrates Pound's belief that "the involved forms and veiled meanings in the 'trobar clus' . . . played a very real part in love intrigue and in the intrigue preceding warfare." (LE, 94)

St. Leider: Guillem de Saint Leidier, in love with the wife of the Viscount of Polignac, "even went so far as to get the husband of his lady to do the seductive singing." (LE, 94)

*Et albirar* . . . : Provençal: "And sing not all they have in mind," from a song of "the sardonic Count of Foix" (LE, 100–01).

heaumes: helmets, crests; see SR, 46: "The count has commanded [me] to make such a chanson as shall cut a thousand shields [whereby] shall be broken and shattered helms and hauberks and hoquetons and pourpoints."

## Part II

*al, ochaisos:* the first two rhyme sounds of "The Borrowed Lady."

a lean man? . . . : Pound describes Bertran as looking rather like himself.

"magnet": Provençal *aziman*.

Aubeterre: east of Altaforte.

Aelis: Lady of Montfort.

Ventadour: Ventadorn, northeast of Altaforte, where Maent's sister lived.

Arrimon Luc D'Esparo: figure in one of Bertran's poems who transmits to him a command for a war song from the Count of Toulouse (see SR, 46). Pound's speaker conjectures that Arrimon alone perceived the "tactic . . . beneath" Bertran's love song, and that it was he who instigated Richard Coeur-de-Lion's attack on and capture of Altaforte in 1183.

The compact . . . driven out!: Cf. Pound's translation of "A Perigord pres del muralh" (SR, 46).

Arnaut: Arnaut Daniel, another Provençal poet (see SR, chapter II, and LE, "Arnaut Daniel"). Daniel lived at Richard's castle between 1194 and 1199. Pound here pictures the two during Richard's siege of Chalus in 1199, just before Richard's death.

leopards: heraldic term for "the lion passant," the device of Richard Coeur-de-Lion.

de Born is dead: Bertran died about 1215, but disappeared from the scene of Provençal politics much earlier, entering the abbey of Dalon near Altaforte.

*trobar clus:* the difficult, intricate Provençal verse forms of which Arnaut, according to Dante, was an incomparable master.

"best craftsman": Dante called Arnaut "miglior fabbro del parlar materno," "the better craftsman of the mother tongue." Pound titled his essay on Arnaut in SR "Il Miglior Fabbro [the best craftsman]," and Eliot later dedicated *The Waste Land*, which Pound helped him to edit and polish, to "Ezra Pound, il miglior fabbro."

his friend's: Bertran's. Pound saw Arnaut's poetry as the standard for Provençal verse (SPr, 43).

Plantagenet: Richard. her: Maent.

sister: Bertran also sang of Elena, Richard's sister and wife of the Duke of Saxony.

had been well received: Bertran and Richard were reconciled after Bertran regained Altaforte.

"I am an artist . . . both métiers": Richard was both warrior and poet, and in this he resembled Bertran more than did Arnaut.

next day: Richard died on 6 April 1199.

"In sacred odour": phrase used in elegies for clergymen.

apocryphal: Pound wrote, "Nor is it known if Benvenuto da Imola speaks for certain when he says En Arnaut went in his age to a monastery." (LE, 109)

*Surely I saw* . . . : Pound translates Dante's description of Bertran in *Inferno*, XXVIII, lines 118–23, 139–42. Cf. lines 21–27.


## Part III

This section originally began with two lines in Bertran's voice, canceled after the poem was published in *Poetry:*

> "I loved a woman. The stars fell from heaven
> And always our two natures were in strife."

Cf. "Or take En Bertrans?" at the end of Part II.

Epigraph: "And they were two in one and one in two" (SR, 45), said by Dante of the headless trunks swinging their heads like lanterns in the Ninth Circle of Hell, and here commenting on the love of Bertran and Maent, pictured as swinging between serenity and turbulence.

Auvezere: a river near Altaforte.

day's eyes: daisies. émail: enameling.

There shut up . . . : Bertran laments his separation from Maent, imagining her only true life as the life she lived with him. The last line betrays this illusion: if she is "A broken bundle of mirrors" to others, then she is no more to him—one moment in "a shifting change." The line also refers to the problem with which the poem begins and ends: that of trying to read the past in the broken fragments which its art preserves.

# Cathay (1915)

Pound's *Cathay* began with a gift of fortune. In 1912, he met Mary Fenollosa, widow of an American scholar of Far Eastern literature, Ernest Fenollosa. Pound at this time was developing Imagist poetics, which has strong affinities with oriental poetics, and had absorbed his share of the taste for things Chinese from the London air. The two soon agreed that Pound should edit Fenollosa's unpublished translations of the Japanese Noh drama and Chinese poetry. From the seventeen-odd notebooks and other manuscripts given him by Mary Fenollosa toward the end of 1913, he brought out *Cathay* (1915), *Certain Noble Plays of Japan* (1916), *'Noh' or Accomplishment* (1917), and *The Chinese Written Character as a Medium for Poetry* (1919).

Pound knew virtually no Chinese at this time, and worked from the notebook texts, which consisted of the Chinese characters beneath which Fenollosa, aided by two Japanese scholars, Mori and Ariga, had written the Japanese pronunciations and rough English translations. He also had available for consultation other English translations by such scholars as Arthur Waley and H. A. Giles. Though, predictably, some Sinologues have raised objections, Pound's translations have a remarkable beauty and ease. Like his "The Seafarer," they carry over the poetry of the original as well as its sense. Whereas other translators had used standard metrical forms, the stylized simplicity of Imagist poetics—direct treatment of the "thing"; no superfluous word; composing by musical phrase rather than metrical line—brought an extraordinary freshness to Pound's translations. Both the Imagist and the Chinese poems embody what might be called an aesthetics of absence or silence, which brings natural objects alive through reticent description. Gombrich quotes a Chinese writer on the analogous aesthetic of Chinese painting: " 'Figures, even though painted without eyes, must seem to look; without ears, must seem to listen. There are things which ten hundred brush strokes cannot depict, but which can be captured by a few simple strokes if they are right. This is truly giving expression to the invisible.'" (208–09) Pound's story of the composition of "In a Station of the Metro" recounts how the poem proceeded from a thirty-line draft to its final two lines, and many of the *Cathay* poems also work by a suppression of signifying language. "The natural object," Pound wrote, "is always the *adequate* symbol." (LE, 5) Pound's poetics, it seems, could compensate in large measure for his lack of Chinese; there is truth in Eliot's claim that Pound is "the inventor of Chinese poetry for our time." (SPF, xvi)

Throughout these notes, I use the Japanese rather than the Chinese pronunciations of the ideograms, since these are used in Pound's source for the poems. Pound himself used the poets' Japanese names; the Chinese names were added later by an editor. The Chinese pronunciations are given by Wai-lim Yip in his much fuller discussion, *Ezra Pound's Cathay*, to which many of these notes are indebted.

# SONG OF THE BOWMEN OF SHU [SP, 49]

The notes to the text Ariga used for this poem record that at the close of the Yin dynasty (1401–1121 B.C.), barbarian invasions of the northern part of China required that the Emperor's troops journey north to subdue them, and that this ode was composed by Bunno, Commander of the Army, to show his sympathy for their sufferings. In return, they fought well, and, in part by their efforts, the Shu dynasty arose.

Pound translated this poem again in ballad form as "Ode 167" in *The Classic Anthology Defined by Confucius* (1954). This version begins,

Pick a fern, pick a fern, ferns are high,
"Home," I'll say; home, the year's gone by

and shows Pound's attempt to mimic the sound structure of the original as he had done in his "The Seafarer" translation. In 1915, however, he had only the Japanese sounds, and was working primarily from the images.

*Cathay* appeared during World War I, and Pound sent this poem along with "Lament of the Frontier Guard" and "South Folk in Cold Country" to his friend the young sculptor Gaudier-Brzeska, who was stationed at the front. Gaudier wrote back from the trenches, "The poems depict our situation in a wonderful way. We do not yet eat the young nor old fern shoots, but we cannot be over victualled where we stand" (GB, 58), and, to another friend, "when you have turned to a warrior, you become hardened to many evils. . . . like the chinese bowmen in Ezra's poem we had rather eat fern shoots than go back now." (Kenner, PE, 203) But such naïve romanticization of the war was not possible for long; Gaudier was killed in 1915, and Pound's bitter hatred of war and the financial interests that foster it informed his work for the rest of his life.

Ken-in: the Huns, or barbarian tribes in the north.

flower: Pound's source omits an answering line, "Flowers of the cherry"; see Yip, 115, 170.

tired: Pound departs from his source, which has "hitched" and "tied." "By heaven" is also his addition.

## THE BEAUTIFUL TOILET [SP, 50]

Pound titled this untitled poem—a version of the "solitary-wife" genre in Chinese poetry—with what is in the original its fifth line, which reads in the notebook:

    beauty of   (ditto)   red powder   toilet
       face

Compare its structure to "The Garden" (SP, 26).

Blue: The ideogram "ch'ing" means blue or green, which the Chinese regard as two shades of one color. While most translators choose "green" here, Pound's "blue" is exotic and suitably melancholy, and saves the line, more "literal" in English than in the Chinese characters, from bathos.

## THE RIVER SONG [SP, 51]

This translation splices together what are actually two poems in the original Chinese. Pound apparently mistook the discursive title of the second—"Poems composed at the command of the Emperor / in I-Chin Park on the Dragon-Pond as the willows are in their fresh green and the new / orioles are singing in their thousand ways" (Yip, 188; cf. ll. 19–22)—for a continuation of the first poem. The original poems are complementary: the first celebrates the "joy" and the permanence of poetry against the transience of earthly delights and kingly glory, and the second commemorates, at the Emperor's command, his pleasure in the delights of spring. Pound, however, has complicated this relation by interpreting the title phrase as the bard's expression of chagrin at his subjection to the Emperor's "order-to-write," in contrast to the birds' "aimless singing." Thus, in Pound's version, the poet no sooner celebrates the power of words than he finds his song in thrall to royal interests, and the last lines (23 ff.) reflect the struggle between the lyric and the official motives for poetry. The error aside, the poem seems less successful than the others in *Cathay*, for the disjunction between the first and second parts makes itself felt in the verse lines and imagery (the "river song" disappears in the last half), as well as the theme, of the translation.

satō-wood: spice wood.

Sennin: The Japanese word for "Chinese spirits of nature or of the air" (SL, 180).

Kutsu: Ch'ü Yüan, a minister. In 1916, Pound published a poem entitled "After Ch'u Yuan" (P, 108) which was based on Giles's version in *A History of Chinese Literature*, but he would not have known from the Fenollosa text that Kutsu is Japanese for "Ch'ü Yüan."

blue islands: "the Fairyland for those who decide to live in seclusion." (Yip, 151).

Han: This river flows south in central China to the Yangtse.

half-blue and bluer: See note to "The Beautiful Toilet."

"Ken-Kwan": onomatopoeic birdsong.

Kō: Chinese Hao, capital during part of the Shu (Chou) dynasty.

Five clouds . . . a-gleaming: In the original poems, the "five clouds" characters also mean "auspicious breath," symbolizing the beneficent influence of the "celestial Emperor"; the "purple sky" symbolizes his dwelling place; and the "imperial guards" are an image of the sun's rays. The ideograms for "Emperor" also mean "sun" and "sky," so that the earthly and celestial emperors become identified.

# THE RIVER-MERCHANT'S WIFE: A LETTER [SP, 52]

This is one of the most delicate poems in *Cathay*, a verse "letter" in which the speaker communicates indirectly, by means of vivid images and shifting tones, the history of her feelings for the absent husband to whom she writes. First, she remembers their friendly play as children. In describing their feelings then as being "without dislike or suspicion," she implies that she did have these feelings at a later time, and they carry over into her description of her unhappiness in their first year of marriage. "At fifteen," she begins to love him, though her imagery and ceremonious language convey a certain reserve: to stop scowling is not to smile, and the image of their mingling dust looks past desire to death. Only in the last section, in which she remembers his departure and voices her present feelings, do we see how that timeless love has changed. In his absence, she has become conscious of time passing and of the preciousness of love in the natural world where nothing can last "forever." Now, his absence makes her miss him, and a language of natural imagery expresses, with eloquent reserve, her desire for his return.

Pound compared the poem to the dramatic monologues of Robert Browning:

> Perhaps the most interesting form of modern poetry is to be found in Browning's "Men and Women." . . . From Ovid to Browning this sort of poem was very much neglected. It is interesting to find, in eighth-century China, a poem which might have slipped into Browning's work without causing any surprise save by its simplicity and its naïve beauty.
>
> ("Chinese Poetry, II," *To-Day*, May 1918, 93-94)

While . . . forehead: This line cost Pound some trouble. The Fenollosa notebook reads, "My hair was at first covering my brows (child's method of wearing hair)." Pound first tried the American "bangs"; Dorothy Pound suggested the English "fringe." Arthur Waley translates it "Soon after I wore my hair covering my forehead," and Amy Lowell and Florence Ayscough, "When the hair of your unworthy one first began to cover the forehead." Yip translates it, "My hair barely covered my forehead."

Chōkan: Chinese Ch'ang-kan, a suburb of Nanking.

Why . . . look out?: Pound omits an allusion to Wi-shang, who "had a date with a girl at a pillar under the bridge. The water came. He died holding tight to the pillar." The remaining image alludes in the original to "a story of a woman waiting for her husband on a hill." (Yip, 192) In Pound's version, the line emphasizes the otherworldly nature of her love during this phase of her marriage, which contrasts vividly with the next section.

Ku-tō-en: Chinese Ch'ü-t'ang, a river of dangerous rocks and impassable rapids. Pound treats the name of the river as the name of a place by the river.

By the gate . . . away: In the original, the mosses have filled his footprints.

Kiang: Ku-tō-en; see above.

Chō-fū-Sa: Chinese Ch'ang-feng-sha or "long wind beach," several hundred miles upriver from Nanking.

# POEM BY THE BRIDGE AT TEN-SHIN [SP, 54]

The sadness of time and the passing of human things, themes that run through *Cathay*, give this poem its subject. Its speaker laments the passing not only of particular things but of better ones: people "of the old days," Ryokushu, Han-rei. Thus, while the opening images of the blown petals might bring consoling thoughts of another spring, they lead instead to the speaker's disenchantment with the present: "But to-day's men are not the men of the old days." Though Pound does not remark its "modernity," as he does that of "The River-Merchant's Wife," this nostalgia exemplifies 4.5.83 one mood of "modern" poetics, the consciousness of a diminished present against a greater past. Its original title, in fact, is "Ku Feng no. 18 (After the Style of Ancient Poems)." (Yip, 196)

Sei-jō-yō: The name of a palace.

court: The original has "capital."

Unwearying autumns: After this line, Pound omits two lines which were unintelligible in Fenollosa's notes: "Mission accomplished, to stay on. Nears, in history, a greater downfall." In the remaining lines, he generalizes the very specific allusions which point this moral in the original poem to a simpler list of paragons of former days. (See Kenner, PE, 205–06, and Yip, 198, for fuller accounts.)

Ryokushu: Chinese Lu-chu, a courtesan who inspired great rivalry.

Han-rei: in the original, a hero for not staying at court once his "mission" was accomplished. Pound's version glorifies his independence.

# THE JEWEL STAIRS' GRIEVANCE [SP, 55]

As Pound's explication shows, part of his attraction to Chinese poetry lay in its finely controlled use of images to evoke and imply rather than to state and describe human emotions. He wrote of this poem, "I have never found any occidental who could make much of that poem at one reading. Yet upon careful examination we find that everything is there, not merely by suggestion but by a sort of mathematical process of reduction. Let us consider what circumstances would be needed to produce just the words of this poem." (*To-Day*, April 1918, 55–56)

my, I: The original does not specify these first-person pronouns. Yip writes that "her/she" could also be used. (66)

# LAMENT OF THE FRONTIER GUARD [SP, 55]

Pound sent *Cathay* to Gaudier-Brzeska at the front in 1915 (see note to "Song of the Bowman of Shu"). Gaudier wrote to a friend, "E[zra] has sent me the Chinese poems. I like them very much. I keep the book in my pocket, indeed I use them to put courage in my fellows. I speak now of the 'Bowmen' and the 'North Gate' which are so appropriate to our case." (GB, 68) Yip sees this translation as the triumph of Pound's creative intuition over Fenollosa's misleading notes, though it is also possible that Pound used other translations to decipher them.

Riboku: Chinese Li Mu, a famous general who died in battle against the Huns in 223 B.C. (Achilles Fang, in Brooker, 140).

This elegiac letter from a poet in exile to a friend of bygone days was Pound's favorite of the *Cathay* poems. Seven years away from America, Pound felt an affinity with the exile persona which is not hard to understand. He published it in *Poetry* in March 1915, a month before *Cathay* appeared, and later included it with "The Seafarer" and "Homage to Sextus Propertius" in his list of "major personae." The one Western poem included in *Cathay* was "The Seafarer," which Pound placed after "Exile's Letter" as a contemporary "exhibit." He later explained,

> I once got a man to start translating the *Seafarer* into Chinese. It came out almost directly into Chinese verse, with two solid ideograms in each half-line.
> Apart from the *Seafarer*, I know no other European poems of the period that you can hang up with the "Exile's Letter" of Li Po, displaying the West on a par with the Orient.
> (ABCR, 51)

The poem's original epigraph reads: "From the Chinese of Rihaku (Li Po), usually considered the greatest poet of China: written by him while in exile about 760 A.D. to the Hereditary War-Councillor of Sho, 'recollecting former companionship.' "

Wai: the Huai River.

Sen-jō: "City of Immortals."

"True man": i.e., a Taoist hermit.

San-ka: "The Tower of Feasting Mist."

Sennin: air spirits (Pound's addition).

blue jade: See note to "The Beautiful Toilet."

Yō Yū's luck: Yō-Yū (Yang Hsiung, 53 B.C.–18 A.D.) was an author who tried to secure a promotion by offering his prose song on the Chōyō Palace.

There . . . heart: Cf. "now in the heart indestructible," Canto LXXVII (C, 465).

# TAKING LEAVE OF A FRIEND [SP, 59]

Wai-lim Yip singles out this poem to illustrate the affinity between the syntactic simplicity of Pound's translation and the "vigorously unanalytical presentation" of the original Chinese. In both, each line, complete in itself, forms with the others a "counterpoint" of visual images that exist simultaneously in the poem like the elements of a landscape. By contrast, Giles' translation confines the images in a more abstract syntactic frame which disposes them in hierarchical relations and temporal succession:

> Where blue hills cross the northern sky,
> Beyond the moat which girds the town,
> 'Twas there we stopped to say Goodbye!
>
> (Yip, 12–21)

# A BALLAD OF THE MULBERRY ROAD [SP, 60]

Pound translates only the first fourteen of the fifty-three lines of the original, which narrates Rafu's refusal of the Prefect's overtures.

Rafu . . . "Gauze Veil": "Rafu" is a proper name; "Gauze Veil" is Pound's invention.

Katsura: cassia.

green: Yip has "yellow." overskirt: Yip has "jacket."

# Hugh Selwyn Mauberley (1920)

This suite of eighteen short poems marks a crucial turning point in Pound's career: it is a farewell to the aestheticism which has played a large part in his poetry up to this point, and, at the same time, an ironic and bitter indictment of modern society, in which what we now refer to as "Kitsch" has displaced serious art. The tension between these two motives accounts for the poem's complexity of tone. Pound's ironies are directed equally at his own misconceived attempts to "wring lilies from the acorn" and at the social values which provide the artist nothing but acorns. Critics have confused the issue by trying to choose between these positions, imagining that if Pound is criticizing the modern world, then he must be vindicating the artist, or vice versa; but the two coexist in *Mauberley*, the image that "the age demanded." Pound comes to terms with his historical situation not by abandoning his ideal of high art, but by maintaining it in ironic contrast to the products of modern culture. He does not value his own or Mauberley's aestheticist productions, which only affirm the social irrelevance of art; but at the same time he neither denies nor approves a society whose authentic art is on the order of the "prose kinema" and the "mould in plaster."

In ironically measuring modern industrial society—which turns art into a commodity and which, more generally, alienates the human mind from the world of things—against the ancient world that produced the poetry of Sappho, Pound in effect implies the impossibility of a modern "renaissance" without drastic change in the economic and social structures of society. *Mauberley* thus initiates the emphasis in Pound's later work on the necessity of altering the dehumanizing economic system of modern society. In "Murder by Capital" (1933), he explained his position thus: "What drives . . . a man interested almost exclusively in the arts, into social theory or into a study of the 'gross material aspects' vidilicet

79

economic aspects of the present? . . . I have blood lust because of what I have seen done to, and attempted against, the arts in my time." (SPr, 228–29) Though it might be argued that this is only a more militantly aestheticist stance, Pound considered the art of a society to be an index to its vitality. The relationship between Pound and his character Mauberley has been much debated, but what it seems to come down to is that the parody of the aesthete Pound fashions in Mauberley is also a self-parody which exorcises the *fin-de-siècle* decadent who wrote some of his early poems. If, Pound's later work sometimes takes him to solipsistic isles, it is clear at least that these are not his hero's "scattered Moluccas."

*Mauberley's* measuring of the modern world against the past has been termed nostalgic. This, however, is something of a red herring. While Pound clearly values the integration of spiritual and material life in the culture of ancient Greece, it is just as clear from the second part of the poem that an imaginary escape into the past, exemplified in Mauberley's neoclassicism, is neither possible nor desirable. The modern artist cannot escape history by retreating to a subjective tropical island, or by imitating the art of the ancients. The memories of Sappho and Samothrace are not antiquarian trophies but evidence that more strongly life-affirming cultures have existed in the past and might be achieved again. Posing imagery of "to kalon," of beauty and nobility, against the imagery of debased modern culture, *Mauberley* combines what Pound referred to as "the art of cure" and "the art of diagnosis." (LE, 45) In this, it prefigures *The Cantos*.

A major factor in Pound's approach to the turning point of *Mauberley* was World War I. As its fifth poem makes clear, the war brought home to him the contradiction between his idealization of high culture and the historical atrocities committed in spite of culture, or even in its name: "For a botched civilization . . . / For two gross of broken statues, / For a few thousand battered books." The war made him question the value of art and its relation to life as nothing else had; it refocused his career as an "investigation of causes of war, to oppose same." (SP, "Biography") In this, broadly speaking, he conceived himself to be following the example of Henry James, a fellow expatriate from "half savage" America, and a penetrating analyst of lives like those of Mauberley, Mr. Nixon, and the Lady Jane. *Mauberley* was, he wrote, "a study in form, an attempt to condense the James novel." (SL, 180) As John Espey and others have observed, many details of *Mauberley* echo James's novels, and the poem is structured as a series of vignettes which resemble the Jamesian "scene." Most important, however, was the influence of what Pound referred to as "the major James." In his 1918 essay, Pound honored James for "a lifetime spent in trying to make two continents understand one another, and . . . three nations intelligible to one another." No one, he wrote, had "so labored to create means of communication as did the late Henry James"; and "Peace comes of communication": "Henry James' perception came thirty years before Armageddon. That is all I wish to point out. . . . Artists are the antennac of the race, but the bullet-headed many will never learn to trust their great artists." (LE, 296–98) This struggle for communication between different nations, and not the "pettiness" which Pound was "tired of hearing . . . about Henry James's *style*," was the real lesson of the master, the legacy of the major James to the major Pound.

*Mauberley* is divided into two parts. The first part opens with a mock-burial of "E. P.," the aesthete in Pound, followed by eleven London vignettes, and concludes with an "Envoi," or send-off, for the whole. The second part, subtitled "Mauberley," depicts the character, career, and fate of this fictional aesthete in the first four poems, and concludes with "Medallion," an example of Mauberley's art.

# E. P. ODE POUR L'ELECTION DE
# SON SEPULCHRE                          [sp, 61]

In this "Ode for the Selection of His Tomb," Pound buries his former self under an epitaph which sums up his career to the age of thirty-one and finds that it brings no glory to the Muses. Some of his phrases echo early reviewers: Wyndham Lewis called him "a man in love with the past," and others found him "out of date," "out of tune," "an anachronism." Pound is not, as some have thought, parodying his reviewers here but agreeing with them; not to understand this is to project one's own aestheticism upon him. In 1913 Pound had remarked ironically of his early poems, "You were praised, my books, / because I had just come from the country; / I was twenty years behind the times / so you found an audience ready" ("Salutation the Second," *Poetry*, April). Now he again assesses his work, and finds that he had succumbed to the siren song of "Literature": his early poetics was a literary one, modeled on art and not on life. This imaginary funeral marks a break between the early career and the later. The aesthete buried, a reborn E. P. begins his most important work.

The quatrain stanza which Pound uses throughout *Mauberley* is an English version of Théophile Gautier's *Émaux et Camées* (1852) stanza. It is the "Bay Psalm Book" stanza rendered modern and ironic by means of unpredictable, cosmopolitan rhymes (*Troie* / lee-way, *trentuniesme* / diadem) and idiosyncratically paced lines. The effect is deliberately "out of key," as in the over-reaching "Bent resolutely on wringing lilies from the acorn."

Title: Pound adapted his title from an ode of Ronsard's, "De l'Election de son sépulcre"; and built in a pun on "epode," which refers to the concluding section of a Greek lyric ode, following the strophe and antistrophe, and also to the shorter line of an irregular couplet.

three years: Cf. Mauberley's three years as "diabolus in the scale" (SP, 72). The last line indicates that Pound has 1913–16 in mind.

"the sublime" / In the old sense: In the ancient treatise "On the Sublime," ascribed to Longinus, the sublime is defined as "the echo of greatness of spirit," a spark leaping from the writer's soul to the reader's.

half savage country: America, where Pound lived until 1908.

lilies from the acorn: Compare Pound's description of the integrity of the ideas and emotions which make up the image in "The Serious Artist": they "must be in harmony, they must form an organism, they must be an oak sprung from an acorn." (LE, 51)

Capaneus: one of the "seven against Thebes," whose story is told in Aeschylus' play of that title and in Euripides' *The Suppliants*. Seeking to help Polyneices take Thebes from his brother Eteocles, Capaneus boasted that not even Zeus could stop him from gaining the city, and was duly destroyed; he is found unrepentant and scalded by his own anger in Canto XIV of the *Inferno*. In Canto LXXIX (487), Pound again likens himself to Capaneus, defiant in defeat.

Ἴδμεν γάρ τοι πάνθ᾽, ὅσ᾽ ἐνὶ Τροίῃ (Idmen gar toi panth', hos' eni Troie): Greek, translating, with Homer's next line: "For we know all that [the Akhaians and Trojans sweated out] in Troy" (*Odyssey*, XII.189). This is the first line of the song that the dangerous Sirens sing to Odysseus as he sails by strapped to the mast of his ship so as not to give himself up to that fatally alluring song. (His crewmen were oblivious to the song, for he had plugged their ears with beeswax.) Identified with Odysseus (a recurrent alter ego in *The Cantos*), "E. P." succumbs to the lure of the classics, cracking up on their rocks instead of navigating through them to his own language and world.

Penelope: wife of Odysseus, to whom he returns at the end of the *Odyssey*.

Flaubert: Gustave Flaubert (1821–80), the French novelist, greatly admired by Pound, whose advocacy of *le mot juste*—the precise word (or, as Marshall McLuhan translates it, "the most juice")—influenced the Imagist reform of the "slush" which poetic language had become. Odysseus was ten years getting back to Penelope, detained by the goddess Circe and other adventures; and Pound here implies that E. P. lingered too long by the obstinate British isles. Circe, in the *Odyssey*, is a formidable seducer.

"the march of events": Pound disclaims the cliché by placing it in quotation marks. He had written to Harriet Monroe that poetry must avoid "clichés, set phrases, stereotyped journalese . . . by . . . concentrated attention to what one is writing" (SL, 49); here, the cliché is "*le mot juste*" for that to which E. P. has not been paying attention.

*l'an trentuniesme / De son eage:* French: "the thirty-first year of his age," adapted from the first line of François Villon's *Testament:* "En l'an trentiesme de mon age" ("In the thirtieth year of my age"). The thirty-first year of Pound's age was 1915–16. The fact that "E. P." exits under the aegis of Villon is significant; Villon was, Pound wrote, "the

first voice . . . broken by bad economics." (ABCR, 104) The "Ode"
thus ends in an enigmatic irony that partially appeals the case of E. P.,
and leads into the second poem, which treats the failures of the age.


## II                                                    [SP, 61]


Having buried his past, Pound now portrays the antipathy of his
age to serious art. His own art is ironically transformed by his
subject: he answers the age's demand for "an image / Of its ac-
celerated grimace" with the brilliant caricature of HSM itself.

The age demanded . . . : Contrast Pound's elegiac portrayal of Laur-
ence Binyon in *The Pisan Cantos*, whose line "Slowness is beauty"
Pound quotes there several times. Cf. Henry James's remark in *A Little
Tour in France:* "As we all know, this is an age of prose, of machinery,
of wholesale production, of coarse and hasty processes." (32)

accelerated grimace: Pound referred to the Futurist movement as "a
kind of accelerated impressionism," and was "wholly opposed" to its
aesthetic principles and its "curious tic of destroying past glories." (GB,
90)

Attic grace: the pure style of ancient Attica, a region of south-central
Greece dominated by Athens.

Better mendacities . . . : Cf. Pound's reply to a reviewer who objected
to his modernization of Propertius: "there is a perfectly literal and, by
the same token, perfectly lying and 'spiritually' mendacious translation
of 'Vobiscum est Iole etc.' in my earlier volume *Canzoni*." (Homberger,
164; see headnote to "Homage to Sextus Propertius," p. 110 below.)

a mould in plaster: Gaudier, who was always on the verge of starvation
and could rarely afford good stone for his work, proposed plaster for
his famous bust of Pound. Pound bought a half-ton block of marble
instead. (Norman, 135)

a prose kinema: In its early years, cinematography was more a medium
of social history than a serious art, characterized by slapstick and self-

mocking exploitation of its own inherent "realism." Its status as a machine art of instant images opposed it to the more arduous craft of cutting shapes into stone or words.

# III                                                    [SP, 62]

Pound illustrates the "tawdry cheapness" of late capitalist culture by juxtaposing its artifacts, conventions, and spirit against their classic counterparts.

tea-gown: a *haute couture* confection popular in the early 1900s, a long dress adorned with lace, ruffles, tucks, pleats, flounces, sashes, etc. Like the tea-rose, a hybrid miniature rose deemed exceptionally elegant, the tea-gown expresses for Pound decadent triviality. Gautier's *Emaux et Camées* includes a poem titled "La Rose-thé."

mousseline: French: muslin. Cos: Greek island which produced a fine, light cloth for the classic draperies of ancient dress. Cf. "If she goes in a gleam of Cos, in a slither of dyed stuff" (HSP, V.32).

pianola: a mechanical device fed by a roll of perforated paper which turns a piano into a "player piano." Pound considered the piano a decadent instrument: "Once people played . . . gracious, exquisite music . . . on instruments which gave out the players' exact mood and personality. . . . The clavichord has the beauty of three or four lutes played together. . . . [Now] we have come to the pianola." (LE, 433)

barbitos: Greek: lyre. Sappho: (fl. early sixth century B.C.) the great Greek lyric poet whose verse, which survives only in fragments, exemplifies the classic love lyric, expressing intense passion in perfectly controlled meter. In her time the lyric was sung or chanted to the accompaniment of the lyre. Music and language were thus fused intellectually and sensually. Pound observed that "both in Greece and in Provence the poetry attained its highest rhythmic and metrical brilliance at times when the arts of verse and music were most closely knit together." (LE, 91) The fragmentary remains of Sappho's lyrics influenced the Imagist poetics of Richard Aldington, H. D., and Pound. Cf. "Imerro" (SP, 37).

Christ follows . . . : Pound contrasts the ancient ecstatic rites of the Greek god Dionysos, god of wine, music, and tragedy, with the derivative Christian rite of "macerating" Christ's body in the symbolic communion wafer.

Caliban, Ariel: in Shakespeare's *The Tempest*, "a savage and deformed Slave" and "an airy Spirit," respectively.

Heracleitus: Greek philosopher (540–480 B.C.) who taught that all things in the universe are constantly changing. Pound insists ironically on the durability of the "tawdry cheapness" he is describing,

the Christian beauty: The great art to which the Christian religion gave rise—for example, Italian Renaissance poetry, painting, sculpture, and architecture—is no longer produced; it is as much a part of the past as the famous "Winged Victory" statue, made on the Greek island of Samothrace where Dionysiac rites were practiced, and which St. Paul visited, spreading the Christian word. Pound later wrote that he was doubtful "whether you can attain a living catholicism save after a greek pagan revival. That again is why Christianity is tolerable in Italy and an offence in England, France, and most of Russia." (GK, 191)

τὸ καλόν (to kalon): Greek: nobility, goodness, beauty (see GK, 316).

Faun's flesh: i.e., the ecstatic Dionysiac rites.

the press . . . franchise: Pound here implies the degeneration of Christianity from mystical vision to modern materialist culture, in which revelation is the province of journalists, tradition is bought by franchise, and the ritual of communion centers on the daily newspaper.

Pisistratus: (605–527 B.C.) Athenian tyrant who gained popularity by liberal laws, encouraged Dionysiac worship, and nurtured the arts. Pound ironically contrasts beneficent tyranny with ineffectual democracy.

Apollo: Greek god of poetry.

τίν' ανδρα, τίν' ἤρωα, τινα θεόν, (tin' andra, tin' heroa, tina theon): Greek: "What man, what hero, what god," adapted from Pindar's Olympian Ode II.2: "What god, what hero, what man shall we loudly praise?" Pound points out "the gulf between TIS O SAPPHO ADIKEI, and Pindar's big rhetorical drum TINA THEON, TIN' EROA, TIN D'ANDREA KELADESOMEN, which one should get carefully fixed in the mind," in a letter to Iris Barry (SL, 91).

tin wreath: in contrast to the ancient tradition of the laurel wreath. Pound puns on "tin' " in line 26, suggesting by his cheap tin wreath the degradation of the arts in the machine age, and leads ironically into the fourth poem, in which he crowns not "heroes" but the naïve youths who lost their lives in World War I.


# IV                                                          [SP, 63]


There were ten million casualties in World War I, a castastrophe so overwhelming that it seemed to attest, as Virginia Woolf put it, that "After 1910 human nature changed." This poem exemplifies the bitter disillusionment which blighted Western consciousness after this grueling four-year slaughter, and reflects Pound's view that the war was perpetuated by the lies, stupidity, and financial interests of those in power.

in any case: This phrase registers the moral ambiguity of the war, and contrasts ironically with the rhetorical heroics of Pindar's "big rhetorical drum" at the end of III.

pro domo: Latin: "for home."

Some quick . . . : a catalogue of the young men's naïve expectations of the war.

pro patria . . . "decor": The Latin words come from Horace's famous line, "Dulce et decorum est pro patria mori" ("It is sweet and fitting to die for one's country"; Odes XII.ii.13), which Pound negates: "It is not sweet and not fitting."

eye-deep in hell: World War I, with its seemingly interminable trench warfare, frequently inspired comparisons to hell in its literature. Gaudier had described it thus to Pound in letters, writing that the trenches were "a sight worthy of Dante, there was at the bottom a foot deep of liquid mud in which we had to stand two days and two nights, rest we had in small holes nearly as muddy, add to this a position making a V point into the enemy who shell us from three sides, the close vicinity of 800 putrefying German corpses, and you are at the front in the marshes of Aisne." (GB, 59)

usury: the practice of lending money at exorbitant interest rates, "without regard to production; often without regard to the possibilities of production." (C, 230) Pound judged financial interests, not patriotism, to be the real cause of the war; hence the necessity of "liars in public places." Cf. Cantos XIV, XV, XXXVIII, XLV, LI.

## V                                                   [SP, 64]

Pound's small, bitter elegy for the war dead looks deceptively simple. Though he deliberately does not name any of the "myriad" war dead, lines 5–6 recall his descriptions of Gaudier-Brzeska, and the poem as a whole recalls his memoir of Gaudier, which opens with the statement, "It is part of the war waste. Among many good artists, among other young men of promise there was this one sculptor already great in achievement at the age of twenty-three, incalculably great in promise and in the hopes of his friends." (GB, 17) They died, he says, not for honor or freedom but for "a botched civilization . . . two gross of broken statues, / For a few thousand battered books." The very fact of the war, Pound implies, is evidence of the failure of Western cultural traditions. The idealism of the young who went off to fight was inspired by those traditions (see Gaudier's comparison of the trenches to Dante's *Inferno* above), but this idealism obscured the brute fact of the war, and the end result was the sacrifice of the living present to an illusion thrown up by the past. Pound's bitterness about culture arises from the discrepancy between its illusions and the actual values which direct the course of history; he sees the glorification of war as a screen, a lure, which obscures the true interests of power and facilitates the manipulation of the people to the service of those interests.

It is worth remarking that in the two war poems, IV and V, Pound abandons his ironic quatrains for sparely carved free-verse lines, which express more subtly the complex tones of elegy and irony this subject requires. Compare its treatment here with Canto XVI.

Quick eyes . . . lid: Pound is recalling line 23 of the Old English poem "The Wanderer," in which earth's lid covers a dead companion. (Robinson, 204)

## YEUX GLAUQUES [SP, 65]

Pound continues the theme of the hypocritical schism between social realities and what is officially admitted to be the case in this poem about Pre-Raphaelite art and its reception in mid-nineteenth-century England. The title, "Grey Eyes," refers to a painting by the Pre-Raphaelite artist Edward Burne-Jones, "King Cophetua and the Beggar-Maid," now in the Tate Gallery in London. Elizabeth Siddal, who married Rossetti, modeled for this painting and many others by Rossetti, Hunt, and Millais; her life was difficult and miserable, and she eventually committed suicide. Pound sees her image as expressing the moral and social malaise of mid-Victorian England, of which Pre-Raphaelite art is both critique and symptom. Official "morality," represented by Gladstone and Buchanan, is posed ironically against the sentimental aestheticism of the Pre-Raphaelite artists, who turned the misery of the prostitute into beautiful images. (David Cecil records that Burne-Jones said he was concerned in "King Cophetua" "to represent the beggar maid as convincingly poverty-stricken without introducing the ugliness of poverty" [147].) The woman's glazed eyes, alienated from body, sensual joy, and love, become a focal point for the malaise of a culture that condemns her while exploiting her for its own purposes.

Gladstone: William Gladstone, British Chancellor of the Exchequer and then Liberal Prime Minister during the period 1859–94. Pound later wrote that "in any international light of the 1930s Russell and Gladstone are, personally, comics, but given the proportion of their own time they were serious matters. . . . Their general attitude toward life [was] ridiculous. But Gladstone did not like Bomba's treatment of political prisoners." (GK, 262–63)

John Ruskin: (1819–1900), art historian, social critic, and champion of the Pre-Raphaelite artists. In his "Of Kings' Treasuries" (*Sesame and Lilies*, 1865), he inveighs against his compatriots for despising literature, science, art, nature, and compassion, and argues that it is this perversion of national values which permits capitalists to exploit unjust wars for profit, and to divert national treasure and energies from humane and constructive purposes to "ten thousand-thousand-pounds' worth of terror a year." (*Works*, XVIII, 104)

Swinburne: Algernon Charles Swinburne (1837–1909), English poet, who was considered and rejected for the office of poet laureate by Gladstone. Pound points to the irreconcilable differences between the best art of the period and the innocuous official images demanded by the state.

Rossetti: Dante Gabriel Rossetti (1828–82), poet, painter, and founder of the Pre-Raphaelite circle; and an important influence on Pound's early work (see Pound's parody of his "The Blessed Damozel," "Donzella Beata," CEP, 26). "Yeux Glauques" at once honors and takes leave of the Pre-Raphaelite tradition.

Buchanan: Robert Buchanan (1841–1901), a poet and reviewer whose famous attack on the Pre-Raphaelite movement, "The Fleshly School of Poetry" (1871), did Rossetti considerable harm. Pound attacks his hypocritical moralizing, which refused to admit that so unpleasant a fact as prostitution could be a fit subject for poetry, without abandoning his own critical stance toward the aestheticist art that made "a pastime" of such subjects.

hers: Elizabeth Siddal's, the model for the painting (see headnote); but also, more generally, the women whose degradation and victimization helped to sustain the Victorians' fine illusions of themselves.

cartons: drawings for paintings.

English Rubaiyat . . . : Edward FitzGerald's creative translation of *The Rubáiyát of Omar Khayyam*, published in 1859, languished un-read until Rossetti discovered it, "remaindered / at about two pence" (Canto LXXX), the following year. The indifference which greeted this poem celebrating the joys of the earth seemed to Pound an ironic testimony to the denial of the body and sensual life encouraged by "offi-cial" post-Victorian morality.

poor Jenny's case: Rossetti's "Jenny" is a poem about a prostitute, in which the phrase "poor Jenny" recurs. The poem regards the different fates of the prostitute and the men who abuse her with irony; she is another evidence of "a botched civilization":

> Jenny, looking long at you,
> The woman almost fades from view.
> A cipher of man's changeless sum
> Of lust, past, present, and to come,
> Is left. A riddle that one shrinks
> To challenge from the scornful sphinx.

maquero: (French: maquereau) pimp. (But cf. GK, 330: "The greeks, being *maqueros* (happy men) with no moral fervour, left . . . a sense of lack [into which] poured a lot of crass zeal.")

## "SIENA MI FÈ; DISFECEMI MAREMMA" [SP, 66]

Another vignette presenting the end of the aestheticist period which Pound is leaving behind him. "Monsieur Verog" (whose name seems to have been inspired by the exigencies of rhyme) is a fictional name for Victor Plarr (1863–1929), Librarian of the Royal College of Surgeons, whom Pound met in 1909. John Espey glosses many details of this poem from Plarr's *Ernest Dowson*, which Pound reviewed in 1915 (93–96). Plarr, who was born in Strasbourg, came to England in 1870. He was a member of the Rhymers' Club during the nineties, and reminisced obligingly in Pound's attentive company. "Old Plarr has let loose on subject of Strasbourg, 11 stanzas in yesterday's *Times*," Pound wrote his mother in 1918. "He was on the wall there in '70 at the age of seven and saw the Galliffet charge." The atmosphere of his present milieu, "the pickled fœtuses and bottled bones," ironically reflects the "pastness" of the era Pound memorializes in him.

Title: from Dante's *Purgatorio*, V. 134: "Siena made me; Maremma undid me," said by "La Pia dei' Tolomei," murdered by her husband in a castle in the Maremma marshlands; used as the subtitle of Rossetti's painting of La Pia. La Pia's one-line history designates this poem as an epitaph for the nineties, personified in the lone survivor "Verog."

Galliffet: a French general in the Franco-Prussian War, which drove Plarr's family from Strasbourg. Galliffet led his troops in a virtually suicidal charge in the Battle of Sedan.

Dowson: Ernest Dowson (1867–1900), a fellow member of the Rhymers' Club about whom Plarr wrote a book of reminiscences titled, *Ernest Dowson 1888–1897*. Pound judged him "a very fine craftsman" who "epitomized a decade" and earned "a very interesting position, strategically, in the development of the [poetic] art." (Tanselle, 118)

Rhymers' Club: poets' circle founded by Yeats, Rhys, and Rolleston in 1890–91, which included Dowson, Johnson, Symons, Plarr, and Image. Pound observed that "the whole set of 'The Rhymers' did valuable work in knocking bombast, & rhetoric, & victorian syrup out of our verse" (Tanselle, 118).

Johnson: Lionel Johnson (1867–1902), English poet. Pound edited his *Poetical Works* in 1915. Johnson, an alcoholic, was famous for his falls, but the story of his death is not true. It epitomizes, however, the Decadent poets' association of the bohemian life with "purity" of craft.

Newman: Cardinal John Henry Newman (1801–90), Catholic theologian and leader of the Oxford Movement. Johnson and Dowson converted to Catholicism.

Headlam: Rev. Arthur C. Headlam (1849–90), Bishop of Gloucester, forced to resign after lecturing on theater and dance at a club. He pursued his dual interests, founding the Church and Stage Guild with Selwyn Image (1849–1930), whom Pound met in 1909 and found one of "the most worth while" people in London. (Stock, 78)

Bacchus: Roman name for Dionysos, the god of wine, music, ecstasy, and tragedy. Terpsichore: the Muse of Dance. the Church: i.e., the Roman Catholic Church.

"The Dorian Mood": Plarr's book of poems, *In the Dorian Mood* (1896).

## BRENNBAUM [sp, 66]

This poem depicting the deracinated Wandering Jew participates in the racial prejudice which blights much modernist iconography, including works of Henry James, W. B. Yeats, T. S. Eliot, Wyndham Lewis, and Djuna Barnes. Pound eventually repudiated as his "worst mistake" "that stupid suburban prejudice of antisemitism" (Reck, 28–29); he was aware, even as he committed it, that "race prejudice is red herring" (SPr, 299n). It can at least be noted that this is one of the two briefest poems in *Mauberley*, and quite gratuitous. It is neither deeply thought nor deeply felt, and may in fact have originated in imitation of some of the poems that Eliot was producing at the same time (e.g., "Burbank with a Baedeker: Bleistein with a Cigar"):

> At a particular date in a particular room two authors, neither engaged in picking the other's pockets, decided that the dilutation of vers libre, Amygism, Lee Mastersism, general floppiness had gone too far and that some countercurrent must be set going. . . . Remedy prescribed, *Emaux et Camées* (or The Bay State Hymn Book). Rhyme and regular strophes. Results: Poems in Mr. Eliot's second volume . . . , also "H. S. Mauberley."
>
> (*Criterion*, July 1932, 590)

Horeb: the mountain where Moses struck the rock a second time to make water flow for his people, and was punished by God for his lack of faith with forty years of wandering in the desert.

Sinai: the mountain where Moses received the Ten Commandments.

An ironic updating of Henry James's famous story, "The Lesson of the Master," this portrait of the "successful" writer who advises the younger one to abandon serious art and aim for commercial success may be based on Arnold Bennett, an English journalist, editor, and novelist who bought his first yacht in 1912. Pound had alluded to "the click of Mr. Bennett's cash-register finish" in a 1918 review, but noted years later when reprinting it that "E. P. rather modified his view of part of Bennett's writing when he finally got round to reading *An Old Wives' Tale* many years later" (LE, 429). While he scorned Bennett's practical-minded career at first, he later said of him, "I might have made money if my snobbishness, which was at its height, hadn't made me sneer at this commoner"; and "we were so aesthetic that Arnold Bennett got on my nerves, and I lost great opportunities." (Olson, 78, 142) At the time he composed "Mr. Nixon," however, Pound associated commercial art with slovenly work, as the mockingly irregular stanzas, lines, and rhymes of this poem imply.

Dr. Dundas: fictional name for a powerful figure of the literary establishment.

Blougram: an allusion to Robert Browning's "The Bishop Orders His Tomb," in which Bishop Blougram is shown to have lost all glimmerings of the divine light in the zealous pursuit of his worldly interests.

Don't kick . . . : Christ tells Paul before his conversion in Acts 9:5, "it is hard for thee to kick against the pricks." Pound probably takes it via Whistler's *The Gentle Art of Making Enemies* (1890): "I feel the folly of kicking against the parish pricks." (225)

This contrasting portrait of the literary "stylist" is based on an interlude in the life of Ford Madox Ford, author of *The Good*

*Soldier,* who retreated in 1919 to a picturesque cottage with a big hole in the roof where he wrote, gardened, and cooked masterpieces of various genres.

## XI                                                                      [sp, 68]

A lampoon of middle-class sexual mores. Pound found the phrase "des femmes . . . ces conservatrices des traditions milesiennes" ("women . . . these conservers of Milesian traditions") in Remy de Gourmont's short story "Stratagèmes." He quotes it as an example of controlled "tonal variation" (LE, 345), and alludes to it in "Postscript to the *Natural Philosophy of Love*": "Woman, the conservator, the inheritor of past gestures, clever, practical, as Gourmont says . . . has always been the enemy of the dead or laborious form of compilation, abstraction." (PD, 213) "Milesian" is the word which, used as a synecdoche for traditions, gives the "tone": the erotic Greek "Milesian Tales" have not survived, nor has the "tradition" been otherwise conserved. T. S. Eliot's famous modern lovers, the typist and the young man carbuncular of *The Waste Land,* may have been inspired by Pound's suburbanites. Both scenes use rhyme as an instrument of satire.

Ealing: a London suburb, now a borough.

## XII                                                                     [sp, 69]

A portrait of the fashionable London literary salon of the period which institutionalized the belletristic isolation of art from social reality that *Mauberley* condemns. Cf. Pound's "Portrait d'une Femme" (SP, 16) and Eliot's "Portrait of a Lady."

"Daphne . . . hands": Pound translates two lines of Gautier: "Daphne, les hanches dans l'écorce, / Etend toujours ses doigts touffus" ("Le Château du Souvenir," *Emaux et Camées*). In Greek mythology, Daphne, a mortal, fled from the god Apollo, who had fallen in love with her, and was metamorphosed into a laurel tree.

Lady Valentine: fictitious name for a London literary hostess, possibly modeled on Lady Ottoline Morrell.

Knowing my coat . . . : Cf. J. Alfred Prufrock's self-consciousness about his dress.

vocation: Pound elaborates in *Patria Mia:* "It has been well said of the 'lady in society' that art criticism is one of her functions. She babbles of it as of 'the play,' or of hockey, or of 'town topics.' " (SPr, 122)

the Lady Jane: the name of the literary hostess in Henry James's "The Figure in the Carpet."

"Which the highest cultures . . .": Pound translates Jules Laforgue's "Menez l'âme que les Lettres ont bien nourrie" from "Complainte des Pianos." (Espey, 65)

Fleet St.: a street in London where writers such as Samuel Johnson "flourished" in the eighteenth century, now a center for journalism.

Pierian roses: Pieria in Greece is in legend the birthplace of the Muses. Pound alludes to one of Sappho's lines, which translates "for you hold no claim to the Pierian roses" (fragment LXXI).

ENVOI (1919)                                                      [SP, 70]

An envoy is an author's parting word to a literary composition, often, as here, addressed to the book itself. On one level, this "Envoi" is a send-off to Part I of *Mauberley.* On another, it is a new version of Edmund Waller's seventeenth-century song, "Go, Lovely Rose," which was set to music by the English composer Henry Lawes (1596–1662); and on another, it is an example of the aestheticist poetics which Pound has been criticizing throughout *Mauberley.*

As an envoy, the poem reverberates with ironies. Pound judged that poetry reached its highest achievements in language bound up with music. In English poetry, the "great lyric age lasted while Campion made his own music, while Lawes set Waller's verses, while verses, if not actually sung or set to music, were at least made with the intention of going to music" (ABCR, 60–61). In 1918 he expressed his "desire to resurrect the art of the lyric, I mean words to be sung. . . . there is scarcely anything since the time of Waller and Campion. AND a mere imitation of them won't do." (SL, 128) The "Envoi" surpasses imitation, as we see from Waller's first stanza:

> Go, lovely rose!
> Tell her that wastes her time and me
> That now she knows
> When I resemble her to thee,
> How sweet and fair she seems to be.

Pound's song is in a sense about the fact that song is absent from *Mauberley* as a whole; its graceful free verse, archaic diction and syntax, and traditionally "poetic" sentiments and imagery reproach the age in which such graces are anachronistic. At the same time, though lovely in itself, the poem is "out of key" with its time; it is beautiful, but dumb-born. In the duplicity of its motives, the "Envoi" is a brilliantly contrived exit from the double bind Pound represents in *Mauberley*, though also a one-time solution.

The "Envoi" has, understandably, generated a certain amount of critical confusion. While it is obviously an extraordinarily accomplished poem, it is at the same time about its own out-of-placeness in the very world *Mauberley* portrays. In being about that, however, it reinstates itself as a contemporary poem which does not merely imitate Waller's song but self-consciously "modernizes" it. It is at once critical and self-critical, like *Mauberley* as a whole. Its date and its placement here at the end of Part I mark it as a transitional poem which embodies all the contradictions of the poet's position in modern society.

*dumb-born:* Cf. "still-born" in "Yeux Glauques."

*her:* Asked "Who sang you once that song of Lawes?" Pound objected that the question was out of order, but Jo Brantley Berryman has shown that it was Raymonde Collignon, who sang some troubadour lyrics that Pound had collected in London in 1918; Pound reviewed this concert and two of her later ones.

*I would bid . . . braving time:* that is, by writing songs to immortalize them.

*gain her worshippers:* a compounding of several senses: first, that a future singer will replace her, thus "gaining her worshippers"; second, that this singer will sing the "Envoi" itself, whose "magic amber" preserves the former's graces, thereby gaining her new worshippers; and finally, that song itself, the "Beauty" that is left of their "two dusts," will find new worshippers in future.


## Part Two

The last five poems were originally subtitled "Part II. / 1920 / (Mauberley)," and the first poem was "I."


## MAUBERLEY (1920)　　　　　　　　　[SP, 71]


The first question this poem raises is the central one of who Mauberley is, and what his relation to Pound is. Pound remarked that "Mauberley buries E.P. in the first poem; gets rid of all his troublesome energies" (Connolly, 59). Mauberley appears to be another kind of aesthete, one who has "turned from" the ethereal productions of Pound's early Pre-Raphaelite aestheticism, but whose own engraver's art is but a soul-less antiquarianism. "His true Penelope," like E. P.'s, "Was Flaubert"; but as E. P. falls for the sirens' lure, Mauberley becomes a lotus-eater. Though Pound remarked, "Of course, I'm no more Mauberley than Eliot is Prufrock," it is probably true that he invented Mauberley at least in part to exorcise this aspect of himself. As John Espey puts it, Mauberley is not

Pound but "a mask of what he feared to become as an artist by remaining in England." (83) The first poem, a companion piece to the "E. P. Ode," sets out Mauberley's aesthetic program along with its limitations.

Epigraph: "He bites at the empty air," adapted from Ovid's *Metamorphoses*, VII.786, which describes Cephalus' dog as he tries to bite the monster that was ravaging Thebes. The dog pursued the monster, and both were turned to stone. The line is an ironic image of Mauberley, whom Pound here turns to stone in the poem, as it were, capturing the futile gestures of his art. Cf. the end of poem II.

eau-forte: French: etching.

Jacquemart: Jules Jacquemart (1837–80), Parisian artist who did an etching of Gautier for the frontispiece of the 1881 edition of *Emaux et Camées*.

Messalina: Valeria Messalina, the profligate wife of the Roman emperor Claudius, who had her murdered in 48 A.D. Her image was engraved on Roman coins.

"His . . . Flaubert": Cf. the "E. P. Ode." Mauberley's art, like "E. P." 's, was based on artistic models and not on life.

Pier Francesca: Piero della Francesca (1420–92), Umbrian painter renowned for innovations in perspective and for mastery of light and atmosphere.

Pisanello: Antonio Pisano (1395–1455?), Italian Renaissance artist from Verona whose medals are valued as historic memorials of the period. Pound wrote that medallions and seals indicate a high level of civilization, "carried down and out into details." (GK, 159) Cf. Canto LXXIV (C, 447).

# II                                                      [SP, 72]

This poem is a fable of Mauberley's uncomprehending response to the urgings of Eros, which confuse his perception and interfere with his artistic application. By the time he wakes up, both Eros and his Muse have fled. Pound was much occupied with the theme of the connection between sexual and creative power. His "Postscript" to Gourmont's *The Natural Philosophy of Love* indulges in flights of pseudoscientific whimsy, and returns at the end to Propertius: "Perhaps the clue is in Propertius after all: *Ingenium nobis ipsa puella fecit*" ("My genius is only a girl"; PD, 214).

Epigraph: "Caid Ali" is a Persian pseudonym of Pound's, carrying associations of FitzGerald's *Rubáiyát*. The French translates: "What do they know of love, and what can they know? If they do not understand poetry, if they do not feel music, what can they know of that passion beside which the rose is crude and the scent of violets a thunderbolt?"

For three years: cf. "E. P. Ode."

diabolus: The "devil" in the musical scale is the augmented fourth, a dissonant interval forbidden to medieval academic composers (an example is the first two notes of Leonard Bernstein's "Maria" in *West Side Story*). Yeats remarked on the Imagists' "devil's metres." (LE, 378)

ambrosia: the food of the gods.

ANANGKE: Greek: fate or necessity.

Arcadia: an image of earthly paradise in Greek, Roman, and Renaissance poetry, named for a pastoral district in ancient Greece.

He had . . . phantasmagoria: The phrase has an antecedent in James's *The Ambassadors* (1903), in which Strether tells Maria Gostrey, "Of course I moved among miracles. It was all phantasmagoric." (Kenner, PEP, 176) Pound adapted it to his own purposes, writing in 1918, "certain men move in phantasmagoria; the images of their gods, whole countrysides, stretches of hill land and forest, travel with them." (SPr, 424) See also Ian F. A. Bell, "The Phantasmagoria of Hugh Selwyn Mauberley," *Paideuma*, V (1976), 361–85.

NUKTIS 'AGALMA: Greek: night's jewel, from Bion's apostrophe to Hesperus, the evening star, in Poem IX.

orchid: the Greek word "orchis" means "testicle." Pound's metaphor for Mauberley's sexuality comments sardonically on his "phantasmagoria."

TO AGATHON: Greek: the good.

sieve . . . seismograph: two of Pound's "scientific" figures for the artist's powers. He writes elsewhere of the artist as a "talented sieve" (PD, 213) and of a necessary (Jamesian) sensitivity to "vibrations" (LE, 331).

verbal manifestation: Pound wrote in 1934, "The art of a period is what the artists make during a period, apart from that there are, in Foch's magnificent phrase, 'merely verbal manifestations.'" (GB, 140).

irides: in Greek, the plural form of iris; here, both the iris of the eye and a complementary symbolic flower to Mauberley's "orchis."

botticellian sprays: an allusion to Botticelli's sublimely erotic "The Birth of Venus."

diastasis: the divided stance of the eyes, or their dilation in erotic invitation. Cf. Canto LXXXI (C, 520).

affect: emotion or feeling, with a pun on his "affecting," or pretending, to be unaffected. Cf. Canto XXXVI (SP, 126).

mandate of Eros: Mauberley's failure to hear and obey the command of the god of love results in its withdrawal, making it "a retrospect."

Mouths biting . . . : Cf. epigraph; these "epilogues" attest the power of the "gods" whose mandate Mauberley ignored.


# "THE AGE DEMANDED" [SP, 73]


Mauberley, like "E. P.," is "unaffected by the 'march of events,'" and retreats into solipsistic preoccupation with his own sensations. Pound's diction throughout the poem is Latinate and analytical, distancing the speaker from the Mauberley he dissects. But the minute interest in Mauberley's "case" bespeaks a certain identification.

this agility: that is, the ability to produce an image of the age's "accelerated grimace."

As the red-beaked . . . bit: In Greek legend, the goddess of love Aphrodite was brought to the island of Cythera following her birth from the sea. Her chariot was pictured as drawn by doves and swans.

The glow . . . inconsequence: Mauberley's interest in beauty and art is antiquarian. Contrast Pound's various early defenses of poetry in "The Serious Artist": "Beauty in art reminds one what is worth while"; "the arts provide data for ethics"; "the individual cannot think and communicate his thought, the governor and legislator cannot act effectively or frame his laws, without words, and the solidity and validity of these words is in the care of the damned and despised *litterati*." (LE, 45, 46, 21)

The coral isle . . . : Cf. the "scattered Moluccas" of IV.

neo-Nietzschean clatter: Pound's interest in poetry, which he defined as "the art of getting meaning into words," was fundamentally opposed to Nietzsche's articulation of the groundlessness of language, though the language of *The Cantos* enacts the dissolution of Western metaphysics which Nietzsche described.

these presents: these circumstances. Pound implies that Mauberley's withdrawal is somewhat understandable, given the circumstances from which he withdraws.

Minoan undulation: the Minoan period, named for King Minos of Crete, was the high civilization of the Bronze Age (3000–1200 B.C.)

doctrine of chances: Pound perhaps has Darwin's evolutionary theory in mind here.

Olympian *apathein:* Greek: the gods' indifference toward humanity.

imaginary . . . sea-surge: Here, Pound has said, he was striving for an onomatopoeic effect, like that of Homer's "untranslated and untranslatable" *para thina poluphloisboio thalasses* ("by the shore of the many-voiced sea"; *Iliad*, I.34).

susurrus: a low soft sound, as of whispering or muttering, the sound of Mauberley's self-absorbed degeneration.

This poem portrays Mauberley's end as he drifts off to the oblivion of his own interior paradise island. Cf. Homer's Lotus-eaters (*Odyssey*, IX) and Canto XX.

Moluccas: spice-growing islands in the Malay Archipelago.

Simoon: the hot, dry, sand-laden wind of African and Asian deserts (which does not, in fact, reach the Moluccas).

Coracle: a small rounded boat of wickerwork covered with skin.

Then on an oar . . . : a parody of Elpenor's fate in Homer's *Odyssey*, XI, translated in Canto I.


# MEDALLION                                                                   [SP, 77]


"Medallion" is usually taken to be a specimen of Mauberley's art. Its interpretation, like that of the "Envoi," has generated a certain amount of confusion due to the fact that critics persist in projecting upon Pound the aestheticism to which *Mauberley* pays farewell. Like the "Envoi," "Medallion" is unquestionably an accomplished poem; but like the "Envoi," it too is limited, in the larger terms *Mauberley* sets up. Whereas the "Envoi" represents the lyric mode, "Medallion" represents "Imagist" poetics, a visual or "phanopoeic" mode in which, Pound said, "painting or sculpture seems as if it were 'just coming over into speech.'" (GB, 82) It has "the sculpture of rhyme" and sharply "engraved" imagery, but it also parodies Mauberley's self-absorption both in its choice of subject and in its dispassionate tone. "Luini in porcelain!" recalls the critique of Mauberley's social obliviousness in the third poem, and the belabored connoisseuristic comparisons to other works of art reflect his inability to draw "from life."

To perceive "Medallion's" limitations, however, is to perceive *Mauberley's* strength. Pound himself valued *Mauberley* rather lightly: "Mauberley is a mere surface," he wrote to a friend, "Again a study in form, an attempt to condense the James novel. Meliora speramus" (SL, 180); and he told Thomas Hardy, "the Mauberley is thin—one tries to comfort oneself with the argument that the qualities are inherent in the subject matter." (Hutchins, 99) His disclaimers are too modest, for he not only creates in *Mauberley* an enduring image of a crucial historical moment but, by its ironic depiction of the alienation and "inconsequentiality" of poetry in its primary function as a social act, forges the link between his poetry and social concerns which will direct the course of his work from this point on. "I am certain of *Mauberley*," T. S. Eliot wrote in 1928; "This seems to me a great poem . . . a document of an epoch; it is . . . in the best sense of Arnold's worn phrase: a 'criticism of life.' " (SPF, 19–20)

Luini: Bernardino Luini (1480–1532), Lombard painter, of whom Reinach wrote, "his elegance is superficial, his drawing uncertain, and his power of invention limited." (*Apollo*, 191)

porcelain: Jo Brantley Berryman links this image with Pound's pseudonymous review of Raymonde Collignon's singing in *The New Age*, 15 April 1920: "As long as this diseuse was on the stage she was nonhuman; she was, if you like, a china image: there are Ming porcelains which are respectable; the term 'china' is not in this connection ridiculous" (397–98).

Anadyomene: Greek: "rising from the sea," an epithet describing Aphrodite's birth. Praxiteles' head of Aphrodite is reproduced in Reinach's *Apollo*, and "Medallion" makes use of it in describing the singer, echoing Reinach's language in the words "suave," "honey," "face," and "oval."

Reinach: Salomon Reinach (1858–1932), French archaeologist and art historian, and author of *Apollo* (1904), a book on ancient sculpture.

King Minos: ancient King of Crete after whom the high civilization of the "Minoan period" is named. Cf. "The Age Demanded."

amber: Cf. the "magic amber" of the "Envoi." metal: Pound used this word to describe the writing of fellow modernists like James Joyce and Wyndham Lewis; see *The New Age*, 29 January 1920, 205, and PD, 73.

topaz: the transparent yellow color of the semiprecious stone. Cf. "gold-yellow," "honey-red," and "amber," colors associated with Aphrodite.

# FROM *Homage to Sextus Propertius*
## *(1918 / 1919)*

The elegant ease of this title immediately suggests a formal, "classical" poetic decorum in the verses to follow. We are startled, then, upon glancing through the poem, to find such lines as these:

> Out-weariers of Apollo will, as we know, continue their Martian
> generalities,
>
> . . . .
>
> My cellar does not date from Numa Pompilius,
> Nor bristle with wine jars,
> Nor is it equipped with a frigidaire patent;
> Yet the companions of the Muses
>     will keep their collective nose in my books,
>
> . . . .
>
>     Out with it, tell it to me, all of it, from the beginning,
> I guzzle with outstretched ears.

—lines in which erudite allusions to Roman history and mythology jostle against colloquial speech, anachronistic images, and parodic "translatorese," all loosely deployed in sauntering rhythms which have no antecedent in classical poetry. What kind of voice is this, and who is speaking in it? This is a question which leads to the heart of the poem, and it requires a somewhat leisurely answer. To begin: Sextus Propertius was a Roman poet of the first century B.C. A contemporary of Virgil, Horace, and Ovid, he was considered by Quintilian one of the two most accomplished Roman elegists. (Sullivan, 3) Little is known of his life apart from what we can gather from his poems, which are mostly love lyrics about his passionate affair with "Cynthia." And this is where Pound's treatment of Propertius comes in, for his "Homage"—an estimable English poem in its own right—was nothing less than a landmark reinterpretation of the Latin poems which created a new Propertius for the twentieth century. Pound's "Homage," as Sullivan puts it, discovered the "vital strength" of the poems beneath the scholarly dust, and presented for the first time "the only part of Propertius which lives for the common reader in the way a poet would wish to live." (22)

The question of what made so radical a reinterpretation possible and necessary calls for a glance at the history of the "Homage." Its immediate instigation seems to have occurred in 1916 when, recommending some reading to Iris Barry, Pound wrote, "And if you CAN'T find *any* decent translations of Catullus and Propertius, I suppose I shall have to rig up something." (SL, 91) The lack of any translations that Pound could consider "decent" had to do, in a very direct sense, with the politics of classical scholarship. Mackail's influential *Latin Literature* (1895), for example, which Pound read, characterizes Propertius as a "neurotic young man" whose poems reflected "the abandonment to sensibility, the absorption in self-pity and the sentiment of passion." (125–26) An author who cared less for producing heroic poetry about the imperial affairs of the Empire than for composing love poems, Propertius was viewed by the classics scholars as a "genius of great and, indeed, phenomenal precocity" (124) who had died before he reached a mature style. Pound—not a classicist, but a true "philologer" or lover of words—saw the case in more complex terms. His anti-establishment politics put him in sympathy with the disaffected Roman, and enabled him to detect in Propertius what the scholars had blindly missed: an ironic tone which gave weight and significance to Propertius' refusal to enshrine the power of the Empire in epic glory, and a public, anti-epical dimension to his extolling of love and love poetry. Taking his cue from several passages in the poetry—the "Ride to Lanuvium" (Propertius IV.8; "Homage" II, not included in SP), and "the juxtaposition of the words 'tacta puella sono' and 'Orphea delinisse feras' " (IV.1; "Homage" I; Homberger, 163)—Pound pursued the subtler resonances of this irony throughout Propertius' poetry.

Selecting from the poems with this interest in mind, he con-
structed the twelve-part "Homage," which is at once a "tribute,"
as its title suggests; a translation, since, with the exception of a few
lines here and there, Pound adds little to what he finds in the Latin;
a paraphrase or imitation, since his "translation" is nonetheless in-
formed by a particular interpretation of Propertius which his own
version emphasizes; and a new English poem, with a structure and
a coherence not given by the original. It is, further, as T. S. Eliot
wrote, a "criticism" of Propertius "which in a most interesting way
insists upon an element of humour, of irony and mockery in
Propertius, which Mackail and other interpreters have missed."
(SPF, 19) And finally, it is, in Pound's words, a "major persona."
In capturing "the spirit of the young man of the Augustan Age,
hating rhetoric and undeceived by imperial hog-wash" (SL, 150),
Pound was portraying himself, writing in an England which was,
like Propertius' Rome, an imperialist nation engaged in a senseless
war. The "Homage," Pound wrote in 1931, "presents certain emo-
tions as vital to me in 1917, faced with the infinite and ineffable im-
becility of the British Empire, as they were to Propertius some
centuries earlier, when faced with the infinite and ineffable im-
becility of the Roman Empire." (SL, 231) In the last analysis, the
"Homage" is a classic/modern palimpsest, a harmonizing of Pro-
pertius and Pound into the dissenting voice of the alienated artist
in any imperialist age.

As Pound's reinterpretation of Propertius was based not on dis-
covering new lines or words but on an ironic *tone* which changed
the significance of the words without affecting their literal mean-
ing, his problem in translating the Latin was to bring out that tone.
Pound's word for Propertian irony was "logopoeia,"

> "the dance of the intellect among words," that is to say, it em-
> ploys words not only for their direct meaning, but it takes count
> in a special way of habits of usage, of the context we *expect* to
> find with the word, its usual concomitants, of its known accept-
> ances, and of ironical play. . . .
>
> *Logopoeia* does not translate; though the attitude of mind it
> expresses may pass through a paraphrase. Or one might say, you
> can *not* translate it "locally," but having determined the original

author's state of mind, you may or may not be able to find a derivative or equivalent.

(LE, 25)

What distinguishes Pound's translation from previous ones, then— apart from the fact that, as Sullivan puts it, it "offers poetry for poetry" (95)—is that, attempting to render this elusive and "un-translatable" quality, he sometimes departs from the literal mean-ings of Propertius' words toward "a derivative or equivalent" which captures the ironic tone. It is this which accounts for the peculiar decorum we noted at the beginning of this discussion. To illustrate how decorum determines "tone" and, thereby, meaning, we may compare two translations of the same passage, one by Pound and one by the Loeb translator, H. E. Butler. Take, for ex-ample, part V.1 of the "Homage," in which Propertius attempts to oblige his patron by tuning his lyre to epic themes. The Loeb trans-lation (II, X) runs as follows:

> But now 'tis time with other measures to range the slopes of Helicon; 'tis time to launch the Haemonian steed o'er the open plain . . . and tell of my chieftain's Roman camp. But should strength fail me, yet my daring shall win me fame: in mighty enterprises enough even to have willed success. Let early youth sing the charms of love, life's later prime the storm of war: war will I sing, now that I have set forth all my mistress' charms. Now would I go my way with grave frown stamped on serious brow; my Muse now bids me strike another lyre. Awake, my soul! Ye Pierid maids, leave these humble strains and take a stronger tone; the work that waits you needs a mighty voice.
>
> Now does Euphrates deny that the Parthian aims his backward shaft, and grieves that ever he cut short the return of the Crassi. Nay, even India, Augustus, bows her neck to grace thy triumph, and the house of virgin Arabia trembles before thee; and if there be any land withdrawn upon earth's furthest rim, captured here-after let it feel thy mighty hand.
>
> This be the camp I follow. Great will I be among singers by singing of thy wars. Let destiny keep that glorious day in store for me.

Even an uninitiated reader might observe a certain ironic resonance here, to which these leaden cadences and elaborately formal idiom are not altogether inappropriate. Pound's version, however, brings it across much more vividly. Pound uses quotation marks to distinguish between Propertius' own sentiments and those he has been instructed to utter. He sometimes bends the sense of the original toward secondary meanings of the Latin words (as in "Now . . . it is time to cleanse Helicon" and "I with my beak hauled ashore"). At other times, he selects bathetically literal meanings for words that have metaphorical possibilities (as in "Now for a large-mouthed product" and "It is India which now gives necks to your triumph"), in so doing making felt the pompous inhumanity of Roman imperialism and its exaltation in poetry. Other choices he makes—as in translating the Latin *quando* as "*when* this matter of a girl is exhausted," where the Loeb translator has "now that [i.e., since] I have set forth all my mistress' charms" (both are correct) or in curbing the tone of the last line to imply an ironic dread rather than star-struck hope—strengthen the feeling of Propertius' inner resistance to the assignment he is outwardly performing. Throughout the "Homage," the note of the poet's true feelings sounds with disturbing dissonance beneath the brassy, "official" chords. Denying seriousness to the rhetoric of imperialism, Pound makes striking the one thing he does take seriously: the absurdity of the self-important seriousness that leads men to make wars and to glorify warmaking.

It is no wonder, given this decorum of dissonances, that some classics scholars had problems understanding the "Homage," for its celebration of Propertian irony was lost on those whose literary perspectives were refracted through establishment politics. Pound had some trouble getting it published, and when in March 1919, Harriet Monroe printed, as Pound put it, "the left foot, knee, thigh and right ear"—that is, four of the portrait's twelve sections—in *Poetry* (Chicago MSS, December 1918), its appearance initiated a storm of protest which continued to rage into the fifties, beginning with William Gardner Hale's critique in the April issue of *Poetry*. He spoke of numerous errors and "howlers" in the "Homage," and concluded that

> Mr. Pound is incredibly ignorant of Latin. . . . For sheer magnificence of blundering, this is unsurpassable. . . . If Mr. Pound

were a professor of Latin, there would be nothing left for him but suicide. I do not counsel this. But I beg him to lay aside the mask of erudition. And if he must deal with Latin, I suggest he paraphrase some accurate translation, and then employ some respectable student of the language to save him from blunders which might still be possible.

(Homberger, 156-57)

The key word here is "respectable," and, at bottom, it is not the respectability of Pound's knowledge of *Latin* that is Hale's real target. No merely erroneous translation could have inspired thirty-odd years of what Brooker calls "unimaginative and self-congratulatory carping" (151) on the part of the classicists. The offensiveness of the "Homage" ran much deeper, and was not semantic but linguistically political. Donald Davie has acutely analyzed the language of the "Homage" as an affront to the "Babu"—or colonized—classicism of the scholars: "Every white-skinned English-speaker, however used he may be to regarding himself as a *colon* (colonist), has also been *colonisé* (colonized). The evidence is in our language, as soon as we set it beside Latin." (EP, 57–58) Pound in the "Homage" contrives at times to mock Babu "translatorese" by exaggerating it ("Gods' aid let not my bones lie in a public location / With crowds too assiduous in their crossing of it") and at times to elude it altogether ("Avernus lusts for the lot of them"), but he no longer plays it straight—as he had earlier done, for example, in his translation of the prayer for Cynthia's life:

> Here let thy clemency, Persephone, hold firm,
> Do thou, Pluto, bring here no greater harshness.
> So many thousand beauties are gone down to Avernus
> Ye might let one remain above with us.
>
> (CEP, 149; cf. "Homage" IX.2)

The linguistic politics of the "Homage" explain why Pound's attempts to clarify what he was doing had little effect. His thesis that

> Mackail (accepted as "right" opinion on the Latin poets) hasn't, apparently, *any* inkling of the *way* in which Propertius is using Latin. Doesn't see that S. P. is tying blue ribbon in the tails of Virgil

and Horace, or that sometime after his first "book" S. P. ceased
to be the dupe of magniloquence and began to touch words some-
what as Laforgue did.

(SL, 178)

met with more scorn than curiosity. He pointed out errors in
Hale's catalog of "blunders," objecting, and with justice, that
"Hale's 'criticism' displayed not only ignorance of Latin but igno-
rance of English" (SL, 231). All the caviling about blunders finally
drove him to deny that the "Homage" was a translation at all:

> No, I have not done a translation of Propertius. That fool in
> Chicago took the *Homage* for a translation, despite the mention
> of Wordsworth and the parodied line from Yeats. (As if, had one
> wanted to pretend to more Latin than one knew, it wdn't have
> been perfectly easy to correct one's divergencies from a Bohn crib.
> Price 5 shillings.)

(SL, 178)

Brushing aside the term "translation," Pound located the "scho-
lastic value" of his "Homage" elsewhere. "The philologists," he
wrote, "have so succeeded in stripping the classics of interest that
I have already had more than one reader who has asked me, 'Who
was Propertius?' As for my service to classical scholarship, presum-
ably nil, I shall be quite content if I induce a few Latinists really
to look at the text of Propertius instead of swallowing an official
'position' and then finding what the text-books tell them to look
for." (Homberger, 164) His real aim, as he conceived it, was not to
"translate" Propertius but "to bring a dead man to life." (SL, 149)

It took several decades for the brilliance of the "Homage" to be
appreciated, but Pound would, in the end, have been satisfied.
Sullivan judges that the "Homage" had a crucial, if belated, effect
on the twentieth-century view of the Latin poet: "Propertius *re-
quired* Pound's reinterpretation (and even distortion) to bring him
within our own frame of reference" (22); and discusses its impor-
tance for later translations such as Robert Lowell's "The Ghost
(After Sextus Propertius)." (173–83) And J. P. McCulloch, a re-
cent translator of Propertius, pays homage to Pound's "masterly
and extraordinary translation," "itself a great English poem." (6)

As for its importance for Pound's own work, the congenially "modern" temperament which Pound discovered in Propertius helped him to establish the critical, alienated, dissident stance which would make his own epic poem possible.

One last word on how to read: the "Homage" is a wonderful, and wonderfully funny, poem, with a tonal range that accommodates Propertian tenderness ("The moon will carry his candle / the stars will point out the stumbles") as well as sardonic mockery ("And my ventricles do not palpitate to Caesarial *ore rotundos*"). It is a poem to be enjoyed, but its plethoras of allusions may somewhat dampen the pleasure of it; as when reading Aristophanes, we sometimes have to turn to the index to find out what makes the joke. This being the case, it is worth noting that Pound himself treated the poem's allusions in the poem rather cavalierly. He makes a number of errors—for example, Oetia's gods for Oeta's god, Achenor for Archemorus, the attributing of Galatea's horses to Polyphemus. When a reviewer complained of this last, he replied,

> As for Polyphemus' livestock, he had, by tradition, sheep; but as he never existed, and as Propertius certainly had no more belief in the existence of Polyphemus than I have, I cannot be expected to dig up . . . an accurate list of his bloodstock. . . . did Propertius who brought a new and exquisite tone into Latin care a damn about these things; or did he tremendously care for writing a language that was not stilted Horatian peg-work or Georgian maunder of Maro?

> (Homberger, 164)

Often enough, we can gauge the tone without a clear idea of the allusions, and that, finally, is the poem's genius. A couple of readings should suffice to get one's bearings; it is a poem not to be missed.

Finally, readers who wish further information will find it in Ruthven, who reprints the Latin texts which Pound used from Lucian Mueller's 1892 edition of Propertius, along with the Loeb translations; in Sullivan's full-length study, *Ezra Pound and Sextus Propertius;* and in the commentaries of Davie, Kenner, and Richardson.

Title: When Pound showed the poem to Thomas Hardy, Hardy suggested that "Propertius Soliloquizes" would have been a more suitable title, and Pound agreed that such a title would have turned "the reader's attention to the reality of Propertius" rather than focusing it on the treatment. He explained, however, that he used the term as Debussy had in his "Hommage à Rameau": "a piece of music recalling Rameau's manner." (Hutchins, 99)

I                                                        [SP, 78]

Propertius describes his poetic intentions, distinguishing his love lyrics from the works of more "public" poets which "expound the distentions of empire." He mocks heroic poetry as a glorification of unheroic and forgettable histories, and claims immortality for his own "soft songs." His animadversions on the theme of the superiority of genius to any worldly wealth or fame include a thrust at bourgeois accouterments, which he lacks, and a dig at Jove as the *haut bourgeois* pacesetter, with his fancy residence at "East Elis."

Callimachus: (*ca.* 305–240 B.C.) Greek elegiac poet known chiefly for his love lyrics. He debated the merits of heroic and lyric poetry with Apollonius Rhodius, and is said to have argued, "*mega biblion mega kakon*" ("the greater the book, the greater the evil") (Brooker, 159).

Philetas: (*ca.* 330–275 B.C.) Greek lyric poet from the Aegean island of Cos. Coan: from Cos.

Grecian orgies: Latin *orgia*, "mysteries." It's more likely that Pound intended by his diction to restore something of the sense of "mysteries" to the modern idea of "orgies" than to imply a simple degeneration from the one to the other. Cf. his view that "we should consider carefully the history of the various cults or religions of orgy and of ecstacy, from the simpler Bacchanalia to the more complicated rites of Isis or Dionysus—sudden rise and equally sudden decline." (SR, 95)

Apollo: Greek god of the sun, light, harmony, and poetry, whom, Pound pictures as "wearied out" or bored stiff by the heroics of war poetry.

Martian generalities: Mars is the Roman god of war.

We have kept . . . order: Pound diverges from the Latin, which translates, "Let verse run smoothly, polished by fine pumice."

Celebrities . . . Trans-Caucasus: Pound takes liberties with lines that translate: "O Rome! Many will add your praises to their histories / who will sing of the Empire's bounds extending to Bactra," in order to comment sardonically on Rome's annexation of Bactria in 20 B.C. As he later put it in *The Cantos*, "Art is local." (C, 678)

distentions: ironic diction expressing antipathy to imperialism.

forked hill: i.e., Parnassus; cf. Pope's "Epistle to Dr. Arbuthnot" (l. 231).

deal-wood horse: the Trojan horse which enabled the Greeks to take Troy.

Achilles . . . Simois: Achilles battles the raging Scamander River in Troy, of which the Simois is a tributary, in *Iliad* XXI.

Hector . . . wheel-rims: After vanquishing the great Trojan hero Hector, Achilles tied his body to his chariot and dragged him three times around Troy. (*Iliad* XXII) More generally, chariots running over slaughtered men in battle "spattered wheel-rims" with blood.

Polydmantus: i.e., Polydamas, a Trojan hero. Helenus and Deiphobos: brothers of Hector. Paris: the Trojan hero whose abduction of Helen brought about the Trojan War.

Ilion: the Greek name for Troy. Troad: the Latin name of the district around Troy.

Oetian gods: Propertius has "Oetia's god," i.e. Hercules, so called because he died as a mortal on Mount Oeta.

Homer: the Greek epic poet who immortalized the story of the Trojan War.

vote: a joke inspired by the Latin *vota* ("wish, vow"). Phoebus . . . Patara: Apollo as sun-god was called Phoebus; he was worshipped at Patara, in the province of Lycia.

devirginated young ladies: Pound brings out a pun latent in Propertius' *tacta*, which means both "touched" in the sense of "moved" and the opposite of *intacta* ("virginal"). Hale and others were scandalized at this "peculiarly unpleasant" rendering, and heaped abuse on Pound. Pound, quoting the line in context, countered that "if this sequence of clauses is wholly accidental, and if the division of *in* and *tacta* is *wholly* accidental, then Propertius was the greatest unconscious ironist of all time." (Homberger, 170) Other classicists, such as Richardson and Sullivan, have defended Pound's reading on the grounds that the pun occurs elsewhere in classical Latin. See also SL, 149-50.

Orpheus: In Greek legend, a poet whose song, accompanied by a lyre which Apollo gave to him, enchanted all living creatures.

Threician: Thracian; Propertius applies the word to Orpheus' lyre, not to the river.

Citharaon . . . pleasure: In Greek legend, the musician Amphion enchanted the very stones of Mount Cithaeron with his melodies so that they followed him to Thebes, where they were used to fortify the wall.

Polyphemus . . . Galatea: Polyphemus, the Cyclops, fell in love with Galatea, a sea-nymph. Aetna was his home. The horses in the original belong to Galatea; see above, p. 112.

Taenarian columns: columns of black marble, quarried at Taenarus in Sparta (Laconia). The glosses which follow are Pound's addition, parodying the academic approach to the classics.

Phaecia: i.e., Phaeacia, the wealthy island where Odysseus meets Nausicaa in *Odyssey* VII. Ionian: Pound's geography is a little muddled; Ruthven suggests that he confused Phaeacia with the Ionian town of Phocaea.

Marcian vintage: The Latin translates: "nor has art built me grottoes watered by the Marcian fount." The "Marcian fount," Hale pointed out, was actually the Marcian aqueduct which carried the Roman water supply. This was the only correction Pound accepted: "Do him the justice to say that the bloody Marcian aqueduct is very very familiar, and that it was a thing I might very well have remembered." (SL, 149)

Numa Pompilius: the second king of Rome, and Pound's addition, alluding to other ancient vintages which Propertius' wine-cellar does not contain.

frigidaire patent: Pound's interpolation, the implications of which eluded those critics who raised a hue and cry about the inaccuracy of his translation.

Jove . . . East Elis: Zeus's temple was at Olympia in Elis.

Mausolus: owner and occupant of a magnificent tomb, the Mausoleum at Halicarnassus, one of the seven wonders of the ancient world.


# III                                                    [SP, 80]


Propertius, receiving a summons from Cynthia at midnight, soliloquizes on the dangers of walking alone at night, and on the equally dreadful consequences if he does not go to her. He tries to banish his worries by invoking the "sacred" status of lovers at nighttime— a frequent assertion in Latin love poetry—and, failing to convince himself, concludes by fantasizing the picturesque mourning rites Cynthia will perform for him after he is killed.

Tibur: now Tivoli, a suburb northeast of Rome.

"Bright tips . . . pools": In the Latin, these images are embedded in the previous sentence, thus: " 'Twas midnight when a letter came to me from my mistress bidding me come without delay to Tibur, where the white hills heave up their towers to right and left and Anio's waters plunge into spreading pools." (Loeb) Their sexual overtones were not lost on Pound, who emphasizes them by carving them away from their grammatical context and setting them in quotation marks.

Anienan: the river Anio (now Aniene), a tributary of the Tibur.

lamentations: Cf. IX, 10ff.

me-ward: Pound allows Propertius' ironic diction to soften comically into Pre-Raphaelite glamor as he thinks of Cynthia.

Via Sciro: Sciron's Road. Sciron in Greek legend robbed travelers on the road from Athens to Megara, pushing them over a cliff in conclusion.

Scythian coast: Scythia was the country north of the Black Sea, peopled by nomads.

Cypris: Aphrodite, the goddess of love. cicerone: guide.

as yet uncatalogued sand: another jibe at Roman imperialism. The Latin translates: "heaps of nameless sand."


# IV  DIFFERENCE OF OPINION
# WITH LYGDAMUS                    [SP, 82]


Propertius, having sent his regrets to Cynthia by his servant Lygdamus, questions him upon his return as to how Cynthia took his refusal. He simultaneously warns Lygdamus not to lie and demands an account which flatters himself: Cynthia lonely and desolate, inveighing jealously against the other woman she imagines has kept him away.

our . . . lady: Pound notes "Propertius' delicate use of 'nostra,' meaning 'my' as well as 'our,' but in a stylist how delicately graduated against 'mihi' by Propertius. Heine's poem ending, 'Madame, ich liebe Sie' is clumsy by comparison" (SL, 149). The ironic "nostra" implies that Cynthia has been unfaithful to Propertius with Lygdamus.

And may . . . shoulders: Pound's addition.

Much conversation . . . home: Pound inserts a line inspired by line 22 in the Mueller text: "*Aequalem multa dicere habere domo!*" (repeated below). The Loeb text has "*Et qualem nolo dicere habere domo!*" ("To keep in his house the sort of woman I wouldn't speak of!"). Pound's improvisation highlights Propertius' complex requirements from his slave: while warning Lygdamus not to lie in one breath, he reminds him with the next that he had better bring the news Propertius wants to hear, even if he has to make it up.

gawds: ornaments. orfevrerie: wrought gold.

escritoires: writing boxes.

the desolated . . . dreams: Cf. Yeats's "The Withering of the Boughs": "The boughs have withered because I have told them my dreams." In 1922 Pound asked Harriet Monroe whether Hale had "yet discovered that my introduction of Wordsworth's name and my parody of Yeats were not produced . . . in an endeavor to give a verbatim rendering of the Latin text?" (Chicago MSS)

rhombus: The rhombus wheel was spun to cast a spell to bring a lost lover back. Propertius imagines Cynthia imputing witchcraft to her imaginary rival and retaliating with curses of her own.

V                                                              [SP, 84]

Pound splices together two elegies (II.x and II.i), showing Propertius first attempting to oblige his patron Maecenas with the war poetry he has asked for, only to produce, in mock incompetence, comic bombast edged with anti-imperialist irony; and then explaining to Maecenas how the inspiration for his love poems works.

Helicon: mountain in central Greece, home of the Muses.

Emathian: Macedonian.

"The bare . . . sufficient": Pound uses quotation marks to show Propertius responding under duress to the demands of his patron.

when . . . exhausted: The Latin *quando* means "when" or "since"; Pound's choice emphasizes Propertius' reluctance.

I . . . beak hauled ashore: The idiomatic translation of the Latin would be "with knitted brow"; Pound's image is inspired by the nautical usage of *subducto*, and represents more vividly the appropriation of the poet's talent for the interests of patrons and states.

gamut: the musical scale. gambetto: Italian: "gambit." Pound substitutes both for the Latin *citharam* (lyre) to emphasize the foreignness to Propertius both of heroic poetry and of writing to order.

cantilation: chant, i.e., the wonted love songs.

Pierides: the Muses, who lived at Pieria on Mt. Olympus before moving to Helicon.

Now . . . product: Pound emphasizes the bathos latent in *magni nunc erit oris opus*.

Euphrates . . . Crassus: The incident ironically represented here involved Crassus' crossing of the Euphrates River to invade Parthia.

It is . . . triumph: Again, Pound translates literally the Latin *tuo dat colla triumpho;* contrast the Loeb translation: "bows her neck to grace thy triumph."

Augustus: the Roman emperor.


2

you: i.e., Maecenas, a powerful figure in the affairs of Rome and the patron of Propertius, Virgil, and Horace.

My genius . . . girl: a favorite line of Pound's, quoted in SR, 96; PD, 214; and LE, 103, 151, 343. See his "Postscript" to Remy de Gourmont's *Natural Philosophy of Love* (PD, 203–14).

gleam of Cos: the island of Cos was famous for the sheer silks it produced.

Iliads: i.e., many analogues to Homer's epic of the Trojan War.

Titans: the children of Heaven and Earth who rebelled against the Olympian gods and were defeated.

Ossa . . . Pelion: Otus and Ephialtes tried to storm heaven by piling up mountains: Pelion upon Ossa upon Olympus.

Thebes: the city where Oedipus killed his father and married his mother and where Pentheus' mother tore him limb from limb in Dionysiac frenzy.

Pergamus: Troy, whose destruction was, of course, the making of Homer's "reputation."

Xerxes: Persian king who, in a military campaign, had a channel dug across the Isthmus of Actium in order to avoid Mt. Athos.

Remus: co-founder of Rome with his brother Romulus, who murdered him.

dignified Carthaginian characters: such as, for example, Dido, who killed herself in despair after falling in love with Aeneas when he left her to found a new city. Rome had destroyed Carthage under Hannibal in the Punic Wars two centuries earlier.

Welsh mines: Pound puns on the Latin "Cimbrorumque minas" ("Cimbrian threat"), confusing Cimbri with Cumbria (Wales); and interprets Propertius' "Cimbrorumque minas et benefacta Marus" to emphasize the benefits that accrued to Marius himself (rather than to the state) from defeat of the invading Cimbrians. The mangling of the Latin sense seems a deliberate expression of Propertius / Pound's boredom with the affairs of the Empire, and also reflects Pound's growing awareness of the economic abuses of imperialism.

Callimachus: see I, note to line 1.

Theseus: legendary Greek hero whose exploits included slaying the Minotaur.

an inferno: the *nekyia*, or descent to the underworld, is a conventional episode in the epic genre.

Achilles: Greek hero whose skill as a warrior was essential to the Greek victory over Troy.

Ixion: legendary king of Thessaly who was enamored of Hera. Zeus had him bound to a wheel of fire in Hades to punish him.

sons of Menoetius: i.e., Patroclus, Achilles' companion in the *Iliad*, whom Hector kills. The characters of Greek epic are often referred to indirectly by means of genealogical formulations.

Argo: the ship in which Jason and the Argonauts sailed in search of the Golden Fleece.

Jove's grave . . . Titans: Propertius refers to "the strife between Jove and [the Titan] Enceladus on Phlegra's plains."

Caesarial *ore rotundos:* imperial round-mouthedness, that is, bombastic rhetoric.

the Phrygian fathers: i.e., the fathers of Augustus.

she speaks . . . "unsuitable": Cynthia disapproves of Homer's Helen, who left Menelaus for Paris, married Deiphobus after Paris died, and returned to Menelaus when the Greeks took Troy.


# VI                                                    [SP, 86]


Pound arranges passages from several poems (III.v, IV.iii, IV.iv) into a soliloquy about death, which mocks the vanity of emperors as surely as it stops the mouth of the lyric poet.

Acheron: a river in Hades over which the dead are ferried.

Marius and Jugurtha: The Roman consul Marius (see V) captured and killed Jugurtha, king of Numidia, and later died insane. Propertius' evocation of death as the "great leveler" points to the vanity of human ambition.

Caesar . . . religion: Caesar was planning an invasion of India at his death, which would have led to the consequences listed.

lares: in Roman religion, the household gods.

Atalic: Attalus invented the technique of weaving cloth of gold.

Persephone: queen of the underworld. Pound used the line *quos ego Persephonea maxima dona feram* ("that I may offer them to Persephone as my most precious gift") as the epigraphs to *Canzoni* (1911) and *Ripostes* (1912).

Syrian onyx: embalming oils from Syria, kept in an onyx container.

Adonis: Adonis, whom Venus ("the Cytherean") loved, was killed by a wild boar as he hunted near Idalium in Cyprus.

# VII                                                              [SP, 88]

Propertius forgets about the Empire and the demands of the heroic, and sings his true subject. James Laughlin judges this poem "the best piece of free verse written in the XX century and perhaps one of EP's finest poems."

Me happy: Pound's partly parodic, partly whimsical rendering of *O me felicem!*

Endymion . . . Diana: The moon goddess Diana fell in love with a shepherd, Endymion, and descended every night to embrace him while he slept.

# IX                                                               [SP, 89]

Cynthia is ill, and Propertius prays to Zeus, Persephone, and Dis to save her.

# 1

rhombs: The rhombus wheels (see IV), used to cast spells over lovers.

scorched . . . fire-dust: i.e., as the remains of a sacrifice propitiating the gods for Cynthia's recovery.

The moon . . . heaven: i.e., in the form of Cynthia (whose name is one of several belonging to the moon-goddess).

Avernus: a lake near Naples, thought to be the entrance to the underworld. Cf. Elpenor's speech in Canto I.

Cerulean: cerulean (deep blue).

Great Zeus . . . troubles: Pound adapts the Latin, which translates,
" 'The woman is saved by the might of Jove'; she herself will sit at thy
feet and tell of the long perils she has passed."

## 2

See headnote, p. 112, for a quotation from Pound's earlier transla-
tion which he judged "a perfectly literal and, by the same token,
perfectly lying and 'spiritually' mendacious translation of 'Vobis-
cum est Iope' . . . for whomsoever wants the humorless vein,
which vein, in this particular poem, makes it utterly impossible to
translate the 'Votivas noctes mihi' at its termination." (Homberger,
164)

Persephone and Dis: Dis (Pluto) carried Persephone off to Hades while
she was picking flowers one day in the valley of Enna in Sicily. Her
mother Ceres (Demeter) searched for her and finally sued Zeus for her
return, and he arranged for her to spend half the year in Hades and half
(spring and summer) on the earth. Propertius propitiates them as king
and queen of the underworld.

Iope: Theseus' wife or Aeolus' daughter. Tyro: mortal woman loved by
the sea-god Neptune (Poseidon), who came to her as the river Enipeus
(see Canto II). Pasiphae: wife of Minos, who conceived the Minotaur
by mating with a bull. formal . . . Achaia: i.e., the beautiful girls of
Achaia, in the Peloponnesus.

Troad: the district surrounding Troy. Campania: a fertile district south
of Rome.

## 3

Dian: i.e., Diana, goddess of the moon and of chastity.

and unto me also: Pound adapts the Latin, which translates, "and sacri-
fice ten nights to her in my name"—a finer irony than Pound's.

Cynthia has Propertius kidnapped by a crowd of small boys and brought to her.

what boys . . . arrows: The idea is that a gang of Cupids waylaid Propertius; Sullivan notes that the image is "a highly artificial genre-picture." (57)

given to lust: Pound translates the Latin *lascivior* (playful, impudent) by way of its modern descendant "lascivious," joking with the Cupid imagery.

Sidonian night cap: one from Sidon in Phoenicia, famous for its purple dyes.

incumbent . . . incubus: The pun is Pound's addition, not suggested by Propertius' Latin. "Incumbent" (one holding office) descends from *incumbere* (to lie upon); its perfect tense (*incubui*) suggests *incubus*, a demon imagined as engendering monstrous births upon sleeping women. (Ruthven, 119–20)

temple of Vesta: implying that Cynthia adopts the role of a vestal virgin, which accounts for Propertius' nocturnal misery henceforth.

Propertius rebukes his friend, the minor poet Lynceus, for making love to Cynthia. This reproval becomes the occasion for another discourse on the greater merits of love poetry over epic, as Propertius mocks Lynceus for imagining that he can win lovers by writing on heroic subjects. The poem thus brings the sequence to a symmetrical close, with Propertius "taking his stand" with the Roman love poets. Pound departs from Propertius in his treatment of this poem, for, as Sullivan points out, Propertius does admire Virgil and discusses his pastoral poems in order to show the likeness between himself and Virgil. (76)

A Trojan: i.e., Paris, who ran off with Helen, Menelaus' wife.

Colchis . . . woman: Medea, of Colchis, where Jason sought the Golden Fleece, gave help to and fell in love with Jason, who treated her shabbily and drove her to desperate deeds.

Lynceus: Lynceus was one of Jason's Argonauts; Propertius here satirically appropriates his name for the friend, minor poet, and rival to whom he is speaking.

She was not . . . fidelity: Pound departs from the Latin, which translates, "What if she hadn't been so constant and true?" (a line which, McCulloch notes, testifies to Propertius' sense of humor).

Achelöus . . . Hercules: Achelöus, a river-god, "contended" with Hercules for Deianira ("Daysair"; see "from *Women of Trachis*," SP, 183–84), whom both loved.

Adrastus: King of Argos, one of the seven against Thebes, whose horse had the power of human speech.

Achenor: The Latin has "Archemorus," at whose funeral Adrastus' horse spoke his first words. Ruthven suggests that Pound deliberately misquotes to show Propertius' boredom with the absurdities of epic machinery.

Aeschylus: the great Greek tragedian.

Antimachus: author of a fifth-century Greek epic about Thebes.

And still . . . importance: Propertius tells Lynceus that his pompous heroics will not buy him any lovers. The Latin here is rather more subtle than Pound's translation.

Actian: of Actium, where Octavian defeated Antony and Cleopatra in 31 B.C., marking the end of the Roman Republic and the beginning of the Empire.

Virgil: the Roman poet, Propertius' contemporary, whose *Aeneid* is a nationalist epic depicting Aeneas' journey from Troy to Italy (Latium) to found the city that became Rome.

Phoebus: Phoebus Apollo, the sun-god, whose temple was at Actium; he supposedly helped Octavian defeat Antony and Cleopatra.

chief of police: Propertius has *custodis* (guard).

Ilian: Trojan.

Lavinian: Lavinia, princess of Latium, was betrothed to Turnus. After Aeneas killed him in battle, she became Aeneas' destined bride.

larger Iliad: Virgil's *Aeneid*. Pound adds "(and to Imperial order)," and changes *nascitur* (comes to birth) to "is in the course of construction," making much of what he considered to be the nationalistic lumber of Virgil's poem. Propertius' *nescioquid* (something or other) invites satiric interpretation.

Phrygian . . . Daphnis: Virgil also wrote pastoral lyrics; in his *Eclogues* (Book VII), the shepherds Thyrsis and Daphnis participate in a singing contest. "Phrygian," referring to the ancestry of Caesar, evokes the archaic settings of pastoral verse.

Tityrus: a shepherd in the *Eclogues*. the same vixen: i.e., one who sells her love for apples.

Corydon . . . Alexis: Corydon is a shepherd in the *Eclogues* who falls in love with Alexis.

Hamadryads: tree nymphs.

Ascraeus: i.e., Hesiod (fl. eighth century B.C.), who lived in Ascra and composed a realistic handbook for rustic life, *Works and Days*. Wordsworthian: Pound's anachronistic comparison of Hesiod and the English Romantic poet Wordsworth expresses an equal boredom with the animadversions of pastoral; he considered that Wordsworth drowned out his great genius in a chorus of "bleatings."

ladies . . . character: suggested by Propertius' *conviva puellas* (guest . . . women).

I shall be honored . . . marrow: The Latin translates, "Be it for me to lie among the garlands of yesterday, for the god [Cupid] has stricken me to the bone," implying that Propertius' songs earn him love and "pleasant nights."

Like . . . tortoise: Pound's image is inspired by the Latin *testudo* (meaning both "lyre" and "tortoise"); the rest of the sentence is Pound's invention.

your: i.e., Virgil's and Lynceus'.

One . . . goose: Pound's formulation, inspired no doubt by his own literary milieu. Propertius' lines mention the goose, but otherwise differ completely.

Varro . . . Leucadia: Varro (b. 82 B.C.) translated the story of Jason and the Argonauts and wrote love poems to Leucadia.

Catullus . . . Lesbia: Catullus (84–54 B.C.) wrote love lyrics to Lesbia.

Calvus . . . Quintilia: Calvus (82–47 B.C.) wrote love poems mourning his wife Quintilia.

Gallus . . . Lycoris: Gallus (69–26 B.C.) wrote love poems to Lycoris.

Styx: the river of forgetfulness in Hades. At the time Propertius writes, Gallus has recently died, and is pictured bathing his lover's wounds in the waters of the underworld.

# *Cantos*

## CANTO I (1915/1925) [SP, 96]

The first canto takes us back to the beginnings of Western litera-
ture as Pound translates a passage from Homer's *Odyssey*. This pas-
sage, he later wrote, "shouts aloud that it is *older* than the rest."
(SL, 274) In Book XI, Odysseus leaves Circe's island and voyages
to Hades, the realm of the dead, to learn from the prophet Tiresias
how to find his way home to Ithaca. This descent to the under-
world, or *nekyia*, is a crucial episode in the Western epic, and has
roots in an ancient ritual which sought to bring past, present, and
future together in a symbolic moment of knowledge.

This is all well and good; but we must ask, how does this passage
come to be the beginning of a twentieth-century epic? Why does
Pound choose to open his long poem with a translation from a
poem that already exists, about a ritual long dead? Our questions
only multiply when we learn that what is now Canto I was origi-
nally the end of the third *Poetry* canto (published in 1917 and
later radically revised), where it functioned as an exhibit having
to do with the Renaissance Latin from which it is translated. What
invisible transformation occurs in its removal from this context
to become the first canto? Though it appears at first that what
began as translation becomes a *trouvaille*, a lucky find, the disjunc-
tion here is less drastic than it might seem; for, as the translation
began as a stylistic exhibit in "Three Cantos," it retains this im-
portance in its new location. In *The Cantos*, Pound has no story—
no single story could be adequate to the modern world. Rather,
the poem is a collage of fragments, of which Odysseus' descent

to the underworld is the first, and it is style, language itself, which becomes the poem's story and history. The language of Canto I is not simply a translator's modern English version of the ancient Greek, but folds together, ply over ply, Homer's Greek, the Latin of the translator, Andreas Divus, whose text mediates between Pound and the Greek, and echoes, too, of Pound's freely alliterative "Seafarer" English. All these are woven into its linguistic texture, and this weaving, heavy with history, tells more than the old story and the ancient ritual it narrates. The poem's modern story inheres in the very substance of the words, rather than being "told" by them. For our archaeological civilization—which contains not only ourselves, and our idea of a Greek beginning, but strata of centuries in between—Pound has imagined a four-dimensional language, which registers the depths of time as well as the world of objects.

In its peculiar substantiality, this language itself performs a ritual of descent and knowledge; the *nekyia* becomes a journey into a language which is no longer familiar and transparent, a simple surface whose parts exist in one-to-one correspondence with things and ideas. The meanings of words belong to history, and are half obscured by time's passing; yet their style records the past, as in the *nekyia* which "shouts aloud that it is older than the rest." Canto I, then, is not only the narrated descent of Odysseus but Pound's own linguistic descent to the depths of the Western literary past to seek direction for his own journey "home" to a language that belongs to the twentieth century as Homer's did to the ancient world and Divus's to the Renaissance.

Odysseus, in Homer's *Odyssey*, learns in the ritual of the *nekyia* that he will "return through spiteful Neptune, over dark seas, / Lose all companions." For Pound's poem, too, the prophecy holds true: his epic venture creates a powerful image of our linguistic "home." The journey, never to be completed, is yet accomplished in the very movement of the words. And the poet, the Odyssean voyager, will indeed "lose all companions": the prophecy of loneliness will come true for Pound at the end of his life in a silence that comes not only because there is no one left to talk to or "to share a joke with"—his old friends Yeats, Ford, Williams, Eliot, Joyce, all dead—but because the old poet ends wrecked in a sea of words that have broken apart from their meanings. Even then, however, the language he has reached has life and gaiety; it dances amid the wreckage of the old order in new rhythms, as though to a music just beginning to be heard: "paw-flap / wave-tap / that is gaiety." Cutting through time, deep into the past and also forward into the future, Pound's first canto "translates" the ancient ritual moment of visionary knowledge into its modern dimension. It speaks no word *about* the twentieth century, yet catches its own historical moment in the body of its speech. It would be hard to imagine a more brilliant beginning for a modern "poem including history."

Circe: a goddess and sorceress who turns Odysseus' shipmates into swine and keeps him with her for a year on her island, Aeaea. When he requests to be allowed to return home, she directs him to seek prophecy for his journey from Tiresias in the underworld.

Kimmerian lands: the mist-shrouded home of the legendary "Winter People," located at the entrance to Hades.

the place: that is, Hades.

rites: Odysseus and his companions make a blood sacrifice to summon the ghosts.

pitkin: a small pit, Pound's coinage for Divus' *foveam*.

Ithaca: Odysseus' rocky island kingdom in the Aegean. In the original poem, Odysseus promises to sacrifice his best heifer once he gets back home.

Tiresias: the blind Theban prophet who retains the gift of prophecy even when dead.

fosse: ditch, pit.

Erebus: the darkness through which souls pass in journeying to Hades.

dreory: Pound's coinage from the Old English word *dreorig* ("bloody") which occurs in "The Wanderer"; see "Patria Mia" (SPr, 123), where Pound translates it as "blood-bedaddled."

Pluto . . . Proserpine: the immortal rulers of the underworld.

Elpenor: Odysseus' youngest companion, who fell off Circe's roof when he woke from a drunken sleep to hear the men departing. They had not missed him before his shade appeared, and it is to perform his funeral rites that they sail "outward and away and unto Circe" at the end of the canto.

ingle: inglenook, or hearth.

Avernus: a small lake in Italy, in legend the entrance to Hades.

*A man . . . to come:* In the *Odyssey*, the epitaph reads "And with a name *among men* to come"; for the Greeks, immortality consisted in the name that endured after death. Elpenor's epitaph recurs in Cantos LXXIV and LXXX.

Anticlea: Odysseus' mother, who died during his absence, and whom he fends off because Circe had warned him that no spirit should drink the blood before Tiresias.

A second time?: Pound translates Divus' *iterum*. Robert Fitzgerald clears up the confusion that has accumulated around this point in explaining that *iterum* translates Homer's Greek *aute* as "again," but in the Greek, the meaning *is* "twice"—once now, and again after death. "*Aute*," he says, "is subtle enough to have this meaning, though *iterum* does not."

"Lose all companions.": Tiresias prophesies that Odysseus will lose all his men in his struggle to get home. Cf. Canto LXXIV, in which Pound-Odysseus after half a century remembers his own lost companions (C, 432–33).

bever: drink.

Neptune: god of the sea who caused Odysseus no end of trouble in revenge for his blinding of the Cyclops, Neptune's son.

Andreas Divus: translator of Homer into the Renaissance Latin text from which Pound translates his Canto I version. Pound found Divus' *Odyssey*, published in 1538, in a bookstall on the Paris quays "in 1906, 1908, or 1910" (LE, 259).

in officina Wecheli: "in the printshop of Wechelus," printed on the title page of Divus' *Odyssey*.

Homer: legendary author (ca. eighth century B.C.) of the earliest epics in the Western tradition, the *Iliad* and the *Odyssey*.

Sirens: singing mermaids who lure sailors to their doom. Odysseus gets by them by blocking his sailors' ears with wax and having himself tied to the mast so that he can hear their singing without being destroyed.

Venerandam: Latin: "venerable." Pound translates from the Second Homeric Hymn to Aphrodite as translated by Dartona from the Greek into Renaissance Latin.

Cretan: Georgius Dartona of Crete. His Latin translation of the Homeric hymns (two addressed to Aphrodite) were bound into the volume along with Divus' *Odyssey*.

Aphrodite: goddess of love and beauty, a recurrent figure in *The Cantos*.

Cypri . . . est: "She was allotted the defenses of Cyprus." oricalchi: of copper, referring to her earrings.

Bearing . . . Argicida: Pound translates this line from the First Homeric Hymn to Aphrodite, which tells the story of how she seduced Anchises, Aeneas' father, by claiming to be a mere mortal spirited away from her playmates by the god Hermes "with his golden wand."

Argicida: "Slayer of Argus," an epithet for Hermes, god of thieves and Olympian messenger. It can also mean "slayer of Greeks," alluding to the Trojan War, for which Aphrodite was responsible by way of the Judgment of Paris, and in which she helped the Trojans, especially her son Aeneas, against the Greeks.

# CANTO II (1922/1925)  [SP, 98]

The first two lines of this canto originally opened the "Three Cantos" which Pound published in *Poetry* in 1917. The body of the canto first appeared as Canto VIII in 1922 and was resituated only in 1923, when Pound arranged *A Draft of XVI. Cantos* (1925). Pound had read Robert Browning's *Sordello* in 1915. He thought it "the best long poem in English since Chaucer" (L, 18 December 1918), and it was his first inspiration for his long poem. Canto II begins with an homage to Browning, expressing Pound's frustration that he cannot do again what Browning has already done so well. As it proceeds, however, Pound makes an implicit distinction between Browning's poetics and his own. Whereas Browning fictionalizes Sordello (a troubadour poet) to suit his own purposes, Pound's "poem including history" questions, from the outset, the relationship of poetry to history.

In a sense, this question informs the whole of Canto II, which plays manifold fictions against a substrate of "fact." The images which follow exemplify imaginative representations of the sea, which symbolizes the "literal" constant underlying the images which form and dissolve on its surface. The So-shu image, an invented Orientalism, personifies the moon and the shaft of light it casts down to the ocean. Pound mimics it in the seal image. The words heard in the wave rush allude to a line in Aeschylus' *Agamemnon* which puns on Helen's name: "Helen" sounds like the Greek *helenaus* ("destroyer of ships") and *heleptolis* ("destroyer of cities")—Helen of Troy being, of course, the legendary cause of the Trojan War. Pound imagines the blind poet Homer also transmuting the sound of the sea into the voices of his poetry. He then moves from *melopoeia*, or the music of poetry, to *phanopoeia*, or images: the wave with its moving ridges of water recalls the Greek myth of Tyro and Neptune, and the "naviform rock"—the rock in the shape of a ship—recalls Acoetes' story of Dionysos' miracle. Pound mimics these images in his invented "Dafne of sea-bords." The recapitulation at the end of the canto moves from the Orient to Greece and Rome and into the present, where the sea becomes "quiet"—description rather than myth, with the literal frogs drowning out the fauns in the "half-light" left behind the departed gods.

A certain ambivalence about history and poetry comes through in all this: poetry, the imagination, is uneasy with history, which seeks facts. Wallace Stevens reconciled these contradictory needs in his idea of the "supreme fiction," an abstract ideal which would satisfy the need to believe without presenting itself as truth. But Pound wants more: he seeks a common ground in all the fictions, the literal, historical rock and water that underlies them all. This seems to be the import of the central myth of Dionysos in the canto, which affirms a natural world that transcends cultural variations and gives all human beings a common bond underlying their different languages and cultures. This natural bond is implicitly conceived in the myth as the ground not only of aesthetics but also of ethics, and Pound's belief in it presides over the *paradiso terrestre*, the earthly paradise, which his long poem imagines.

In *The Pisan Cantos*, Pound reminisces, "To break the pentameter, that was the first heave." (C, 518) The composition of Canto II was an important stage in the progress toward a new poetic line. Its hung-over free verse line is recognizably a development from the two-part, four-stress alliterative line Pound used in "The Seafarer" and from its freer descendant in Canto I; thus

> Sea-fowls' loudness was for me laughter ("The Seafarer")
> Sun to his slumber, shadows o'er all the ocean (Canto I)
> Safe with my lynxes,
> feeding grapes to my leopards (Canto II)

Canto II continues Pound's forging of "a language to think in." (LE, 194)

Robert Browning: the Victorian poet (1812–89) whose long poem *Sordello* (1840/64), about the Italian troubadour Sordello (1180–1255), was a crucial inspiration for *The Cantos*.

Lo Sordels . . . : Provençal: "Sordello comes from Mantua," from a troubadour biography of Sordello. Pound quotes the line and translates Sordello's brief biography in "Troubadours—Their Sorts and Conditions" (LE, 97).

So-shu: The name Pound first used in this image, which is his own invention, is "Ka-hu." (Yale MSS) He probably preferred "So-shu" because of its onomatopoeic sound rather than for the sake of any allusion.

Lir: a Celtic sea-god.

Picasso: Pablo Picasso (1881–1973), whose eyes Pound thought resembled a seal's. Pound saw a good deal of his work while living in Paris, and admired it.

"Eleanor . . . : The Chorus in Aeschylus' *Agamemnon* puns on Helen's name, describing her as *helandros* (man-destroying), *helenaus* (ship-destroying), and *heleptolis* (city-destroying). Eleanor, a French form of "Helen," refers to Eleanor of Aquitaine, who, like the legendary Helen, was a powerful influence on the events of her time.

Ear, ear . . . : Pound considered one quality of Homer's poetry "untranslatable": "the magnificent onomatopoeia, as of the rush of the waves on the sea-beach and their recession in 'para thina poluphloisboio thalasses.' " (LE, 250)

"Let her go . . . : This passage is freely translated from Homer's *Iliad* (III.139ff.), in which the Trojan elders on the wall, seeing Helen, speak of her dangerous beauty and of sending her back to the Greeks in order to end the war. Pound discusses several other versions of this passage in "Translators of Greek: Early Translators of Homer" (LE, 249–55).

Schoeney's daughters: Pound alludes here to Golding's translation of Ovid's *Metamorphoses*, VIII.427–35, in which Atalanta, daughter of Schoeneus, is "one/Of Schenyes daughters." Pound quotes the passage in "Notes on Elizabethan Classicists" (LE, 236).

Tyro: In Book XII of the *Odyssey*, Tyro is one of the ghosts Odysseus sees in Hades. The sea-god Poseidon was smitten with her.

Scios: Aegean island northeast of Naxos.

Naviform: shaped like a ship.

The ship landed . . . : Pound translates Acoetes' story of Dionysos' revenge on his kidnappers from Book III of Ovid's *Metamorphoses*.

young boy: Dionysos, Greek god of wine, music, tragedy, and ecstasy, in disguise. vine-must: new wine. The imagery in this passage—wine, grapes, leopards, ivy, lynxes, panthers—is of the natural things sacred to Dionysos.

Naxos: island in the Cyclades famous for its wine, where Dionysos was worshiped.

I: Acoetes, the ship's pilot, who recognized Dionysos' divinity and was spared. He tells the story as a warning to King Pentheus to honor Dionysos and allow the Thebans to worship him. Pentheus does not heed it, and is himself torn limb from limb by the Theban women in Dionysiac frenzy. The story is dramatized in Euripides' *The Bacchae*.

ex-convict: Lycabus (Lycabs), a pirate.

Lyaeus: another name for Dionysos, meaning "soother of troubles."

Olibanum: the Latin word for the frankincense used in Dionysiac rites.

Medon: one of the shipmates.

Tiresias: Theban prophet who warned Pentheus of Dionysos' divinity and foretold his death. Cadmus: Pentheus' grandfather, founder of Thebes, who also warned his grandson to worship the new god.

Ileuthyeria: an invented name. Looking at the coral, Pound imagines a myth which would make it a sign of the animate natural world portrayed in Acoetes' story. His model is the myth of Daphne, who, fleeing Apollo, was transformed into a laurel tree. (Cf. "The Tree" and HSM, XII, SP, 6, 69.)

Poseidon: the sea-god who fell in love with Tyro.

Hesperus: the evening star.

fauns: forest deities, half man, half goat.

Proteus: a sea-god who had the power of metamorphosis. He was almost impossible to catch because he was always changing his shape, but once caught he could predict the future. (Cf. *Odyssey*, IV.365f.) Here he personifies the secret of nature's metamorphoses, the sameness that underlies the differences.


# CANTO III  (1925)                                        [SP, 103]


Like Canto II, Canto III begins in dialogue with Robert Browning. In *Sordello*, the poet-narrator, in Venice, intrudes himself into his poem to consider how he can make his poetry a force for social change and a solace to the suffering humanity he sees around him. Eighty years later, when Pound remembers his own experience of Venice, Browning's vision of history as a progress led and inspired by poetry appears unfulfilled. The past exists in tatters and fragments, and the modern epic—which Pound defined as "a poem including history"—must represent it as such, "with neither hope nor fear." The modernist collage of the third canto creates the sense of a past which has crumbled and decayed, which frustrates nostalgia at the same time that it denies Browning's vision of progress. In suggesting its failure, Pound again raises the problem of a "poem including history." Browning's progressive vision and the risk of its denial create a dialectic which informs the half-century-long struggle of *The Cantos*.

I sat . . . : In *Sordello*, Browning writes, "I muse this on a ruin'd palace-step / At Venice" (III.676–77); Pound answers with his own situation. The Dogana is the old customs house in Venice, located at the entrance to the Grand Canal.

"those girls": Pound quotes from *Sordello*, III.698.

Buccentoro: The *bucintoro* was a beautiful rowing boat from which, in the early history of Venice, the Doge, or mayor, used to cast a ring into the water to "marry" the city to the Adriatic. Mary de Rachewiltz suggests that Pound may be applying the word to one of the pleasure boats on which singers rode on the Grand Canal. Alternatively, the rowing club of that name near the Dogana. "Stretti": Italian: "in close embrace," from a popular song. Cf. Canto XXVII (C, 129-30).

Morosini: the Palazzo Morosini in Venice.

And peacocks . . . : translation of a line in Gabriel d'Annunzio's *Notturno* (1921), mentioned by Pound in his "Paris Letter," *The Dial*, November 1922: "La casa di Core è abitata dai pavoni bianchi" ("White peacocks now live in Kore's house"). D'Annunzio laments the fall of a Venetian palace into commercial use. Koré: Persephone (Proserpine), daughter of Demeter.

Tuscan: Tuscany is the region surrounding Florence in northern central Italy.

Panisks: little Pans, woodland gods. dryas: tree-nymphs. maelid: meliad, a fruit-tree-nymph.

the lake: Lake Garda, home of the Latin poet Catullus and one of the sacred places of *The Cantos*.

Poggio: Gian Francesco Poggio Bracciolini (1380–1459), Renaissance Italian Papal Secretary and humanist. Pound's image appears to have been inspired by a letter of Poggio's about visiting the baths at Baden, Switzerland, but he was not quoting from him. See "Aux Etuves de Weisbaden" (PD, 98–103).

My Cid . . . Valencia: Pound freely translates the opening of the Spanish epic *Poem of the Cid* (*ca.* 1140); he praised its "swift narration, its vigor, the humanness of its characters, . . . its inability to grow old." (SR, 66) My Cid ("My Lord") is Rodrigo Diaz de Bivar (*ca.* 1040–99), the hero of the epic. Burgos: the Castilian city where the Cid lived.

Una niña . . . : Spanish: a little girl nine years old. The town is closed against the Cid, and only she dares to tell him that his enemy Alfonso VI has vowed to punish anyone who assists him. Pound had imbibed enough of the spirit of romance to recognize her in "a pair of very big black eyes and a very small girl tugging at the gate latch" when he visited Burgos in 1906. See "Burgos: A Dream City of Old Castile," *Book News Monthly*, October 1906. voce tinnula: Latin: "with ringing voice"; from Catullus LXI.

Bivar: the Cid's estate.

Raquel and Vidas: moneylenders tricked by the Cid into lending him money in exchange for a chest of gold as security. He tricked them by filling the chest with sand and insisting they not open it.

menie: army.

Valencia: a region of Spain which the Cid took in 1094.

Ignez da Castro: a fourteenth-century Spanish noblewoman secretly married to Pedro, heir to the Portuguese throne. She was murdered by King Alfonso IV; when Pedro succeeded him, he had her body exhumed and enthroned beside him, demanding that his court pay her homage. Pound thought her story one of "the splendid horrors of the Spanish past," and unsuitable for art because "No poem can have as much force as the simplest narration of the events themselves." (SR, 218–19)

Mantegna: Andrea Mantegna (1431–1506), Renaissance painter whose frescoes for the Gonzaga family in Mantua survive, documenting a period when, as Pound thought, a sound economic system made possible a great civilization. Cf. Canto XLV, the Usura Canto.

"Nec Spe Nec Metu": "with neither hope nor fear"; motto in Isabella d'Este's rooms in the Ducal Palace in Mantua.

## *from* CANTO IV   (1919/1925)   [SP, 105]

Despite its number, Canto IV was the first to reach final form, and its beginning is a kind of invocation. Whereas Canto 1 goes back to the earliest Western literature, the image of burning Troy which opens Canto IV imagines an even earlier origin in the historical event that inspired Homer's *Iliad:* "The silver mirrors catch the bright stones and flare." But poetry is never a simple mirror of history. It represents desire as well as fact, as we see from the other images in the passage: cries of passion, visions of gods, a landscape of imagination. The black cock crowing in the sea-foam parodies the birth of Venus, ironically picturing the origin of beauty in what Yeats called the "rag-and-bone shop of the heart."

The next image is a complex one which shows the power of the imagination to form "history" in the image of desire. The old poet droning his story is actually several poets who all tell the same story; he weaves them together into what Pound called a "repeat in history," a "subject rhyme." The first is the Greek myth of Procne and Philomela, in which Procne's husband Tereus, King of Thrace, rapes her sister Philomela and cuts out her tongue to keep her silent. Philomela, however, weaves a narrative tapestry which reveals his crime, and in revenge, Procne kills their son Itys and serves his heart to Tereus for supper. He draws his sword upon the two women in anger, and as they flee from him, they metamorphose into a swallow and a nightingale. The second story comes from the biography of a troubadour poet, Guillem de Cabestan. Cabestan fell in love with Soremonda and was killed by her jealous husband, who cut out his heart and served it to her in revenge. When she learned this, Soremonda leapt to her death. The likeness in the external events of these two stories is obvious. But

Pound saw something more, which his conflation of them brings out. Soremonda, in his version, merges with Procne and Philomela. She seems not so much to fall as to float; her sleeve catches the wind like the swallow's wing, and the swallow's cry, " 'Tis. Tis. Ytis!" affirms this miraculous metamorphosis.

In the "subject rhyme," Pound sought a recurrent structure or pattern as a symbolic constant of poetic imagination. It is not the literal truth of the paired events he is claiming, but the continuity of spirit which underlies both stories and causes them to take similar shapes. As he wrote in "Psychology and Troubadours," "That the spirit was, in Provence, Hellenic is seen readily enough by anyone who will compare the *Greek Anthology* with the work of the troubadours. They have, in some way, lost the names of the gods and remembered the names of lovers." (SR, 90) Canto IV is a poetic restatement of this idea that a common religious sensibility links apparently different poetic forms.

ANAXIFORMINGES: Greek: "Lords of the lyre," an epithet of Apollo. The word opens Pindar's second Olympian Ode, and exemplifies what Pound disparagingly called Pindar's "big rhetorical drum." (SL, 91)

Aurunculeia: the bride in Catullus' epithalamium (LXI).

Cadmus of Golden Prows: Cadmus is the legendary founder of Thebes, a creative exile who left his homeland to found a new city. Cf. Canto XXVII (C, 132).

Choros nympharum: chorus of nymphs. Alan Peacock notes that Pound picks up "choros" from Horace's Ode I.iv.5, where it is an accusative plural, so that this phrase is not quite the linguistic hybrid it seems.

Ityn: the Latin accusative form of Itys' name from Horace's Ode IV.xii.5, which Pound keeps for the pun on "eaten!"

Et ter flebiliter: And thrice with tears, referring to the swallows' cry: "Ityn!" and " 'Tis." "Flebiliter" comes from Horace's Ode IV.xii.5.

Rhodez: old spelling of Rodez, a region in the troubadour country of central France.

Ytis: another pun on Itys' name heard in the swallows' cry.

# CANTO IX (1923)                    [SP, 106]

Canto IX is one of Pound's four "Malatesta Cantos" (VIII–XI), a
series based on the life and times of an Italian lord and condottiere,
or professional soldier: Sigismondo Pandolfo Malatesta (1417–68).
Pound's attraction to this obscure Renaissance hero arises from the
fact that, while actively and riskily engaged in the political in-
trigues of the Italian city-states, which finally led to his excoriation
by Pope Pius X, Sigismondo also managed to "gather the artists
and savants about him" (Canto XIII) at his court and to leave be-
hind him a work of art—the Tempio Malatestiano in Rimini,
Italy—which registers the complex historical temper of his time. In
the midst of political turmoil, Sigismondo created in Rimini a little
"civilization," to which his Tempio (Temple) enduringly testifies.
He brought to his court the Renaissance humanist Basinio, who
"argued down the anti-Hellene"—that is, defended the revival of
Greek, which created the Renaissance; Piero della Francesca, who
painted the Tempio's frescoes; Matteo de' Pasti and Agostino di
Duccio, who did its carvings and sculptures. The monument (un-
finished) which resulted is quintessentially Renaissance: half Chris-
tian, half pagan in its concept, its symbolism, and even its name:
the Tempio, dedicated to Sigismondo's beloved third wife Isotta,
is officially called the Church of St. Francis. It marks, Pound wrote,
a "cultural 'high' . . . a state of mind, of sensibility, of all-round-
ness and awareness." (GK, 159) Pound's interest in it stemmed in
part from his conviction that "Only in basically pagan Italy has
Christianity escaped becoming a nuisance." (GK, 300) In many
respects, it is an analogue for *The Cantos*, which also composes an
unfinished image of its time. Both are monuments to values which
oppose the prevailing powers of their ages—Sigismondo's, the
monotheistic church; and Pound's, the usurious economic system.
Both are "examples of civilization" which show both high aware-
ness and, as Pound says in another context, "the defects inherent
in a record of struggle" (GK, 135). And each might be judged to
be, as Pound said of Sigismondo, "a failure worth all the successes"
of its age. (GK, [2]) "You can contrast it with St. Hilaire. You can
contrast it with ANY great summit done WITH the current of
power." (GK, 159–60) In the same way, you can contrast *The*

141

*Cantos* with poems that accept rather than resist the dominant forces of their time.

Pound recreates the atmosphere of Sigismondo's struggle in the manner in which he represents his "life and contacts." The Malatesta Cantos are anything but a chronological narrative. Pound wanted a form that would directly express what he judged most important about his subject: struggle, the one constant in Sigismondo's life. "All that a single man could do," wrote Pound, "he managed *against* the current of power." (GK, 159) Canto IX employs several techniques to this end. An important unpublished source for the series was the "Chronicle" of Gaspare Broglio, a soldier in Sigismondo's army, preserved in the Gambalunga Library in Rimini. It partly inspired Pound's first-person narrator, a composite voice of the chronicler, of Sigismondo's brother Domenico ("And the emperor came down and knighted us"), who served in his army, and of the poet imaginatively remembering. Looking back on the past, this narrator tells Sigismondo's story not as a historian would reconstruct it but as someone who had witnessed and survived that eventful confusion might remember it: in fragments, half erased by time, with what was most important, most memorable, standing out from the rest. Five centuries later, this broken form is an appropriate image for the only way *we* can know Sigismondo's story. Hardly anyone would care to commit the chronicle of Sigismondo's adventures to memory; even in more conventional histories, such as Charles Yriarte's *Un Condottiere au XVe siècle* (Paris, 1882), his life appears a tangle of events, not an orderly succession with causal links intact. As Pound later wrote, "We do NOT know the past in chronological sequence. It may be convenient to lay it out anesthetized on the table with dates pasted on here and there, but what we know we know by ripples and spirals eddying out from us and from our own time." (GK, 60) The narrator's retrospective monologue, for all its prosiness, embodies its material rather than merely containing it; it is an organic, not a conventional, form, and its disrupted surface allows for "blanks in the record" for things the author doesn't know (Canto XIII). To these techniques of history-writing, Pound adds another: he translates fragments of the surviving documents, particularly, in Canto IX, a collection of letters which were found in Sigismondo's postbag and preserved in the library at Siena. These letters, received by Sigismondo during his military campaigns, convey his wide and various involvements in creating a "civilization." They bring him to life as a "factive personality."

Pound's use of documents in the Malatesta Cantos is an innovation important to understanding his purposes in *The Cantos*. In the Malatestas, Pound does not simply "include" history; he actually revises it. In 1922, when Pound began the sequence, the official view of Sigismondo was of a ruthless heretic who, having committed the most atrocious crimes imaginable, finally got himself publicly vilified by the Pope himself. Pound, studying the documents in the libraries at the Vatican, in Rimini, and elsewhere, saw a different picture. He concluded that Sigismondo's crimes had been greatly exaggerated by Pope Pius II for his own political purposes, and that the distorted image he recorded in his *Commentaries* had perpetuated itself. Pound aimed to restore a truer picture of Sigismondo; more recent historians, such as Philip J. Jones, have followed Pound's lead in reinterpreting the struggle between the Pope and the condottiere and have confirmed his revision, as Michael F. Harper has shown. This historical reconstruction, besides serving Pound's idealization of Sigismondo's character, also reflects his resolve to make poetry a mirror of history, not a fictional transcendence of it—as the sequence's opening lines about Truth and Calliope emphasize.

It is not, then, the local issue of Sigismondo's character which is Pound's main interest, but rather how the language of art—of style and rhetoric—expresses its own historical context. He allows the Pope's pompously distended Latin to speak for itself, its rhetorical excesses redounding upon its author, and the homelier affectations, errors, and endearments in the letters from Sigismondo's associates to project a composite portrait of their addressee. He ends Canto IX in his own voice, "reading" the design of history in the style of the Tempio: " 'Past ruin'd Latium' / The filigree hiding the gothic, / with a touch of rhetoric in the whole."

Sixty years later, we can hardly avoid seeing problematic complications in the value Pound placed on Sigismondo's high "cultural awareness"—hero worship being chief among them. In 1923, Pound could discount Sigismondo's violence and immense egotism for the sake of the great value he attached to the triumphant embodiment of his antimonotheistic sensibility in the Tempio, "against the current of power." Looking back from the second half of our century, however, it is no longer possible to overlook the ruthless acts of barbarism on which this "cultural high" was raised. While we may still be moved by the eloquent "record of struggle" Sigismondo left in the Tempio, we must judge this Renaissance record of struggle, as Pound himself could not, within the context of the record of struggle Pound's poem has left for our own time, which mirrors the still unresolved crisis of the heroic values on which Western civilization is founded.

Astorre Manfredi: Lord of Faenza and archenemy of the Malatestas, who ambushed Sigismondo when the latter was crossing his territory. Sigismondo escaped by losing Astorre's hounds in the marsh.

Fano: town in the Marches south of Rimini, part of Sigismondo's inheritance, later lost to the Pope.

Emperor: Sigismund V (1368–1437), crowned Holy Roman Emperor in Rome in 1433, who knighted Sigismondo and his brother Domenico on his way home to Luxembourg.

Basinio: Basinio de Basinii (1425–57), Italian poet who argued the value of Greek studies for the writing of Latin poetry with Porcellio Pandone (the "anti-Hellene") in a ceremonious debate at Sigismondo's court in 1456.

lists: the boundaries of the battlefield.

Madame Genevra: (1418–40); daughter of Parisina and Niccolo d'Este, Sigismondo's first wife. She died at age twenty-two, and Pope Pius accused Sigismondo of having poisoned her.

Rocca: Italian: "Rock," Sigismondo's impressive fortress at Rimini.

Monteluro: village near Florence where Sigismondo won a victory for his second father-in-law, Francesco Sforza (1401–66), with whom he quarreled soon after when Sforza failed to help him keep Pesaro.

And old Sforza . . . : Sforza arranged with Federigo d'Urbino and Galeazzo Malatesta that the city of Pesaro would go to his brother Alessandro Sforza in an underhanded deal involving a marriage between

Galeazzo and Alessandro's granddaughter. In the same deal, Fossembrone went to Federigo.

*bestialmente:* Italian: in a beastly manner. *per capitoli:* Italian: by contract. Both quotations are from Broglio's "Chronicle."

And the King o' Ragona . . . : After having agreed to fight for Alphonse, King of Aragon (Ragona) against the Florentines and having accepted three fourths of his pay for the job, Sigismondo changed sides and fought for the Florentines instead.

Valturio: Roberto Valturio, author of *De Re Militari*, advised Sigismondo to change sides and keep the money.

*haec traditio:* Latin: this treachery, which Pound translates "changeover."

old bladder: Pope Pius II (1405–64); the nickname alludes to his windbag rhetorical style. *rem eorum saluavit:* Latin: saved their [the Florentine] cause. Pound is quoting from Pius' *Commentaries*.

Polixena: Polixena Sforza, Francesco's daughter and Sigismondo's second wife. Sforza had promised him Pesaro on his marriage to her, and he grew disaffected when Sforza betrayed his promise. She died in a convent in 1449, and Pius later accused Sigismondo of having murdered her.

Venetians: Sigismondo fought for the Venetians in 1449.

Wattle-wattle: Sforza, who married the daughter of the Duke of Milan and succeeded him in 1451.

Foscari: Francesco Foscari, Doge of Venice, 1423-57. *Caro mio:* Italian: my dear.

Classe: Sigismondo stole marble from the Byzantine cathedral San Apollinare in Classe, Ravenna, to use in the building of the Tempio.

*Casus est talis* . . . : Latin: The case is this: Doge (mayor) Foscari. The citizens of Ravenna complained to the Doge of Venice about Sigismondo's attempt to pillage their cathedral.

Filippo . . . : Pound quotes from documents showing that Sigismondo did not exactly steal the marble but concocted a shady deal "one night" with Filippo Calandrini, Cardinal of Bologna and "Commendatary" of

San Apollinare, to buy the stone for four hundred ducats. The Tempio was built over the Church of Santa Maria in Trivio. *abbazia:* the Abbey of San Apollinare. plaustra: oxcarts. Sigismondo carted the stone away under cover of night, doing some damage in the process, and paid the abbot Purtheo two hundred ducats for all the toes he had stepped on.

German-Burgundian female: Sigismondo was accused by the Venetians of raping and killing a German noblewoman on her way to Rome in 1450. Neither his guilt nor his innocence was ever established, but the Pope took his guilt for granted and added this fuel to his rhetorical fires.

messianic year: that is, his thirty-third year of age. Poliorcetes: Pisanello (cf. HSM) cast medals for Sigismondo which read, "*Poliorcetes et semper Invictus*" (Latin: Taker of cities and always invincible).

Polumetis: Greek: manyminded, Homer's oft-employed epithet for Odysseus.

Broglio: Gaspare Broglio, one of Malatesta's soldiers who wrote a chronicle of his life and times.

*m'l'a calata:* Italian: "he put one over on me," or "I'm the goat" in Pound's onomatopoeically inspired translation.

Istria: Istrian marble was used for the Tempio's facade.

silk war: between Venice and Ragusa, competitors in the silk industry.

Milan and Florence: Sigismondo fought with them against Venice and Naples in 1452.

Vada: village in Livorno with a fortress which Sigismondo captured by means of his bombards from Alfonso.

Siena: Siena gave Sigismondo the "small job" of attacking Count Pitigliano, who had seized some Sienese lands. His heart was not in it, and they suspected him of treachery and tried to arrest him. He escaped, but left behind his post-bag, containing about fifty letters he had received during the five-month service. If the Sienese expected to find evidence of treachery, they found instead that Sigismondo's mind had been on other matters.

*Ex Arimino* . . . : Latin: "From Rimini on the 20th day of December/ My most excellent, magnificent, and powerful lord." Excerpt from a letter of Matteo Nuti, an architect called in to interpret Alberti's plans for the Tempio when Alberti was called back to Rome. Alwidge: Luigi Alvise, a builder.

"*Magnifico* . . .": excerpt from a letter written by Giovane Alvise on behalf of his father Luigi; he begins by blessing his "magnificent most excellent lord" and ends by proposing an excursion to Rome for himself. Genare: Pietro di Genari, Sigismondo's secretary.

Sagramoro: Jacopo Sagramoro da Soncino, an adviser to Sigismondo.

"Illustre . . .": "My excellent lord." Battista: Alberti di Battista. This letter is from Pietro di Genari to Alberti. danar: unit of money.

"Monseigneur . . .": letter from "D[omenico?]" written at Isotta's direction. *Mi pare* . . . : Italian: It appears to me that she said everything. Lucrezia: Sigismondo's daughter.

"Magnificent Lord. . .": Lunardo da Palla, the tutor of Sigismondo and Isotta's son Sallustio, writes a thank-you note on his behalf. Rambottom: Giorgio Ranbutino, a stonemason working on the Tempio.

"*Malatesta* . . .": letter from "Malatesta of the Malatestas" [i.e., Sallustio] to his "magnificent lord and father," the "Most excellent lord and lord without lord Sigismondo, son of Pandolfo, Captain General of the Malatestas." Gentilino da Gradara: agent of Sigismondo. ronzino baiectino: Italian: little bay pony.

"Illustrious Prince . . .": excerpt from Trachulo, Sigismondo's court poet, advising him to take over the city of Siena himself. This is just what the Sienese feared, and the letter must have confirmed their suspicions when they found it in the post-bag. Canto X refers to it as "Trachulo's damned epistle." Hannibal: the great general, from whom Sigismondo claimed descent.

"*Magnifice ac potens* . . .": letter from Sigismondo's secretary beginning "Magnificent and powerful lord, my most excellent lord, permit me this humble advice." defalcation: embezzlement. aliofants: elephants, a favorite symbol of Sigismondo, much used in the Tempio. Antonio: Isotta's brother. Ottavian: painter who illustrated the papal bull authorizing the church. Agostino: A. di Duccio, sculptor for the Tempio.

"*et amava* . . .": Pound quotes from several documents in Latin and Italian: "And he loved so much as to endanger his soul Isotta degli Atti" [from Pope Pius's *Commentaries*] and "she was worthy of it"; "constant in purpose" [from Horace's Ode III.iii], "pleasing the prince's eye, beautiful to see, beloved by the people (the grace of Italy)" [from Broglio's "Chronicle"].

"Past ruin'd Latium": Pound echoes Landor's "Past ruin'd Ilion Helen lives" in "To Ianthe"; as Helen "lives" in Homer's style beyond the ruin of ancient Greece, Isotta "lives" in the Tempio's style beyond the ruin of Latium, the legendary name of Italy before Aeneas' conquest. The reference connotes the revival of ancient (pagan) culture in the Renaissance.

sarcophagi: The Tempio has sarcophagi resembling the Roman ones on the grounds of the sixth-century Church of San Vitale in Ravenna.

# CANTO XIII (1925)   [SP, 114]

Canto XIII is a collage of excerpts from the sayings of the Chinese philosopher Confucius, or Kung (551–479 B.C.), taken from three Confucian classics which Pound translates as *The Great Digest*, *The Unwobbling Pivot*, and *The Analects*. Pound first composed them in a prose anecdote in "Imaginary Letters" (PD, 72–73); Canto XIII rewrites this letter in verse. In the dramatic frame of a conversation, he imagines Confucius' words in their historical context, for Confucius himself did not write; his wisdom, like Socrates' and the Buddha's, was recorded by his disciples. Confucian thought became one of the ethical poles of *The Cantos*, which move, as Pound says, "Between KUNG and ELEUSIS" (C, 258). He wrote Canto XIII near the beginning of what would prove to be a life-long study of Confucius and Chinese, and it expresses the crucial aspects of his attraction to the old sage.

The key concept, in a word repeated ten times in the poem, is "order," defined by Confucius as a quality which begins in the sincere heart and radiates into the world. It is opposed to the worldly values of fame, pretension, and ambition. The foundation of this order is, Kung implies, nature itself: " 'They have all answered correctly, / That is to say, each in his nature.' " Confucian ethics is eminently social and this-worldly: Kung "said nothing of the 'life after death.' " His teaching is not for the sake of gaining heaven but for the sake of a well-kept state—orderly in its defenses, its government, its ritual observances, with its wealth directed toward spiritual riches rather than material excess: " 'When the prince has gathered about him / all of the savants and artists, his riches will be fully employed.' "

This social ideal, Pound thought, had much to recommend it. His attraction to Confucian order may be understood as a reaction against the ethical relativism which succeeded the decline of the ethical foundations of Western culture, the Judeo-Christian tradition and the Enlightenment faith in reason. Pound had no wish to revive the exhausted Occidental traditions of transcendence and redemption; instead, he sought in Confucius a model for an alternative social order. Confucian ethics, based on the principle of *jen* or sympathy between oneself and others maintained by means of mutual respect within all social relationships, had underwritten many centuries of Chinese civilization (though, by the twentieth century, its principle of respectful relationship had been corrupted to the maintenance of arbitrary and unjust power relations). Its attraction for Pound lay not only in its assumption of the natural goodness of human nature, but also in the Chinese ideographic language which Pound, through Fenollosa, saw as inscribing collective metaphors drawn from natural process. Such a language, he thought, could mediate between the "sincere heart" and the social order, reconciling differences in an ultimate "natural" common ground.

This appeal to the absolute of a common nature, of course, no longer carries much conviction. As James Legge, a translator of the Chinese classics, puts it, "Proceeding from the view of human nature that it is entirely good, and led astray only by influences from without, the sage of China and his followers attribute to personal example and to instruction a power which we do not find that they actually possess." (I, 31) Nature is bound up with change, destruction, and death; no ruler is infallible; no metaphor commands universal acceptance. Pound too was well aware that the simple and beautiful social philosophy expressed in Canto XIII has its limits. In the "Imaginary Letters," his Walter Villerant remarks, "Good art weathers the ages because once in so often a man of intelligence commands the mass to adore it . . . . I am merely defining a process. I do not protest against the leaves falling in autumn." (PD, 56) He closes Canto XIII with a similar image not found in the Confucian texts: " 'The blossoms of the apricot / 'blow from the east to the west, / 'And I have tried to keep them from falling.' " With this conclusion, Pound obliquely acknowledges the futility of attributing to nature a less complex order than it has. Canto XIII ends with its own critique of the interpretation of nature it presupposes.

Khieu, Tchi, Tian, Tseu-lou, Thseng-sie, Kong-Tchang, and Nan-Young were all disciples of Kung. Yuan Jang was an old friend. Wan, or Wu Wang, was king from 1169–15 B.C. The original passages in Pauthier's French translation, from which Pound translated these excerpts, are given in Terrell's *Companion*. Angela Jung Palandri relates the last image to Chapter 31 of the *Chuang Tzu*, which refers to an apricot orchard in which Kung lectured, now marked with a stone reading "Apricot Temple," near the Confucian Temple in Shantung. The apricot blossoms, she writes, "symbolize cultural florescence and Confucian teachings." (301)

## from CANTO XIV (1925)                    [SP, 117]

Pound's Hell Cantos (XIV and XV) seem at first a startling swerve from the preceding ones, yet on closer attention we see many connections. Pound is drawing, of course, on the tradition of Dante's *Inferno*, an epic which ranges its historical and mythological characters on a scale of evil defined by Christian theology. But Pound's Inferno differs from Dante's in being a hell of the living, not of the dead (though Pound read Dante's Hell too as a portrait of "the world, blind with its ignorance, its violence, and its filth" [SR, 131]). He portrays his sinners *in vivo*, intending, as he put it, "a portrait of contemporary England, or at least Eng. as she wuz when I left her" (SL, 191)—the England to which he had bidden an ironic farewell in *Mauberley*.

Pound had expressed his disaffection for England earlier in both *Mauberley* and "Homage to Sextus Propertius." Still, the Hell Cantos require some explanation. Between *Mauberley* and the Hell Cantos (composed in 1923), Pound had met the theorist of Social Credit, C. H. Douglas, and had conceived the idea of a causal relationship between economic corruption and cultural decay (a connection already implicit in *Mauberley*). The Hell Cantos portray perverters of language, of nature and the body, and of money as the mutual creators of an earthly Inferno which he hoped, by noticing, to help change. The Hell Cantos, then, tie in with Canto II, in which the sailors abuse a natural human bond for money; with Canto III, in which the Cid foils the moneylenders; with Canto IX, in which the Tempio stands as an image of what was possible in "a Europe not YET rotted by usury"; and with Canto XIII, which connects the well-kept state with language that does not lie ("blanks in their writings / . . . for things they didn't know").

Pound's imagery in the Hell Cantos is so potent that many readers turn away in dismay. The vision is angry, not analytic; in contrast to Dante's Hell and to the moral beauty of its gradations of evil, Pound's is a place where no clarity, no distinctions, no understanding, are possible. What is "rotted by usury" is the moral faculty itself. Whereas Christian theology had provided an ethical framework within which individual moral struggle became meaningful, Pound sees modern capitalism as having eroded the moral faculties of those who live under it to the point that even its worst exploiters are its mere victims. Marx defined a capitalist as a personification of capital; similarly, Pound could write of the munitions profiteer Basil Zaharoff, "I doubt if Zaharoff knew much of what he was doing." (GK, 302) Hence the anonymity of those who exist in his living Hell. Eliot's objection in *After Strange Gods* that Pound's "is a Hell for the *other people*," then, mistakes Pound's entire perspective. He was writing not about individual vice and virtue but about the evils of an economic system under which, after Calvin, the very distinction between virtue and vice which Eliot is assuming have been obliterated. "I am writing for humanity in a world eaten by usury," Pound later explained. "I write for a cultural heritage that includes centuries of anti-usurious doctrine and results thereof in cathedral building." (PE, 55)

Pound takes risks in completely abandoning story, characterization, dramatic interest, pathos—the means by which Dante rivets his readers' attention to the horrors he depicts—but there is point in this refusal. Hannah Arendt has said that evil, in the twentieth century, is banal; Pound's slum owners and liars, his obstructors of knowledge and distribution, are an image of this impersonal banality, as is his "unpoetic" language. "There is," Pound wrote, "the art of diagnosis . . . and the art of cure. They call one the cult of ugliness and the other the cult of beauty." (LE, 45) The diagnostic Hell Cantos deliberately withhold literary satisfactions in their attempt to erase the boundary between poetry and history. They aim to represent the banal horror of the spiritual desert that late capitalism has created, aspiring not to literary closure but to the abolition of the social evils they portray. To Eliot's criticism that "a Hell altogether without dignity implies a Heaven without dignity also," Pound might have replied, to quote Canto XIII, that he had "said nothing of 'the life after death.' "

pets-de-loup: wolf-farts; French slang for academics.

Invidia: allegorical figure of Envy.

corruptio: Latin: corruption.

. . . . .m Episcopus: Bishop ———m. Pound wrote, "the XIV–XV has individuals in it, but *not* worth recording as such. In fact, Bill Bird rather entertained that I had forgotten which rotters were there. In his edtn. he tried to get the number of . . . . . . correct in each case. My 'point' being that not even the first but only last letters of their names had resisted corruption." (SL, 293)

# CANTO XVII (1925)                    [SP, 118]

The delicate music of this canto and its many mythological allusions almost obscure the personal experience at its core. The canto was composed in 1924, the year that Pound and his wife Dorothy left Paris to settle in Rapallo, Italy. From that time until the war, Pound spent winters in Rapallo with Dorothy and summers in Venice with the American violinist Olga Rudge, whom he had met in Paris about 1920. The canto seems to record the personal conflict which this arrangement eventually resolved: "As shaft of compass, / Between them, trembled." Pound veils the literal situation under a cover of mythological personae. For example, the figure of Hermes recalls the last line in Canto I (as does the "So that" which opens the canto); his significance here is as the bringer of Aphrodite to Anchises. Later in *The Cantos*, Aphrodite is often a figure for Olga Rudge, and Hermes here more subtly refers to her. Athena, as Odysseus' protector, guides him safely home to Penelope. The canto's imagery evokes both Rapallo—a beautiful little town of tile roofs and cypress trees with the Mediterranean before it and steep, wooded hills, covered with vines and olive trees, rising behind it—and Venice, a city of cut stone set in the Adriatic.

Pound once wrote, "I believe that Greek myth arose when someone having passed through delightful psychic experience tried to communicate it to others and found it necessary to screen himself from persecution"—that is, by inventing a story to express the experience indirectly. His use of mythological imagery in this canto leaves aside literal representation, and recalls his definition of myth as "explications of mood" (SR, 92). The first image of metamorphosis and fruitfulness—"So that the vines burst from my fingers"—suggests a mythologizing of sexual experience as sacred renewal (which is explicated elsewhere in *The Cantos* by Pound's high regard for the ancient Greek rites of Eleusis). Dionysos (Zagreus), god of wine, ecstasy, and tragedy, presides. The power of love is also linked with poetic power by the imagistic play of silence against sounds and voices. Venice, as the scene of the literal metamorphosis of marble, formed of organic matter by time and pressure, represents art's power to transform the vital, natural world into permanence and formal beauty. But the beautiful city is also a scene of disaster, as the canto's last images recall. They seem to allude to the darker aspects of both sexuality and the mythological imagination—Anchises' fear of the immortal goddess, the awesome destructive power of Dionysos.

ZAGREUS: Dionysos, god of wine, ecstasy, and tragedy. 10: Hail.

goddess: Artemis (Diana), goddess of chastity and the hunt.

palazzi: the palaces along the Grand Canal in Venice.

Chrysophrase: chrysoprase, a light green, semiprecious stone.

Nerea: a Poundian composite of Thetis, daughter of Nereus, whose sea-cave was at Thessaly, and Aphrodite (Venus), born of the sea-foam, whom Botticelli depicts being borne to shore on a great curved shell.

porphyry: purple semiprecious stone.

malachite: green semiprecious stone.

panthers: associated with Dionysos; cf. Canto II.

*choros nympharum:* chorus of nymphs; cf. Canto IV.

*sylva nympharum:* wood of nymphs.

Memnons: perhaps Memnon, son of Eos and Tithonus. A legendary statue of him near Thebes was said to respond with a musical tone when touched by the morning light. Cf. PVA, 213.

Borso: Borso d'Este (1431–71), son of Niccolo d'Este; lord of Ferrara (a small city-state near Venice), patron of the arts and a peacemaker between Sigismondo Malatesta and Federigo d'Urbino (see Canto X).

Carmagnola: Francesco da Carmagnola (1380–1431), Italian militarist executed for treason in Venice.

*i vitrei:* the glassmakers of Murano, an island near Venice. Crystal is a recurrent image in *The Cantos.*

"In the gloom . . .": Pound paraphrases a line from Canto XI, where it alludes to Malatesta's creative efforts amid the gloom of fifteenth-century Italian politics. Here it alludes to such Venetian splendors as Saint Mark's Cathedral with its gold mosaics.

Now supine . . . : In Books IV and V of the *Odyssey,* Odysseus' raft breaks and, after a hard two days at sea, he washes up on the beach of Phaiakia. Exhausted, he makes himself a bed in a burrow and falls asleep. He wakes when the Phaiakian princess Nausikaa happens by with her maidservants. Nausikaa falls in love with Odysseus, but he declines her invitation to marry and forges on home to Penelope.

Zothar: invented name.

sistrum: Egyptian ceremonial rattle.

Aletha: invented figure.

Koré: In Greek mythology, Persephone, Demeter's daughter; after Hades abducted her, Demeter, the goddess of grain and fertility, withheld her gifts from the earth and the land turned cold and barren. Zeus arranged for Persephone to return to the earth for all but four months of the year, restoring fruitfulness to the land for the eight months of her return.

brother of Circe: Probably not Circe's literal brother; perhaps a reference to Pound himself.

fulvid: tawny.

Sigismundo: Malatesta; see Canto IX. Dalmatia: Adriatic shore east of Venice which Venice controlled after 1420.

## *from* CANTO XX  (1927)                    [SP, 121]

This passage portrays the "lotuseaters," the opium-smoking hedonists whom Odysseus encounters on his way home from Troy, as men who have fallen victim to the sirens' song (see *Odyssey* IX.82f. and XII.183f.). Odysseus, in order to pass the Sirens' rocks safely, plugs the ears of his crewmen with wax and has himself lashed to the mast so that he can hear the fatally alluring song without succumbing to its power. The lotuseaters' speech attempts to justify their "dropping out"; but the "ligur' aoide" line marks their anti-heroics as a song and dance learned from the Sirens. In a letter to his father, Pound said that Canto XX presents a "sort of paradiso" (L, May 1925); but the bones of thousands of dead and the siren tag render this an ironic paradise, like the one which was Mauberley's fate. The passage as a whole elaborates the opening of the canto, which is based on a Provençal phrase of uncertain meaning: "e l'olors de noigandres," which Emil Lévy, maker of a Provençal dictionary, emended to "d'enoi gandres" ("and the smell wards off boredom"). Pound's association of this phrase with the lotuseaters again implies another link between the classical and troubadour imaginations (cf. Canto IV), and the canto is another example in Pound's argument for a continuous imaginative thread running from the ancients through medieval times to his own.

incense: i.e., opium smoke.

lotophagoi: the Greek word for lotuseaters.

With silver spilla . . . : a description of the opium plant; the spilla is the stalk.

Voce-profondo: in a deep voice.

the clear bones . . . : In Book XII of the *Odyssey*, Odysseus recounts how his hungry crew disobeyed his orders and slaughtered the sacred cattle kept by Helios, or Apollo the sun-god, on the island of Thrinakia. The god punishes them by sinking their ship, so that all the sailors except Odysseus die.

the goddess: i.e., Circe; see below, and cf. Canto I.

Elpenor: crewmember who fell off Circe's roof and died. He was given a ceremonial burial, and his oar was set in the sand as a memorial. Cf. Canto I.

Spartha: the Greek city Sparta, home of Menelaus, the Greek king and hero to whom Odysseus tells the story of his travels.

ingle: hearth.

Circe Titania: goddess and sorceress, descended from the Titans, who gave Odysseus' men a potion which turned them into swine. Odysseus was protected from the potion and spent a year with Circe on her island before sailing for home. Cf. Canto I.

Kalüpso: After his men are destroyed for slaughtering the sun's cattle, Odysseus washes up on the island of the goddess Kalypso. He stays for seven years, then sets out for Ithaka on a raft.

"Give! What . . . : Pound parodies Eliot's *The Waste Land: "Datta* [Sanskrit: give]: what have we given?"

*neson amumona:* the Greek words for Apollo's "noble island," Thrinakia.

Ligur' aoide: the Greek words for the "clear sweet song" that the Sirens sing to lure sailors to their destruction.

## *from* CANTO XXV (1928) [SP, 123]

In this meditation on "forms and renewal," Pound imagines a natural history of forms. The documents for the Venetian public buildings record the prosaic origins of the palace's ethereal form; and the Roman poet Sulpicia is imaged as a human flute played by the wind, the rhythms of her lines, "forms cut into time," as enduring as the palace. Her voice is counterposed to those of the damned, who lament in the manner of Dante's damned that they "set nothing in order." Their Hell is one in which forms, words, and concepts have lost all trace of the energies that created them, and loom as deadly shadows over a valley. Tradition, Pound implies, is a danger unless it is continually renewed, as the ghosts are renewed by the blood rite in Canto I.

Pound elaborates on this mystical idea of aesthetic form in his essay on Cavalcanti:

> The god is inside the stone. . . . The force is arrested, but there is never any question about its latency, about the force being the essential, and the rest "accidental" in the philosophic technical sense. The shape occurs.
>
> (LE, 152)

But the modern mind, he writes, has lost this medieval clarity:

> We appear to have lost the radiant world where one thought cuts another with clean edge . . . magnetisms that take form, that are seen, or that border the visible, the matter of Dante's *Paradiso*, the glass under water, the form that seems a form seen in a mirror. . . .

A medieval 'natural philosopher' would find this modern world full of enchantments, not only the light in the electric bulb, but the thought of the current hidden in air and in wire would give him a mind full of forms.

(LE, 154–55)

Pound's nostalgia for the clarity of medieval form is at bottom a nostalgia for the coherent world view provided by Christian theology, which grounded thought and language upon absolutes no longer available to the modern mind; our cosmos is not theirs. As this canto makes clear, his aesthetic idealism attempts to substitute form itself for the Christian Word, attributing to it permanent, noumenal being which the creative mind perceives.

because . . . non sincere: Pound quotes from fourteenth- and fifteenth-century documents relating to the alteration of the Doge's palace in Venice. vadit pars: a Venetian legal term meaning "It was decided" (Terrell, 101). da parte: decided (i.e., 254 votes in favor). de non: against. non sincere: not counted.

murazzi: the walls along the Venetian canals.

Sulpicia: Roman poet (fl. 40 B.C.). Her extant works consist of six brief poems about her love for Cerinthus, printed in volume III of Tibullus, along with five poems composed in her honor by an unknown author ("The Garland of Sulpicia").

green . . . cortex: Cf. Canto LXXXIII (C, 530). cortex: i.e., bark.

"Pone metum, Cerinthe . . . deus nec laedit amantes": Latin: "Put fear aside, Cerinthe . . . the god doesn't harm lovers." Pound quotes from a poem in "The Garland of Sulpicia" about Cerinthus' fear during Sulpicia's illness. Cf. Canto XCIII (C, 630).

Zephyrus: the west wind.

Hic mihi dies sanctus: Latin: This day is holy for me. Pound quotes from a poem in the "Garland" which begins, "Today, the day that gave you to me, Cerinthus, / Shall be a dedicated day, counted among the feasts."

"Sero . . .": Too late, too late; from St. Augustine's *Confessions*, where the line continues, "Too late have I loved you, beauty as ancient as new."

bolge: The eighth circle of Dante's Hell has ten ravines or *bolgias*.

Civis Romanus: Roman citizen.

blood rite: sacrifice by which Odysseus restores speech to Tiresias and hears his prophecy; see Canto I.

vanity of Ferrara: Pound refers to Ferrara as a "paradiso dei sarti [tailors' paradise]" in Canto XXIV (C, 114).

Phaethusa: In Book XII of the *Odyssey*, Circe tells Odysseus about the sacred cattle of Apollo on the island of Thrinakia: "these fat cattle never die. / Immortal, too, their cowherds are—their shepherds— / Phaëthousa and Lampetía, sweetly braided / nymphs that divine Neaira bore / to the overlord of high noon, Hêlios" (tr. Fitzgerald). In Canto XXI (C, 100), she is remembered as "Strong as with blood-drink, once."

Phlegethon: the river of fire in Hades.

Form, forms . . . : Cf. the confused wilderness of renewals in Cantos XX and XXI (C, 92, 100).

Napishtim: Ut Napishtim, wise man in the Babylonian epic *Gilgamesh*.

νοός: nous, the Greek word for mind, or the collective intellectual force of the cosmos. The Platonists, Pound wrote, have brought many minds "to be suddenly conscious of the reality of the *nous*, of mind, apart from any . . . individual mind, of the sea crystalline and enduring, of the bright as it were molten glass that envelops us, full of light." (GK, 44)

"as the sculptor . . . father": Pound quotes himself: first, a line which occurs earlier in Canto XXV (SP, 123); then a phrase from his Cavalcanti essay (see headnote); and then phrases from Canto XXIII (C, 109). The last alludes to Aphrodite's cunning speech to Anchises when she pretends to be the mortal daughter of King Otreus instead of a dangerous goddess. Cf. Canto I and Cantos XXIII and LXXVI (C, 109, 456).


*from* CANTO XXX  (1930)                              [SP, 125]


In this canto Pound parodies Chaucer's "Compleynt unto Pity," in which Chaucer laments that, because Pity is "dead," all the other courtly virtues allied with it—Beauty, Lust, Jolyte, Assurance, Youth, Honesty, Wisdom, Estaat, Drede, and Governaunce—have lost their value. Canto XXX seems to contradict Chaucer's view: Pity, there, is the root of evil rather than the keystone of the courtly virtues. But Pound's "Compleynt" is not as far from Chaucer's as it seems to be, for, as Dekker points out, his point is that Pity is no longer clearly allied to virtue; it is also invoked to protect "foulnesse," decrepitude, "things growne awry." (66) Pound's complaint, then, is rather an ironic complement to Chaucer's than its opposite. It is also closely allied to a moment in Canto XX of Dante's *Inferno* which Pound describes in *The Spirit of Romance:*

> When Dante weeps in pity for the sorcerers and diviners, Virgil shows classic stoicism:
> "Art thou, too, like the other fools? Here liveth pity when it were well dead. Who is more impious than he who sorrows at divine judgment?"

(134–35)

The association with Dante recalls the Hell of Pound's Canto XIV, which represents the evildoers not as dead and suffering for their sins, but as alive and quite enjoying them. In sanctioning evil, Pound implies, pity, "the root and the spring," has been perverted. Pedro with his dead queen is an image of a double perversion of values: on one day, the murder of Ignez; on another, the grotesque homage exacted for "governaunce" that is dead and rotten.

To the question of what to put in place of divine judgment and the rotten corpse of political authority, however, the canto answers only, "Time is the evil." Artemis, who utters the complaint, belongs to the timeless world of myth, of gods that are "eternal states of mind," and not to the historical world of change and death. Although, as the hunt goddess, she is the agent of destruction, she cannot arbitrate it in the human world. Nor has the modern world an equivalent for Dante's ethical scheme, derived from medieval theology, by which evil and its fit punishment could be imagined in accordance with a communal authority. Canto XXX can only be read with uneasiness, presenting as it does a fantasy of destructive power unallied to values which could underwrite its action in the world of history.

phrases correspond to definite sensations undergone." (LE, 162)
Far from being considered inimical to spirit, the body's sensations
were seen as the origin of thought and knowledge; and if the poem
was obscure, Pound thought, this was at least partly because body
and spirit have become so estranged in our time that we can no
longer understand such a language. "We appear to have lost the
radiant world where one thought cuts through another with clean
edge, a world of moving energies," a " 'harmony of the sentient,'
where the thought has its demarcation, the substance its *virtu.*"
(LE, 154)

From this vantage, we can begin to see the point of Pound's
placing an obscure translation of an obscure poem at the heart of
*The Cantos.* To include a modern English image of the canzone
in his twentieth-century epic was to embed in its center a gleam
of the lost radiance Pound associated with Guido's poem. As with
"The Seafarer" and the "Homage," Pound's version is in part
translation and in part a brilliantly impressionistic reading. It is also
a stylistic triumph, for despite its line-by-line opacities, its final
effect is of a mysterious light, "formed like a diafan of light on
shade," an image at once of the loss and the radiance. Compare the
Canto XXXVI version with Pound's earlier translation (P, 248–50)
and with the prose translation of J. E. Shaw in his *Guido Caval-
canti's Theory of Love.*

A lady asks: Guido's canzone was a response to a contemporary poem in
which the persona inquired the nature of love.

affect: feeling. Guido's word is *accidente*, implying the medieval philo-
sophical distinction between essence and accident. Love is an essence;
its instances are accidents, none being necessary to the essence as such.
Pound explained, "I am aware that I have distorted '*accidente*' into
'affect' but I have done so in order not to lose the tone of my opening
line by introducing an English word of *double entente.*" (LE, 159) The
word's lost sense corresponds to the loss of the "radiant world where
one thought cuts through another with clean edge." Pound wrote that
the "definition of 'l'accidente,' i.e. the whole poem, is a scholastic defini-
tion in form, it is as clear and definite as the prose treatises of the period,
it shows an equal acuteness of thought." (LE, 161)

virtu: Pound wrote that this medieval concept "requires a separate

Cf. Cantos LXXVI (C, 460), XCIII (SP, 181), and XCIV (C, 635).

Artemis: virgin goddess of the hunt (Roman Diana). Cf. Canto IV.

Paphos: town on the island of Cyprus sacred to Aphrodite.

Mars: the Roman war-god and lover of Venus (Aphrodite).

doddering fool: Hephaistos, or Vulcan, the god of fire and smithcraft who was lame and unhandsome. Aphrodite was married to him, though she was not, as Pound implies, faithful.

Pedro . . . Ignez: See Canto III.


*from* CANTO XXXVI (1934)                              [SP, 126]


This fragment of Canto XXXVI consists of the second of Pound's two translations of the "Canzone d'Amore" ("Song of Love"; also known as the "Donna mi priegha," "A lady asks me"), a prosodically intricate and philosophically subtle poem by Guido Cavalcanti (1250–1300). The poem has been notorious for its obscurity from Guido's day to our own. Pound's fascination with it was intense and longstanding. Besides making two translations (1928 and 1934), he edited its text and made it the center of a long essay on Cavalcanti composed over a period of twenty years, an indispensable commentary on the translation (LE, 149–200).

   Cavalcanti, and the canzone itself, had a complex significance for Pound. As a "persona," Guido exemplified the "modern" temperament. Against the orthodox Dante, who adhered to the Christian world view as mapped by St. Thomas Aquinas (and who alludes to his old friend Guido's heresies in *Inferno* X), Guido was a religious skeptic, a questioner of authority and "received ideas." Besides his intellectual independence, Pound admired Guido for his opposition to "asceticism and the belief that the body is evil"; this he saw as the basis not only of the canzone's love theme but of Guido's poetic art and the imaginative world it portrays. For Guido, the body was the "perfect instrument of the increasing intelligence" (LE, 152). His supple, sensuous language, Pound thought, was alive with the energies of its origin in sensory experience. "Guido thought in accurate terms," wrote Pound; "the treatise," but offered as a brief definition "the potency, the efficient property of a substance or person" (Tr, 18); an example is the power or "knowledge" of the oak in the acorn. Cf. Canto LXXIV (C, 154).

Where memory liveth: Guido's words, *dove sta memoria,* are remembered by Pound in Canto LXIII (C, 353) and in the Pisan cantos LXXIV (SP, 154) and LXXVI (SP, 160).

diafan: This is Cavalcanti's word for a concept that has no modern equivalent: that of the substance which, as light touches it, makes the light itself visible. In the "Cavalcanti" essay, he compares it to Dante's *Paradiso* X.68–69, which Binyon translates, "Sometimes when vapour has so charged the air / That it retains the thread that makes her zone" (LE, 184). Pound says of Cavalcanti's poem, "It seems to me quite possible that the whole of it is a sort of metaphor on the generation of light" (LE, 161); and he theorized that Cavalcanti might have drawn on the light metaphysics of Bishop Grosseteste (see LE, 160f.).

Cometh from a seen form . . . possible: Pound quotes Spinoza's formulation, "The intellectual love of a thing consists in the understanding of its perfections," in elucidation of these lines (LE, 184).

formèd trace: The "Cavalcanti" essay has an extensive commentary on Guido's "formato locho," which, Pound says, means something like "Determined locus or habitat. . . . As to 'form'; you may here add the whole of medieval philosophy by way of footnote. Form, Gestalt, every spiritual form sets in movement the bodies in which (or among which) it finds itself." (LE, 188)

Beautys be darts: Pound imitates the medieval orthography of his original.

the white light that is allness: Pound relates this line to Dante's *Paradiso* VIII and X (LE, 190).


# CANTO XXXVIII (1933)                    [SP, 129]


Canto XXXVIII is a highly complex ideogram, a "phalanx of particulars" which draws literary allusions together with images of public and private events that were current at its writing. It makes no concessions to the expectation that a poem ought to be made of "beautiful" language and images, and the new reader of *The Cantos* may be tempted to skirt what seems a tangle or barbed wire in search of more pleasing poetry. But no one who wishes to understand the significance of Pound's poetic project can hope to do so by focusing only on the lyric passages, for these luminous fragments must be seen against the darker fabric Pound weaves of the errors and wrecks of history. To grasp the whole, hell, purgatory, and paradise, is the challenge of *The Cantos*.

Pound anticipates our difficulties:

> You might put the question in the following form: What drives, or what can drive, a man interested almost exclusively in the arts, into social theory or into a study of the "gross material aspects" vidilicet economic aspects of the present? What causes the ferocity and bad manners of revolutionaries?
>
> . . .
>
> I do not believe that any oligarchy can indefinitely survive continuous sin against the best art of its time. . . . I have blood lust because of what I have seen done to, and attempted against, the arts in my time. . . . whatever economic passions I now have, began *ab initio* from having crimes against living art thrust under my perceptions.
>
> (SPr, 228–31)

All his political efforts were for the sake of his conviction that creative work is the highest value of human life. "I would put up a dozen brass tablets to one phrase of [the sculptor] Constantin Brancusi's," he wrote. "ONE OF THOSE DAYS WHEN I WOULD NOT HAVE GIVEN UP FIFTEEN MINUTES OF MY TIME FOR ANYTHING UNDER HEAVEN. There speaks the supreme sense of human values. There speaks WORK unbartered. That is the voice of humanity in its highest possible manifestation." (SPr, 283)

In *Mauberley*, Pound had mourned and raged against the death of his friend, the brilliant sculptor Henri Gaudier-Brzeska, who was killed in World War I at the age of twenty-three. After that event, Pound's career changed direction: his autobiography in the

*Selected Poems* includes the datum, "1918 began investigation of causes of war, to oppose same." In a 1928 article titled "Peace," he listed what he believed these causes to be:

1. Manufacture and high pressure salesmanship of munitions, armaments etc.
2. Overproduction and dumping, leading to trade friction, etc., strife for markets etc.
3. The works of interested cliques, commercial, dynastic and bureaucratic.

The useful research, in fact the only research that is not almost a sabotage of intentions of peace foundations would consist in contemporary (not retrospective) i.e. up to the minute gathering and distribution of information re. these activities. . . .

Where retrospection is necessary or commodious, the life of Sir Basil Zaharoff would be a fascinating document, any well-informed record of the exact procedures followed by Vickers or Krupp in getting off their products onto 'les nations jeunes,' of passing the guns into China or other areas of absorption would not need painful distribution.

(SPr, 222)

In Canto XXXVIII, Pound carries out that "research" in the medium at his disposal. In turning the field of his poem over to the political machinations of businessmen he ironically illustrates his own theory of what economic abuses have "done to the arts." It is a daring irony, which risks new kinds of obscurity, and it is a remarkable success in its own terms. Few readers who engage in trying to understand the canto's elements and to puzzle out their connections can avoid being stimulated, irritated, and angered into a keener sense that it is men who make wars, not "history," and that the economic systems that make war inevitable can and must be challenged and changed. It would be too much to claim that the canto completely answers the question of how to prevent wars; but its lesson, in a sense, is the question itself, which has only become more urgent in the fifty years since the canto's first publication.

Still, we must wonder in what sense a poem, and so difficult a poem as this one, can be an effective force for the prevention of war. It is entirely true that poetry is only one kind of force among many necessary for social change. But the relegation of poetry to a detached aesthetic sphere is exactly what Pound feared, and what he most resisted in his own work. Nor is he alone in refusing to serve his lyric gifts at the expense of representing social realities; writers as diverse as Virginia Woolf, Bertolt Brecht, Nadine Gordimer, and Peter Handke have followed similar courses. Pound's cantos on economics, if not *literally* a force for change, mark his refusal to allow the spirit-sustaining and civilizing' function of poetry to become the poet's pretence and the reader's escape while wars—"Murder by Capital"—continue to barbarize body and spirit. In offering up the space of his poem to social concerns, Pound "holds the mirror up to life," and composes a polemical image of the endangered status of mind and creativity in modern society.

The world of Canto XXXVIII resembles that of the Hell Cantos. But, as the epigraph suggests and as Pound tells us explicitly (134), its hell is at the same time a "paradise" which consists in the hope for change that a knowledge of causes makes possible. This point raises the question of how well this hope is grounded in the poem. Here, the value of the ideogrammic method (see Introduction, pp. 7–8 appears, for Pound does not explicitly analyze the economic abuses which lead to war; rather, he represents those causes by allusive vignettes so arranged as to require the reader to think out the connections between them. In engaging the reader with the facts he presents, Pound succeeds in his purpose, and this success is not diminished by the fact that his critique of capitalism, derived from C. H. Douglas' Social Credit theory and Silvio Gesell's theory of money, is limited in scope. The paradisal light into which he seeks to conduct us consists in the belief in our own power to know the world, and to act upon that knowledge to better it.

For more extensive annotation, see Terrell (154–59) and Brooker (276–85), to which these notes are indebted.

Epigraph: Italian: "the woe which falsifying the coinage [counterfeiting] brings upon the Seine [Paris]," from Dante.

An' that year . . . : i.e., 1894, when Bolivia and Paraguay were at war with each other and Zaharoff was negotiating armaments sales to both for Vickers.

Metevsky: Zenos Metevsky was Pound's name for Sir Basil Zaharoff (1849–1938), a Greek-born armaments maven who sold munitions for Vickers, Ltd., and for Maxim and Vickers, and who held interests in the Schneider-Creusot, Krupp, and Mitsui armaments firms as well as in international banks and newspapers. He was knighted in 1918 for his services during World War I. Cf. Cantos XVIII and XCIII (C, 627).

America del Sud: South America.

Pope: Pope Pius XI (1857–1939), whom Pound met in the Ambrosian Library in Milan, Italy, before he became Pope. Pound probably compares his manners to Joyce's, the Marconi anecdote suggests, because of his merely "polite" curiosity as to the material workings of the world. Pound and Joyce were moving in opposite directions as artists in the thirties—Joyce into language as a fabricated world in itself, Pound into linguistic "codes" that could only be broken by the reader's making connections between the words and the world.

Marconi: the Italian physicist who invented the wireless telegraph. Pound later connects Marconi's insight into electricity with the Social Credit insight into money in a Rome Radio Speech: "Then somebody found out they could do without metal counters. Just like Loomis found out . . . electricity would travel thru the air. Nothin' practical came of it, till Sig. Marconi got it into a system. Credit HAD existed just like lightning existed." (EPS, 177) Mahlon Loomis was a paternal ancestor of Pound.

Jimmy Walker: Irish Catholic mayor of New York from 1925 to 1932, involved in the famous Tammany Hall scandals.

Lucrezia: Lucrezia Borgia (1480–1519), who appears as "Madame Hyle [Matter]" in Canto XXX. The rabbit's foot which she lacked is apparently meant to represent her ill-fated reliance on superstition rather than science in dealing with her pregnancies.

cigar-makers: Pound quotes from Dexter Kimball's *Industrial Economics* (1929), pp. 79–80. Cf. Pound: "Civilization means the enrichment of life and the abolition of violence; the man with this before him can indubitably make steel rails, and, in doing so, be alive." (SPr, 199)

Akers: the armaments firm Vickers.

increasing gold imports: See Pound's essay "Gold and Work" (SPr, 336–51) for his critique of the gold standard, especially pp. 348–49, where he again alludes to Dante's lines about falsifying the coinage.

Mr Whitney: Richard Whitney, a New York financier.

two Afghans: Afghanistan made treaties with the Soviet Union and Great Britain in Geneva in 1921 (during the postwar disarmament conference) in order to import arms through India.

secretary of something: Albert B. Fall, U.S. Secretary of the Interior, was bribed to lease oil wells to private companies without competitive bidding. His deals were brought to light in the Teapot Dome scandal of 1929.

D'Arcy: William Knox D'Arcy, Australian oilman who, in 1901, leased most of Persia's oil lands from the Shah for sixty years and founded the Anglo-Persian Oil Co. Cf. Canto XL (C, 197).

Mellon: Andrew W. Mellon, who was Secretary of the Treasury in 1929 when the stock market crashed.

Wilson: Woodrow Wilson, whose presidency of the United States from 1913 to 1921 Pound considered "a period of almost continuous misfortune to the organism of official life in America. Came the war, the ultimate stupidity of Europe, the slow breaking of ignorance in America, the immense engulfments of bunk and sentiment, that would have been spared us, perhaps by an immediate Rooseveltian Fourth of July celebration in 1914." (SPr, 219) Wilson was ill after the Treaty of Versailles in 1919, though not with prostatitis. Pound is satirizing the acclaim Wilson received after Versailles as "the new Messiah."

Her Ladyship: Lady Maud "Emerald" Cunard (1872–1948), mother of Nancy Cunard, whose Hours Press published the first edition of *A Draft of XXX Cantos* in 1930. Agot Ipswich is Margot Asquith.

They began to kill 'em: i.e., World War I began.

louse in Berlin: Kaiser Wilhelm II of Germany.

François Giuseppe: Franz Josef, Emperor of Austria, who declared war in 1914. Cf. Cantos XVI, XXXV, and L (C, 71, 172, 247).

Miss Wi'let: Violet Hunt, English novelist and second wife of Ford Madox Ford.

Mr Gandhi: Mahatma Gandhi, Indian political and religious leader by whose political strategy of *satyagraha* or peaceful resistance India gained its independence from England in 1947. The money saved in not buying English guns and cotton could be diverted to food and peace efforts.

Untel: French slang: "So and So."

Jockey Club: Paris social club. In a 1932 article, Pound wrote, "When somebody, for purely social reasons, hunts up Mr Whatshisname, the French toymaker, and doesn't find him in the Jockey Club, but does ultimately locate him in Japan, some weeks before the Manchurian shindy, this either is, or ought to be, news." (Terrell, 156)

Mitsui: Japanese holding company with interests in armaments and banking, associated with Vickers.

"The wood . . . : In his *Diary*, John Quincy Adams speaks of growing black walnut trees and of seeing walnut gunstocks made in the Springfield Armory (374–75 and 551–52; Terrell, 156). Cf. Canto XXXIV (C, 169, 171).

Muscou: Moscow. Pound is praising constructive industrialization in the Soviet Union following the Russian Revolution.

Italian marshes: Mussolini's draining of the Pontine Marshes in central Italy was one of the constructive acts for which Pound admired him. The project had been attempted repeatedly since the time of Tiberius (Roman emperor, A.D. 14–37). The area now produces wheat, cotton, and livestock.

"Marry . . . : Charles William Beebe (1877–1962), American marine biologist, published his *Beneath Tropical Seas* in 1928. The image here represents natural providence.

Rivera: Miguel Primo de Rivera, dictator of Spain, 1923–30.

Infante: son of Alfonso XIII, last king of Spain.

gothic type: Pound found Vienna "tragicomic" in its use of heavy black-letter type for books and journals, whereas "every shop sign in Vienna that is intended to be read, to convey information to the by-passer that something in particular is for sale, is printed in Roman or block letters." (Terrell, 156–57)

Schlossmann: A survivor of the Austro-Hungarian Empire whom Pound met on a visit to Vienna in May 1928. (Stock, 361)

Anschluss: political merger between Austria and Germany in 1938.

The white man: Leo Frobenius (1878–1938), German anthropologist and author of the seven volume *Erlebte Erdteile* (roughly, "Parts of the World Experienced"; 1925–29), in which he recounts how the Babunda tribesmen in Biembe, at first unfriendly, changed their tune after a thunderstorm which they credited to his powers. Frobenius' interpreters heard drummers beat out a message about "the white man who made the tempest in Biembe" (V, 53). Baluba is an error for Biembe. Cf. Cantos LIII, LXXIV (SP, 147, 156), LXXVII (C, 465).

"The country . . . : Repeated from Canto XXXV (C, 174); Pound was living in Paris in 1923.

Kosouth: Ferencz Kossuth (1841–1914), Hungarian noble and leader of the Independence Party.

1927: Pound misdates his 1928 visit to Vienna.

the Tyrol: Austrian territory, part of which was ceded to Italy after World War I.

Bruhl: Lucien Lévy-Bruhl (1857–1939), French anthropologist and author of *How Natives Think* (1925). Pound misremembers his argument, which is not that the primitive mind does not generalize but that it generalizes according to categories different from those of the European mind.

Romeo and Juliet: In Shakespeare's play, Romeo, mistakenly thinking Juliet dead, kills himself; and she, waking to find him dead, also commits suicide. Brooker (282) points out that Lévy-Bruhl discusses customs of premature burial and widows' suicide in primitive tribes, and Pound relates a contemporary case reported in the newspaper to the literary and anthropological ones.

Green, black, December: Possibly an allusion to Lévy-Bruhl.

Mr Blodgett: Lorin Blodgett, author of *The Textile Industries of Philadelphia* (1880).

Douglas: Major C. H. Douglas (1879–1952), British economist whose theory of Social Credit powerfully influenced Pound's work. Pound quotes first from a serialized essay titled "The New and the Old Economics" and then from Douglas' *Social Credit* (p. 120), paraphrasing the "A + B Theorem" that is the foundation of Douglas' critique of capitalism. The point is that the money paid to the workers is always less than the money required to buy the goods produced. This leads both to underconsumption, which in turns leads to economic depression, and to large profits for the owners and shortages for the workers. See Surette (80–98) and Kearns (92–99) for valuable discussions of Pound's economic ideas; see also Canto XLV.

per forza: Italian: necessarily.

and the light . . . bewildered: Cf. Dante's *Paradiso*, XXVIII.16–19: "I saw a point of light so sharp that I had to close the eyes that it burned, so strong it was."

Herr Krupp: Alfred Krupp (1812–87), Prussian industrialist who founded the world's largest armaments works. Like Zaharoff, he sold arms to both sides impartially, e.g., to Britain and Russia for the Crimean War. He was decorated by both the Russian Order of Peter the Great and the French Legion of Honor. In 1868, Krupp sent the Emperor Napoleon III ("Barbiche") his catalogue of "steel cannon which I have sold to *several powerful European governments*" (emphasis his) and received a polite reply from the war minister, Edmond Leboeuf, a relative of the Schneiders of Schneider-Creusot. Pound takes the information from Richard Lewinsohn's *A la Conquete de la richesse* (1928), Fenner Brockway's *The Bloody Traffic* (1933), and Enrico dall'Oglio's *I Mercanti di cannoni* (1932).

operai: Italian: workers.

Bohlem und Halbach: Gustav von B. und H., Krupp's son-in-law, who took the family name and ran the firm after Alfred.

Eugene, Adolf, and Alfred: Father, son, and son-in-law who founded the Schneider armaments plant at Creusot.

the deputies: Eugene Schneider was elected deputy for the Saône-et-Loire region in 1845.

Schools, churches, [hospitals]: The armament firms took good care of their employees.

Herr Henri: Henri de Wendel, French steel magnate.

Chantiers de Gironde . . . bank: The firms owned interest in the Gironde shipyards and in international banks.

François de Wendel: son of Henri; President of the Comité des Forges, the French steel cartel.

Robert Protot: Robert Pinot, Secretary of the Comité des Forges.

Hawkwood: Sir John de Hawkwood (d. 1394), English soldier of fortune. Pound records the anecdote about Hawkwood and a passing monk, who greets him with "God give you peace" and receives in reply, "And God take away your means of getting a living" (SR, 70).

Journal . . . de Paris: French newspapers controlled by the Comité des Forges, which editorialized against disarmament after World War I.

Polloks: unidentified.

faire passer . . . : French: "putting these concerns above those of the nation."

# CANTO XLV (1936)  [SP, 135]

The traditional definition of usury is the lending of money at exorbitant interest rates. It is this practice which Deuteronomy 23:19–20 forbade in the following terms:

Thou shalt not lend upon usury to thy brother; usury of money,
usury of victuals, usury of any thing that is lent upon usury:
Unto a stranger thou mayest lend upon usury; but unto thy
brother thou shalt not lend upon usury: that the Lord thy God may
bless thee in all that thou settest thine hand to in the land whither
thou goest to possess it.

The Catholic Church outlawed the practice categorically up to the
time of the Reformation, when John Calvin succeeded in over-
turning the ban. Calvin argued that Deuteronomy forbids usury
only insofar as it is "opposed to equity or charity." (Nelson, 78)
Pound's definition is more specific: "A charge for the use of pur-
chasing power, levied without regard to production; often without
regard to the possibilities of production." (C, 230) This definition
makes the legitimacy of interest charges dependent upon the real
increase in value which the lent money, put to use, achieves. Pound
saw the prime offenders against this principle as private banks,
which are empowered to create money, or credit, out of nothing;
and his *Fifth Decad of Cantos* is concerned with legitimate and
illegitimate—or good and evil—banking practices.

In *The Cantos*, the Usura Canto follows the series XLII–XLIV,
which provides a counterexample of usury in the form of a docu-
mentary history of a Sienese bank called the Monte dei Paschi
(Mount of the Pastures), founded in 1624 and still thriving today.
The operations of this bank were quite literally guaranteed by the
principle of natural increase: the pastures of Siena, which caused
the flocks to increase, also underwrote the interest paid and re-
ceived; for to own deposits or shares in the bank was to own
*luoghi* or "places" on the mountainside. The Monte lent at 5½ per
cent and paid its depositors, or shareholders, 5 per cent; the ½ per
cent remaining went for overhead, with any extra profits being
applied to civic works. The Monte, then, was in effect a nonprofit
bank; it belonged completely to its shareholders, and since all its
profits returned to the people, no "clog" in the circulation of
money could occur. (See Canto XXXVIII, Douglas' A + B
Theorem.)

Pound contrasts the Monte with English and American banks,
which are privately held and create large profits for their owners
independent of any actual production. In Canto XLVI, Pound

quotes the founder of the Bank of England claiming that the bank *"Hath benefit of interest on all / the moneys which it, the bank, creates out of nothing."* The creation of money *ex nihilo* by the banks was the outrage against which Pound's entire effort at economic reform was aimed. In his two-page "Introductory Textbook" (1938), Pound quotes the Constitution of the United States: "The Congress shall have power: To coin money, regulate the value thereof, and of foreign coin and to fix the standards of weights and measures"; and notes, "The abrogation of this last mentioned power derives from the ignorance mentioned in my first quotation." His first quotation, from John Adams, is "All the perplexities, confusion, and distress in America arise, not from defects in their constitution or confederation, not from want of honour and virtue, so much as from downright ignorance of the nature of coin, credit, and circulation." (SPr, 159–60) Pound understood (as Marx, "endowing money with properties of a quasi-religious nature" [I, 112], did not) that money is properly neither a commodity nor "congealed labor" but nothing more than a symbolic designation of credit, which by rights belongs to the people of a society, and not to private banks. He saw that if the government had retained control over money/credit (assuming its honest implementation), the interest which now goes to private banks, creating their immense wealth, would instead accumulate as communal capital available for public works. Depending on government expenditure, then, there might be no need to levy taxes; indeed, the government might pay its citizens dividends.

Pound saw, then, that the governments had betrayed the people by authorizing private banks to "create money out of nothing" and then grow rich merely by charging interest on it. Before the thirties, American banks were allowed actually to print money; now, they continue to create money out of nothing by means of "the float": the effective doubling of money during the time it takes the bank to transfer it from one account to another, during which time the bank "hath benefit" of the accruing interest. Though in theory the Federal Reserve now controls the money supply, it is still true that private banks, by virtue of the huge volume of monetary transactions that they control, also exert great power over the circulation of money. In contrast to the Monte, then, the banks practice usury, collecting interest "without regard to production"—a practice Aristotle condemned twenty-three centuries ago as "unnatural" because it "makes a gain out of money itself, and not from the natural object of it. For money was intended to be used in exchange, but not to increase at interest." (*Politics*, I.10) The authorization of this practice by the government is tantamount, Pound perceived, to granting licenses for usury and for the economic disruptions and inequities resulting from the abuse of money/credit; and he could never bring himself to accept the ignorance and apathy of the American people which permitted these abuses to continue.

Pound portrays and excoriates these economic disruptions, and their cultural effects, in his Usura Canto, which he places in the midst of the documentary background on public and private banks in *The Fifth Decad*. Its austere dirge poses Usura against the real human values that it blights, negates, and overrides: good houses, good bread, good art, natural fertility. These things are emblems, for Pound, of human civilization, as the celebration of human life and creativity in harmony with nature. Most of his examples come from the late medieval and early Renaissance periods, before the Reformation, when the Church still banned usury. After the Reformation, "with usura," "the line grows thick"; craftsmanly care languishes because money-lust, not love of the earth and of the communal good life, directs the hand.

The structure of the Usura imagery, in which the personified figure of usury is posed "between" stonecutter and stone, weaver and loom, bride and bridegroom, embodies that "alienation" which Hegel and Marx see as the inevitable condition of human life in capitalist society. In the year of his death, Pound reflected on his economic writings and wrote that, with regard to usury, "I was out of focus, taking a symptom for a cause. The cause is AVARICE." (SPr, [3]) This late distinction marks not a change in thinking but merely a change in tone from anger to despair. His revisionary formulation says, in effect, that it is as difficult to regulate human appetites as to change the massive economic structures which avarice has created. Whatever might be the limitations of his analysis, Pound's Usura Canto remains a powerful protest against a debased culture whose "painted paradise" is mostly commissioned from Madison Avenue.

Compare the 1941 "Addendum for C" (C, 798).

hath no man . . . *luthes:* Pound paraphrases an image from François Villon's *Testament,* "Ballade pour Prier Nôtre Dame," written for his mother, which Rossetti translates as follows:

A pitiful poor woman, shrunk and old,
I am, and nothing learn'd in letter-lore.
Within my parish-cloister I behold
A painted heaven where harps and lutes adore,
And eke an Hell whose damned folk seethe full sore:
One bringeth fear, the other joy, to me.

The "painted paradise" recurs in Cantos LXXIV and XCV (SP, 157, C, 643). Pound had written two years earlier in *ABC of Reading* that

Villon, the first voice of man broken by bad economics, represents also the end of a tradition, the end of the mediaeval dream, the end of a whole body of knowledge, fine, subtle, that had run from Arnaut to Guido Cavalcanti, that had lain in the secret mind of Europe for centuries . . .

The hardest, the most authentic, the most absolute poet of France. The under-dog, the realist, also a scholar. But with the mediaeval dream hammered out of him. (104)

virgin receiveth message: i.e., paintings of the Annunciation.

Gonzaga . . . concubines: i.e., Andrea Mantegna's painting of Francesco Gonzaga and family in the Palazzo Ducale at Mantua.

to sell and sell quickly: Cf. "In Durance" (P, 20); HSM; and Canto LXXIV (C, 448).

thy bread: Cf. Cantos LXXIV and LXXX (C, 428, 493).

the line grows thick: Pound wrote in *Guide to Kulchur,* "I suggest that finer and future critics of art will be able to tell from the quality of a painting the degree of tolerance or intolerance of usury extant in the age and milieu that produced it." (27) Earlier, he had interpreted medieval art—"line, composition and design"—as "the temple of the spirit" (SR, 166), and as early as *Mauberley* had imaged "usury age-old and age-thick" as one of the causes of wars.

Stone cutter . . . stone: This image probably has its origin in Pound's memory of Gaudier, who was too poor to afford more than stray fragments of good stone. Pound himself bought the marble for the famous "hieratic head," the bust Gaudier carved of him.

wool . . . market: In *ABC of Economics*, Pound wrote, "Probably the only economic problem needing emergency solution in our time is the problem of distribution. There are enough goods, there is enough superabundant capacity to produce goods in superabundance. Why should anyone starve?" (SPr, 234)

murrain: plague.

Pietro Lombardo: (1435–1515), Italian sculptor of the family who built the Church of Santa Maria dei Miracoli in Venice with its beautiful mermaid bas-reliefs carved by Tullio Romano. Pound wrote that "A few bits of ornament applied by Pietro Lombardo in Santa Maria dei Miracoli (Venice) are worth far more than all the sculpture and 'sculptural creations' produced in Italy between 1600 and 1950." (ABCR, 151) See also Cantos LXXIV, LXXVI, and LXXXIII (C, 430, 460, 529).

Duccio: Agostino di Duccio (1418?–81), Italian sculptor who carved the bas-reliefs in the Tempio Malatestiano (see Canto IX).

Pier della Francesca: (1420–92), Italian painter who painted a fresco for the Tempio Malatestiano; he also figures in HSM, Part II, I.

Zuan Bellin': Giovanni Bellini (1430–1516), Venetian painter who did a "Pietà" for the Tempio Malatestiano.

'La Calunnia': "Calumny," a painting by Sandro Botticelli (1444–1510) in Florence's Uffizi Gallery. Cf. Canto LXXX (C, 511).

Angelico: Fra Angelico (1387–1455), Florentine painter.

Ambrogio Praedis: (1455–1508), Milanese painter.

*Adamo me fecit:* Latin: Adam made me, from a sculptor's inscription on a hand-hewn column in Verona's Church of San Zeno. Cf. Canto LXXIV (C, 432, 448), GB (96), and "Patria Mia," where Pound opposes the signed columns to what is possible under "industrial conditions" in which "columns are ordered by the gross." (SPr, 107).

St. Trophime: Church in Arles, France, distinguished by its double-columned cloisters. Pound visited it in May of 1919.

Saint Hilaire: Church of St. Hilaire at Poitiers, France, visited by Pound during his tour of Provence in 1919. Cf. Canto XC (C, 605).

cramoisi: crimson cloth.

Memling: Hans Memling (1430?–95?), Flemish painter. Cf. Canto LXXVI (C, 455).

CONTRA NATURAM: Latin: against nature; a phrase Aristotle repeatedly uses to describe usury in the *Politics* (see headnote). Pound wrote, "If there comes ever a rebirth or resurrection of Christian Church, one and catholic, a recognition of divinity as *La somma sapienza e il primo amore* [the highest wisdom and the first love] it will come with a recognition and an abjuration of the great sin *contra naturam*, of the prime sin against natural abundance." (SPr, 265)

whores for Eleusis: Eleusis is the town in ancient Greece where the Eleusinian mysteries were celebrated in ancient times. These fertility ceremonies commemorated the seasonal cycle, and involved the myth of Pluto's abduction of Demeter's daughter Persephone (or Kore— "maiden"), with Dionysos, Hermes, Aphrodite, Athena, and Semele as participating deities. Their celebrants were sworn to secrecy, and very little knowledge of the ancient rites survives. Scholars speculate that they involved a passage through the terrifying darkness of the underworld into a mystical illumination associated with rebirth. Pound wrote that his *Cantos* took shape "Between KUNG [i.e., Confucian ethics] and ELEUSIS" (C, 258), and here counterposes the sacred nature rites of Eleusis with the degradation of sexuality under capitalism, "largely by Xtianity, or misunderstanding of that Ersatz religion." (SL, 303)

Corpses . . . banquet: Cf. the recurring image of Ignez da Castro's corpse, placed on the throne for homage by her husband Pedro, in Cantos III and XXX.

# CANTO XLVII (1937)                              [SP, 137]

In the Usura Canto (1936), Pound denounces the degradation of spiritual values in modern culture: "They have brought whores to Eleusis." But denunciation, however powerful, cannot cure so pervasive an ill, and Pound speculated later in *Guide to Kulchur* that "a modern Eleusis" may be "possible in the wilds of a man's mind only." (294) Canto XLVII (1937), obscure, disturbing, and mysterious, might be taken as such a modern Eleusis. It is intensely personal, yet it seeks common ground in the expression of personal feeling by means of ancient myths. Its dissonant tones, moving between elegy and ecstasy, irony and bucolic simplicity, sound the modernity of its lonely ritual. In a curious way, the canto's subject is just that loneliness, the lost common ground of the experience it records.

The obscurity of this canto is so much a part of its meaning that exegesis is almost antithetical to it, a self-contradictory attempt to turn what is irretrievably private and subjective into common coin. Yet we may trace the poem's main lines of force without dispelling that significant obscurity. Indeed, we must do so, in order to grasp the way obscurity becomes significant in this canto. Pound at once expresses and veils personal feeling in mythical allusion. Here, as in Canto XVII, this use of myth reflects his view of its psychological origins. The Greek word *mythos* can mean a report or story, without distinction as to truth or falsity. Pound's more elaborate idea was that the first myths arose when someone "walked sheer into 'nonsense,' that is to say, when some very vivid and undeniable adventure befell him, and he told someone else who called him a liar. Thereupon . . . he made a myth . . . an impersonal or objective story woven out of his own emotion, as the nearest equation that he was capable of putting into words." (LE, 431) The personal issues in the canto are also universal ones: mortality ("Thy day is between a door and a door"), the measure of a human life ("By this gate art thou measured"), and the creative power that projects that life into the future. The two manifestations of this creativity in the canto, sexuality and poetic power, are in conflict in the canto's beginning; he is with Circe, he is not "at home." That conflict is resolved in the rapturous illumination at the end of the canto, in which the sexual act overcomes the separation between the lone individual and the burgeoning natural world; the "I," the self, is lost in the whole, yet feels its being most intensely: "Io," "I," "Hail."

To use myth and ritual to express fear of time and death implicitly emphasizes the universality of that fear, and draws on the collective resolutions of it which the ancient rites embodied. The three myths which Pound weaves together in Canto XLVII all involve a descent to the underworld, and a progress from terror and darkness to illumination and regeneration. The first, recalling Canto I, is that of Odysseus' journey to Hades to consult Tiresias for knowledge of how to get home to Ithaca. The second is the myth of Ceres and Proserpine (Demeter and Persephone), the basis of the Eleusinian Mysteries (see Canto XLV). These were ancient fertility rituals structured as a progress or quest from the darkness and terror of death to a mystical vision in which the merging of self with the natural cycle of birth and death is illuminated and affirmed. In this progress, the terror of death is transformed into joyous acceptance. (Eleusis, associated with "Elysion," the realm of the blessed, names the underworld as "the place of happy arrival.") The third is the myth of Adonis, or Tamuz, the god of ancient Syrian and Greek fertility cults. Adonis, Aphrodite's mortal lover, was gored by a wild boar while hunting and died. Aphrodite's grief was so great that Zeus granted his return to earth for half the year, having him spend the other half in Hades. Adonis' yearly return to earth in the spring restored fertility, and the Adonis cults performed rituals lamenting his death in the fall and rejoicing in his return in the spring.

The canto superimposes these myths in a progress from the terrifying descent to the land of the dead undertaken in fear and ignorance through the sacrificial death of Tamuz-Adonis, which brings about the renewal of fertility, to the surrender to the power of sexuality by which that fear is transformed into ecstatic illumination. In Canto XLVII, the interweaving of personal utterance and mystical allusion links such myths with the crisis of death that confronts every human being. But, though the poem looks back to a past when the sacred rites which bound the participants to nature and to each other were a communal reality, its own solitary celebration indeed takes place "in the wilds" of its author's mind. It is this which makes it so incontrovertibly modern.

Who even dead . . . knowledge: In the *Odyssey*, X.490–95, Circe tells Odysseus that in order to sail home to Ithaca he must first seek prophecy from the blind Tiresias in Hades, who retains prophetic powers even after his death. Odysseus responds with fear.

Proserpine: Persephone, center of the Eleusinian mysteries, daughter of Ceres (Demeter), the grain goddess. See also Canto XLV.

drugged . . . *thasson:* In the *Odyssey*, X.224ff., Circe's sorcery transforms Odysseus' men into swine. Pound quotes the crewmen's Greek words, meaning "let's hail her"; their clumsy consonants sound like the speech of "drugged beasts."

The small lamps . . . swift seed: The ancient rituals performed for Adonis in Greek villages along the Mediterranean involved casting an image of Adonis and ceremonial "gardens of Adonis" adrift in the sea. In Rapallo in July, Pound would see Italian women cast votive candles adrift in honor of the Madonna, and here he matches this scene with the ancient ritual.

Neptunus: Roman sea-god.

Tamuz: Syrian analogue of Adonis.

Scilla: Scylla, the sea monster who guarded the mainland side of the Strait of Messina and devoured six of Odysseus' crewmen as his ship sailed by.

Τυ Διώνα . . . Και Μοῖραι τ᾽ Ἄδονιν (TU DIONA . . . KAI MOIRAI T᾽ ADONIN): Pound is quoting from the Greek poet Bion's "Lament for Adonis": "They cry more shrilly than even *you, Dione. / The Graces* mourn *Adonis.*" Dione is Aphrodite's mother.

Two-span . . . counting: The misogyny of this passage seems to come from the fear of sexual power as a natural drive which leads one to death. Molü: the herb which Athena gave Odysseus to protect him from Circe's sorcery, so that he could sleep with her without harm. *naturans:* Latin: naturally.

Begin thy plowing. . . drawing down stone: Pound translates freely from the Greek poet Hesiod's *Works and Days*, a didactic text addressed to the poet's brother instructing him how best to live in a world of toil and suffering.

Pleiades: seven stars in the constellation Taurus, identified with the daughters of Atlas.

small stars: the star-shaped flowers of the olive tree.

Tellus: Roman earth goddess.

cunnus: Latin: vagina.

Io: The same word means "Hail" in Greek and "I" in Italian.

Zephyrus: the west wind.

Apeliota: the east wind.

## CANTO XLIX (1937)                    [SP, 141]

Canto XLIX, the Seven Lakes Canto, is a reminiscence of *Cathay*
and an overture to the Chinese Cantos (LI–LXI). But it is much
more than that, for it has a complex thematic and historical sig-
nificance in Pound's work. The poem is a collage of ten sections.
The first six of these are based on texts in an old manuscript book
of Chinese and Japanese poems (accompanied by painted scenes)
which belonged to Pound's parents. The seventh records his own
voice; the eighth consists of an untranslated poem by an emperor
of ancient Japan; the ninth is a peasant song which Pound found
translated in the Fenollosa notebooks; and the last lines are again
Pound's voice.

Pound did a first translation of the eight Chinese poems in the
manuscript book in the spring of 1928, with the help of a Chinese
visitor, Pao-sun Tseng, founder and president of the I Fang
Women's College. Only many years later did he decide to use the
translations in *The Cantos*. He adapted them freely for that pur-
pose, rearranging them and interpolating images from one into
another. In the new frame of Canto XLIX, the poems become
elegiac fragments which "speak as if weeping" not so much of a
lost world as of a lyric beauty lost to the poet and his poem by
the exigencies of his own century. The canto's first line—"by no
man these verses"—emphasizes the voicelessness of the images, in
which bamboos, cinnamon spikes, rooks, and bells sound, but the
human voice is silent. The exquisite Oriental landscapes become
at once an enticement and a rebuke: Pound lures us into a seduc-

tively "poetic" world, only to disturb our pleasure at the end with the shattering of its illusion. "In seventeen hundred came Tsing to these hill lakes." The beneficent governance of Tsing, if it ever was, belongs to the past, and so does the lyric beauty that commemorates it. The state we have in its place hardly inspires such lyricism: with "Geryon," to paraphrase Canto XLV, hath no one such a painted paradise as the manuscript book portrays. The untranslated "KEI MEN RAN" poem underscores our estrangement from that harmony of state and culture; and the "Sun up" song romanticizes a life in which work and rest, food and drink, reflect the rhythms of the sun and the seasons. The last three lines suggest a veiled allusion to contemporary politics, perhaps to the imperialist ambitions of Italy during the thirties. "Imperial power," these lines seem to say, is simply the governance that preserves the "stillness"—peace, the unchanging rhythms of nature. Like Orpheus' song, it is "power over wild beasts." This would be a very different reading of imperialism from that of *Mauberley* and "Propertius," reflecting Pound's growing desperation during the thirties as he struggled to bring together the paradise of words and the potential paradise, as he thought, of the world.

The eight anonymous Chinese poems of the manuscript book describe eight scenes in the lake district of Hunan, China. But the "seven lakes" phrase does not occur in the original eight poems which Pound translated, nor are there seven lake scenes in the poems, or in the Hunan region itself. It evokes a mental landscape, and transforms the historical and literal origins of the poems into a utopia, a "no-place" of past and future. Pound's 1928 translations, given below, have been edited and published by Hugh Kenner from a text Pound sent to his father (see "More on the Seven Lakes Canto").

Rain . . . weeping: Cf. Pound's 1928 translation:
   Rain, empty rain
   Place for soul to travel
         (or room to travel)
   Frozen cloud, fire, rain damp twilight
   One lantern inside boat cover (i.e. sort of
         shelter, not awning on small boat)

Throws reflection on bamboo branch,
causes tears.

Autumn moon . . . the river: Cf. the 1928 version:
West side hills
screen off evening clouds
Ten thousand ripples send mist over cinnamon flowers:
Fisherman's flute disregards nostalgia
Blows cold music over cottony bullrush.

Cloud shuts off the hill, hiding the temple
Bell audible only when wind moves toward one.

Touching green sky at horizon, mists in suggestion of autumn
Sheets of silver reflecting all that one sees
Boats gradually fade, or are lost in turn of the hills,
Only evening sun, and its glory on the water remain.

Where wine flag . . . cross light: Cf. the 1928 version:
Small wine flag waves in the evening sun
Few clustered houses sending up smoke

Comes then . . . leisure: Cf. the 1928 version:
Cloud light, world covered with milky jade
Small boat floats like a leaf
Tranquil water congeals it to stillness
In Sai Yin dwell people of leisure [deleted]
The people of Sai Yin are unhurried.

Wild geese . . . lanthorns: Cf. the 1928 version:
Wild geese stopping on sand [title]
Just outside window, light against clouds
Light clouds show in sky just beyond window ledge [deleted]
A few lines of autumn geese on the marsh.

A light moves . . . south sky line: Cf. the 1928 version:
Fisherman's light blinks
Dawn begins, with light to the south and north
Noise of children hawking their fish and crawfish.

In seventeen . . . hill lakes: Pound, already at work on the Chinese

Cantos, added this line. Tsing, or Ch'ing, is the twenty-second dynasty, 1616–1912; the visitor may be K'ang-hsi, Tsing emperor from 1662 to 1722. His reign is presented in Cantos LVIII–LXI, and his *Sacred Edict* in Cantos XCVIII–XCIX.

State by . . . for pleasure: The "old king" Yang-ti built canals which gave pleasure to his people and also served as useful trade routes. Pound contrasts the conjunction of economic and aesthetic interests in ancient China with the "infamy" of modern states (particularly America) which must "borrow" the money they coin from private banks at interest. Geryon is the monster that symbolizes fraud in the eighth circle of Hell in Dante's *Inferno*. Cf. Canto LI, where Geryon is "twin with usura."

KEI . . . KAI: Pound quotes the Roman transliteration of the Japanese pronunciations of an ancient Chinese poem ascribed to the Emperor Shun (2255–05 B.C.), from the Fenollosa notebooks. (Fenollosa has KEI for KAI.) The English translation given there is extremely rough and obscure. Fenollosa's annotation reads, "The moral of the poem is that ministers working in harmony, as the sun & moon, will enable the state to preserve its glory forever. Sun and moon refer to officials. Clouds represent the world—society in general. Succession of sun & moon may refer to imperial succession at this juncture." (Kenner, 46) Pound later translated the poem as follows:

> Gate, gate of gleaming,
> knotting, dispersing,
> flower of sun, flower of moon
> day's dawn after day's dawn new fire
> Sun up . . . what is it? (Kenner, 46)

Pound translates this peasant song, called the "earth-beating song because old folks beat the ground (for music) in singing [it]," from the Fenollosa notebooks. (Kenner, 45)

power over wild beasts: Cf. the closing line of Canto XLVII.

# CANTO LI (1937)                    [SP, 142]

Canto LI closes *The Fifth Decad* with a recapitulation of the Usura Canto (Canto XLV). This time, however, the usura theme is embedded in a complex of images which gives it a more specifically political interpretation. Having fixed on usury, or avarice, as "the root of all evil," Pound in Canto LI is preoccupied with the question of what kinds of social change might control its influence. Specifically, he seems to be considering Mussolini's imperialist politics as a means of implementing a *"paradiso terrestre."*

The first clue to this theme occurs in the canto's opening imagery of light and mud, drawn, as Terrell notes (197–98), from passages in a canzone by Guido Guinicelli, *"Al cor gentil repara sempre Amore"* ("Love always repairs to the noble heart"):

> The Sun shines on the mud the whole day long: the mud remains vile and the Sun keeps its heat. When a proud man says, "I am noble because of my race," he is like the mud, the true nobility is like the Sun.
>
> (De Sanctis, 32)

Pound, who had inveighed against nationalism since World War I, emphasizes Guinicelli's critique and associates it with the theme of imperialist politics by conflating the mud image with Napoleon's sardonic comment on the greatest impediment to his military campaigns. At this point, Pound repeats the usura litany from Canto XLV, and in fact, the social reforms which Napoleon instituted included the laws against usury. Pound thus presents Napoleon in the highly condensed first section of the canto as the type of the beneficent totalitarian, and the later quotation from Hitler's deputy that "A way of life will be achieved between peoples" reflects Pound's misplaced hopes for a Europe no longer divided by nationalist interests.

History has shown how utterly futile those hopes were. Pound's conception of totalitarian politics involved a fundamental error in the relations he conceived between nature, usury, and the state. In *Guide to Kulchur*, he repeats that "Usura is contra naturam," adding that it is also "antithetic to discrimination by the senses . . . because any perception or any high development of the perceptive faculties may lead to knowledge. The moneychanger only thrives on ignorance." (281) The troutfly passage, adapted from a nineteenth-century treatise on angling, exemplifies both the intelligence of nature, in the trout's canniness about the habits of the insects it eats, and, in the flytier's meticulous simulations, a creative intelligence which is "Godlike in a way" ("Deo similis in quodam modo"). The political empire which Pound imagines would be in the same way the product of a god-like human intelligence, with "the light of the doer . . . cleaving to it." But in light of the subsequent history of Europe, the poet, and the poem, this dream has a terrible irony. The "light of the doer," as history everywhere shows, is never the absolute light that the canto's images of the sun, and of God, invoke. Human constructions are inherently fallible, and not even the linguistic ones can have the precision, the absolute light, claimed by the ideogram which closes the canto: Ch'ing Ming—"precise definition." While there is political truth in Pound's assertion that "The art of not being exploited begins with 'Ch'ing Ming'" (GK, 244), the art of "calling things by their right names" is as much as poetry or painting an art of metaphor. "The light of the doer" indeed cleaves to words as well as to things, making all definitions potentially changeable social agreements and not the absolutes Pound desperately tried to imagine them.

Blue dun . . . Granham: instructions for making and using artificial flies for catching trout, taken from Charles Bowlker's *Art of Angling* (1829). Blue dun and Granham are the names of two troutflies.

That hath the light . . . cleaving to it: Pound explicates this image in *Polite Essays:* "Forma to the great minds of at least one epoch meant something more than dead pattern or fixed opinion. 'The light of the DOER, as it were a form cleaving to it,' meant an ACTIVE pattern, a pattern that set things in motion." (PE, 51)

"Deo . . . adeptus: Latin: "Godlike in a way, this intellect that has grasped," from Albertus Magnus, quoted by Pound in his "Cavalcanti" essay (LE, 186).

Grass . . . place: the same line occurs in Canto XLIII (C, 219) with reference to the Monte dei Paschi, the bank guaranteed by the natural increase of the flocks grazing in the Sienese public pastures. See Canto XLV, headnote.

Thus speaking . . . vivendi: On July 8, 1934, Hitler's deputy Rudolph Hess broadcast the quoted words ("Between peoples a way of life will be achieved") in a speech from Königsberg in East Prussia. (Terrell, 198)

circling . . . basket: another vignette of the usurers' hell, alluding to Dante's *Inferno* in which the monster Geryon takes Dante and Virgil on his back and spirals downward into the eighth circle of Hell. The twelve regents, Pound said, were bankers. (Pearlman, 218n) In Canto LXXIV, Pound wrote, "theatre of war . . . / 'theatre' is good. There are those who did not want / it to come to an end." (C, 477)

A thousand . . . basket: Cf. "Addendum for C" (C, 799). his: Geryon's.

League of Cambrai: A coalition of European states which tried to take Venice in 1508–10, succeeding only temporarily.

The closing ideograms are Cheng[4] ("right") Ming[2] ("name"). One or both recur in Cantos LX, LXIII, LXVI, LXVII, LXVIII (C, 333, 352, 382, 387, 400).

*from* CANTO LIII   (1940)                    [SP, 145]

Canto LIII is one of the ten Chinese History Cantos (LII–LXI) which were published together with the John Adams Cantos (LXII–LXXI) in the 1940 volume *Cantos LII–LXI*. In these cantos, Pound "includes history" more single-mindedly than ever before. The Chinese Cantos consist mainly of translated extractions from and observations upon a thirteen-volume history by Père Joseph-Anne-Marie de Mauriac de Mailla, a French missionary to China, titled *Histoire générale de la Chine* (1777–83). They move chronologically through about five thousand years of Chinese history, from 3000 B.C. to the eighteenth century A.D., at which point Pound turns to the career of John Adams, American revolutionary and a founder of the republic. The shift is not arbitrary: by means of it, Pound traces a current of civilizing energy which arose in ancient China and passed through dynasty after dynasty; made contact with Europe in the eighteenth century when the French began to translate the Chinese texts; and passed through French

Enlightenment thought to revolutionary America, where it mani-
fested itself in the social theory of John Adams. Nor is his interest
merely historical: as Canto LII makes clear, Pound is proposing
the ethics of Confucius and Adams as a radical cure for modern
political and economic systems. The point of the five-thousand-
year chronicle is the peace and stability which this ethics made
possible. His Chinese/American diptych appeals to his American
readers to reclaim the roots of their own cultural heritage as it
existed before the "usurocracy" gained control of the Union (SPr,
161).

Confucius (551–479 B.C.), already presented in Canto XIII, con-
tinues to exemplify Pound's ideal of enlightened rule based on
harmony with nature, the wisdom of the ages embodied in cul-
tural traditions, and "Ching Ming"—"calling things by their right
names." The "record of Confucius," Pound wrote in *Guide to
Kulchur*, "is the record of a great sensibility." (232) He con-
sidered that the Four Books of Confucius and Mencius "contain
answers to all problems of conduct that can arise." (352) Arguing
the superiority of Confucian thought to Western ethics, he wrote:
"As a working hypothesis, say that Kung is superior to Aristotle by
totalitarian instinct. His thought is never something scaled off the
surface of facts. It is root volition branching out, the ethical weight
is present in every phrase." (GK, 279) This last statement sheds
some light on Pound's politics during the thirties and forties. His
casting Confucian ethics in the language of contemporary Italian
politics marks the project of these cantos as Pound's attempt to
find an alternative to the failed Western idea of community that is
no mere utopia, but tested and proven in history.

The Chinese history Pound gives us in Canto LIII seems at first
inexplicably careless of a certain kind of detail which we are ac-
customed to expect in historical writing. He gives us strange
names, few dates, events noted so elliptically that we often cannot
grasp either what happened or its importance. What does he ex-
pect us to learn from it? Why should the legend that Yeou taught
the people to weave huts of branches matter? Pound's interest
seems to be in the significance of *what* a given culture chooses to
remember, to salvage from the losses of time and set up as its own
origins. The legend of Yeou inaugurates a tradition of good gov-

ernors whose beneficence earns them a kind of immortality in the people's memories. It is an example of a constructive act at the beginnings of a civilization; but more important, it is a paradigm for the benign exercise of social authority. In leaving out all kinds of information which we are accustomed to consider indispensable to history-writing, the Chinese Cantos assert the possibility of a radical alternative to the capitalist social values which underwrite the form, as well as the substance, of modern Western history.

Yeou: mythical Chinese king who taught people to build huts of branches.

Seu Gin: Yeou's legendary successor, who introduced the instructor's platform, barter, and accounting by means of an abacus with knotted counters.

Fou Hi: Emperor of China, 2953–2838 B.C.

Chin Nong: Emperor 2737–2698 B.C., remembered for introducing grains, improving agricultural methods, and establishing markets for distributing the produce.

Souan Yen . . . Hoang Ti: Souan Yen was a favored minister under Chin Nong who seized power and ruled as Hoang Ti after 2698. His accomplishments include the training of tigers for military use, the invention of writing (inspired by bird tracks), the invention of money, and the construction of a bamboo organ.

Syrinx: the nymph who was changed into reeds while fleeing from Pan.

Ti Ko: legendary emperor who combined vocal and instrumental music for the people's pleasure and edification.

YAO: Ti Ko's son, a remarkably wise and beneficent Emperor described by de Mailla as being "*éclairé que le soleil . . . aux nuages qui fertilisent les campagnes*" ("bright as the sun . . . with clouds that nourish the fields"), who invented astronomy.

YU: Emperor famous for learning to control the floods of the Huang River, and to channel the water for irrigation. He had his people store their own grain and pay taxes in the resources of their regions.

Ammassi: Pound's use of the Italian word here ("heap" or "pile") compares the Chinese grain tithes to the system of grain stores instituted by

Mussolini to facilitate distribution. (Cf. SPr, 91.) Tsing-mo: sacrificial herb which Pound compares to *molü*, the magic herb that kept Odysseus safe from Circe's spells.

Chun: another wise ruler who sacrificed to Chang Ti (the Great Spirit, i.e., a god).

que vos . . . conforme: French: that your verse expresses your intentions, / and that the music suits it. Chun encouraged music for learning and pleasure.

YAO: The ideogram "yao" means "eminent."

CHUN: The ideogram means "wise."

YU: The ideogram means "insect" or "reptile."

KAO-YAO: The ideogram means "bless kiln."

Tching Tang: emperor from 1766–53 B.C., who made copper money so that his people could buy stored grain during a drought. After seven barren years, Tching offered himself as a sacrifice to the gods on a mountain and a rainstorm obligingly ensued. Pound compares this to Frobenius' experience in Biembe (see Canto XXXVIII, SP, 129).

MAKE IT NEW: Tching inscribed the ideograms "Make it new—day by day—make it new" on his bathtub after the rainstorm ended the drought.

"We are up . . .": Emperor Tching Tang established the Shang dynasty upon the downfall of the Hia dynasty.

Kang: Tching's son, who ruled from 1078–52 B.C., unremarkably.

Tcheou: the Chou dynasty. In *Guide to Kulchur*, Pound quotes Confucius saying he is pro-Chou because the Chou "examined their predecessors," that is, "they examined the civilization and history of the Dynasties which preceded them." (19–20)

Confutzius: i.e., Confucius. See Canto XIII.

Wen-wang: (1231–1135 B.C.), Duke of Chou.

Wu-wang: (1169–15 B.C.), Wen-wang's son, first king of Chou dynasty.

Kang-wang: i.e. Kang, above, who needed help in ruling.

Chao-kong: adviser to Kang.

Kungfutseu . . . Mao: Confucius agreed to serve as minister for his province, Lou, on condition that the corrupt T. C. Mao be executed.

Tsi: The lord of Tsi sent singing girls to Lou to bribe and corrupt its prince; when this ploy succeeded, Confucius retired to a neighboring state.

At Tching . . . correct: When someone, seeing Confucius "wandering like a lost dog," compared his physique to the emperor's, Confucius modestly denied any resemblance except to the lost dog. Cao: i.e., Kao-yao. Tse Tchin: chief minister of Chang.

Yng P: illegitimate son of the Prince of Onei, who refused the succession because of his birth.

Tchin and Tsai: The princes of these states attacked Confucius and drove him into the desert when he was on his way to visit the Prince of Chou in 489 B.C. Chou's troops rescued him.

Tsao: small Shantung state which lasted from 1122 to 501 B.C.

3000 odes: Confucius returned in 493 B.C. to edit the Odes, after the princes refused to follow his advice.

comet . . . 479: Confucius died in the fortieth year of Ouang's reign, an event, legend has it, which was noticed by the heavens.

'Hillock': This was actually a nickname of Confucius, not of his father, Kung Shu Liang-Ho, though it suggests an appropriate body-type for the latter. An officer in Lou's army, he held up a drop gate so that his men could escape during a siege in 562 B.C.

## *from* CANTO LXII (1940) [SP, 150]

Canto LXII opens Pound's ten-canto homage to John Adams (1735–1826), second President of the United States of America and a statesman of extraordinary intelligence, moral spirit, humanity, and courage. The source for the Adams Cantos is Charles

Francis Adams' *Works of John Adams* (cited as W). (See also
Canto LIII, headnote.) The last lines of Canto LXII hail him as

> . . . the clearest head in the congress
> >                   1774 and thereafter
> >         pater patriae
> > the man who at certain points
> >             made us
> >     at certain points
> >             saved us
> > by fairness, honesty and straight moving
> >             ARRIBA ADAMS

The John Adams installment of *The Cantos,* composed in 1939
on the eve of World War II, had a complex significance. Pound
wrote them not only to honor one of America's greatest, and least-
known, statesmen, but to remedy his compatriots' inexplicable
ignorance of this crucial figure in their history. "I do not see," he
wrote in 1938, "a regeneration of American culture while Marx
and Lenin are reprinted at 10 cents and 25 cents in editions of
100,000 and Adams' and Jefferson's thought is kept out of the plain
man's reach, and out of my reach considering that for three years
I have in vain tried to buy John Adams' letters." (SPr, 162) Nor
was he exaggerating Adams' virtual disappearance from the Ameri-
can mind: with unintentional irony, the dust jacket of the first
American edition billed the poem as the "John Quincy Adams
Cantos." Such ignorance, to Pound's mind, implied a disastrous
erosion of a cultural heritage, the "stones of foundation" on which
the American republic was built. In "National Culture: A Mani-
festo," he wrote,

> A national American culture existed from 1770 till at least 1861.
> Jefferson could not imagine an American going voluntarily to
> inhabit Europe. After the debacle of American culture individuals
> had to emigrate in order to conserve such fragments of American
> culture as had survived. It was perhaps no less American but it
> was in a distinct sense less *nationally* American as the usurocracy
> came into steadily more filthy and damnable control of the union.
>
>                                                                 (SPr, 161)

Pound's revival of Adams' thought and work, then, came into being not primarily as an homage to the past but as an attempt to recover its values in order to cure what he saw as the disease of his own time, the betrayal of the founding values of America to mercantile interests. (See his two-page "Introductory Textbook," in which he juxtaposes quotations from Adams, Jefferson, Lincoln, and the Constitution on the economic system of the new republic; GK, 354–55, SPr, 159–60.) He later wrote,

> The clearness of comprehension on the part of the revolutionary leaders is registered in diaries and "memoirs" of the times, and particularly in the notes of John Adams, who among other things, had been sent to Europe to organize the credit for the new State, and who secured the first loan from Holland.
>
> It is to be understood that the experience of John Adams was neither theoretical nor abstract. . . . He convinced the Hollanders of the solidarity of the American guarantees by comparing the insignificant debt of the United States to the great debt of England. . . . The intimate letters and conversations between Adams and his friends contain concrete concepts as, for example: "It is necessary to keep up the idea that this paper is good for something," meaning that the note can be exchanged for actual goods.
>
> . . . at the beginning of the nineteenth century, the "Mercantile" concept still retained traces of decency: Adams judged it "hardly mercantile" to do trade on borrowed capital.
>
> (SPr, 168–69)

The Adams Cantos, then, must be understood in their social and historical context: they are one more episode in their author's untiring campaign to awaken his readers to the economic abuses of their governments and to the consequences of those abuses in wars, the decline of culture and of the quality of life, and the withering of the critical spirit that chose from among the best institutions of previous cultures in creating the new republic.

Given these motives, we might be puzzled as to why the style of the Adams Cantos is as fragmented, elliptical, and, at times, strained as it is, not to mention, as Frederick K. Sanders has shown, rife with errors. What does Pound expect us to make of these broken notations? In a curious way, the hurried, tortured, note-taking style of the Adams Cantos is very precisely expressive of the condition that moved Pound to write the poem. If it is often, as Randall Jarrell and Robert Fitzgerald observe, "eccentric, slangy, illogical," "perfunctory and thoroughly dull" (Homberger, 350, 352), it is also historical, genuine, documentary: it reflects Pound's impatience with the fact that his poem had to try to recover what both he and his American readers should already have known, even as it expresses the urgency of his purposes. John Adams himself, Pound said, "wrote an excellent prose which has not, so far as I know, been surpassed in our fatherland." (SPr, 148) He was not attempting, in these cantos, to surpass it, but rather to provoke his audience to read the original, out-of-print Adams himself. "Not there, the poem ain't, to explain the history but to arouse curiosity," he wrote to one reader. (Yale MSS, to Lewis Maverick, 2 September 1957) Insofar as they succeed in creating that curiosity, sending his readers in search of their history, the Adams Cantos are all that their author would have wished. Paradoxically, then, their unreadable style tends toward a cure even as it is itself symptomatic of the historical situation which provoked them. If the Adams Cantos are *about* American history, they are themselves equally a curious and telling symptom *of* American history.

'*Acquit . . . Europe.*': In his Preface to the *Works*, Charles Francis Adams explained that, while his account would inevitably be found to contain errors, he would correct them "with cheerfulness" when informed of them.

for the planting . . . COMPANIE: from the 1629 Massachusetts Bay Company Charter, signed by King Charles I.

Thomas Adams: a possible Adams ancestor who was made one of eighteen assistants to the first governor of the Massachusetts Bay Company.

Merry Mount: a Henry Adams founded the American Adams family on forty acres at Mount Wollaston, later renamed Merry Mount, and then, Braintree; now Quincy.

Weston's: Thomas Weston (*ca.* 1575–1644) settled near Mount Wollaston (and may have been a maternal ancestor of Ezra Loomis Weston Pound).

Capn Wollanston: English colonist who settled and named Mount Wollaston.

ten head . . . : from Henry Adams' homestead document: "May 24th, 12th month, 1640. Granted to Henry Adams for ten heads (family members), forty acres, upon the same covenant of three shillings per acre." Henry founded a brewery there.

old style . . . new style: The English calendar was changed in 1752 to accord more accurately with the solar year.

its emolument: "His condition, as the teacher of a school [in 1755] was not and could not be a permanent establishment. Its emoluments gave him but a bare and scanty subsistence." (W, I, 22)

'Passion . . . whatsoever: Adams explains his lack of calling to the ministry.

not less . . . liberty: Adams thought that "Parliament could not lawfully tax the colonies. His whole soul was in the case. But to him it was not less the cause of order and of justice than of liberty." (W, I, 80)

Burke, Gibbon: Edmund Burke and Edward Gibbon, eighteenth-century British historians to whose representations of British statesmen Charles Francis Adams objected: "Such a beautifier of imperfect figures is the illusive mirror of national pride!" (W, I, 92)

tcha: the ideogram for tea, introducing the Boston Tea Party theme.

Lord North: English Prime Minister under George III who tried to keep the American colonies under British economic control by means of the Stamp Act and the tea tax. John Quincy Adams held his policies responsible for the revolution, and for turning the British soldiers—the redcoats—from friends to foes.

Rapallo: the Italian seaside town where Pound lived from 1924 to 1945.

Lard Narf . . . impassible: "At about nine o'clock of the night on which Lord North declared himself impassible to menace, a single sentry was slowly pacing his walk . . ." (W, I, 97); this begins Charles Francis Adams' account of the Boston Massacre of March 5, 1770.

Styschire: Pound is parodying the naming of British regiments by counties.

baker's boy: Pound misread his note on the barber's boy who provoked the British sentry and, in doing so, the Boston Massacre.

Capn Preston: The captain of the British troops came with six men to the sentry's aid, which attracted the notice of "forty or fifty of the lower order of town's people, who had been roving the streets armed with billets of wood." (W, I, 98)

force . . . Fwancis: Charles Francis Adams wrote that the incident was "the first protest against the application of force to the settlement of a question of right." (W, I, 98)

so fatal . . . etc.: The crowd threw snowballs and rocks at the guard, who began firing their muskets. Though they claimed the intention of firing over the heads of the crowd, Charles Francis Adams judged that "So fatal a precision of aim, indicating not a little malignity, . . . is one of the most singular circumstances attending the affray." (W, I, 99) He continued, "The drops of blood then shed in Boston were like the dragon's teeth of ancient fable—the seeds, from which spring up the multitudes who would recognize no arbitration but the deadly one of the battle-field." (W, I, 99) Cadmus founded Thebes by slaying a dragon and sowing its teeth, from which sprang up warriors.

patriots . . . knowl-edge: The patriotic party employed John Adams as their legal adviser and "a guide in those measures in which questions involving professional knowledge were to be discussed with the authorities representing the crown." (W, I, 107)

BE IT . . . doggymints [documents]: The form used to enact laws in the colony before 1740 began, "Be it enacted by the Governor, Council, and House of Representatives in General Court assembled, and by authority of the same"; Colonel Bladen, member of the Board of Trade and Plantations, got the words banned because they implied an authority different from the king's. John Adams later helped to reinstate them. (W, I, 108)

Encourage . . . farmin': John Adams served on a committee to encourage "arts, agriculture, manufactures, and commerce." (W, I, 109)

not suggest . . . Bastun: These lines summarize John Adams' defense of the British soldiers after the Boston Massacre, and reflect his determination that law and justice should prevail over the people's vindictive anger. While many considered him a traitor for taking on the case, Adams said in his defense that if "by means of an abandoned administration at home, and the outrages of the soldiery here, the bonds of parental affection and filial duty between Britain and the colonies shall be dissolved," then fighting must ensue; but until then, "we must try causes in the tribunals of justice, by the law of the land." (W, I, 113) Two soldiers, convicted of manslaughter, were burnt in the hand, and let go.

mens sine affectu: Latin: a mind without feeling; Adams urged in his defense of the soldiers that reason should hold sway over emotion. (W, I, 114)

Bad law . . . Burke: " 'Bad laws,' said Burke of his own country, Great Britain, 'are the worst sort of tyranny. In such a country as this, they are of all bad things the worst; worse, by far, than anywhere else; and they derive a particular malignity even from the wisdom and soundness of the rest of our institutions.' " (W, I, 120–21)

disputed . . . king: An anonymous reply to Governor Hutchinson's speech about allegiance to Britain "disputed the right, thus far generally conceded in Christendom, of seizing the lands occupied by the heathen, by virtue of authority vested in the head of the Catholic Church, and granting them to any Christian monarch whose subjects might be the first to discover them." (W, I, 121–22)

If we be . . . people?: John Adams wrote: " 'If our government be considered as merely feudatory, we are subject to the king's absolute will, and there is no authority of Parliament, as the sovereign authority of the British empire.' " (W, I, 126); and: " ' "Every subject is presumed by law to be sworn to the king, which is to his natural person," says Lord Coke. "The allegiance is to his natural body;" and he says: "In the reign of Edward the Second, the Spencers, the father and the son, to cover the treason hatched in their hearts, invented this damnable and damned opinion, that homage and oath of allegiance was more by reason of the king's crown . . . than by reason of the person of the king; upon which opinion, they inferred execrable and detestable consequents." The judges of England, all but one, in the case of the union between Scotland and England, declared that "allegiance followeth the natural person not the politic," and "to prove the allegiance to be tied to the body natural of the king, and not to the body politic, the Lord Coke cited the phrases of divers statutes mentioning our natural liege sovereign." ' " (W, I, 127–28); and " 'The question appears to us to be no other than whether we are subjects of absolute unlimited power, or of a free government formed on the principles of the English Constitution.' " (W, I, 129)

Coke: Sir Edward Coke (1552–1634), English jurist, author of the *Institutes*. Cf. Canto CVII, where Pound calls him "the clearest mind ever in England." (C, 758)

Mercantile temper . . . : "The mercantile and manufacturing temper of Great Britain regarded the people of the colonies not as friends and brethren, but as strangers who might be made tributaries." (W, I, 132)

constitution . . . Oliver: " 'I see,' said the judge to [John Adams], 'you are determined to explore the constitution, and bring to life all its dormant and latent powers, in defence of your liberties, as you understand them.' To which he replied, that 'he should be very happy if the constitution should carry them safely through all their difficulties, without having recourse to higher powers not written.' It was doubtless in this spirit that his advice was taken by his friends, and the necessary measures accordingly prepared, by which to present Peter Oliver, chief justice of the superior court, guilty of high crimes and misdemeanors, as set forth in the proper forms of impeachment. The result was that they were adopted by a vote of ninety-two members of the House against only eight dissentients." (W, I, 138–39)

Oliver: Peter Oliver (1713–91). chief justice of the Massachusetts Colony who was impeached for attempting to have the judges paid by the Crown instead of by the Colony.

no jurors wd / serve: After John Adams' articles of impeachment appeared in the newspapers, those drawn to act as jurors refused to consent on the grounds that "the presiding officer [i.e., Oliver], having been charged with high crimes and misdemeanors in office, by the legislative power of the province, could not be recognized as a suitable person to hold the court, whilst the charges remained unacted upon." (W, I, 139)

# INTRODUCTION TO
## *THE PISAN CANTOS* (1945/1948)

After he completed the Chinese/Adams Cantos, Pound intended to take his long poem in a new direction: he would now, he wrote in 1939, leave economics aside and go on to "questions of BE-LIEF"—"philosophy or my paradise." "From 72 on," he wrote to James Laughlin, "we will enter the empyrean." Then World War II began, blotting out the empyrean. Paradise became unimaginable, and Pound, who had conceived of his work since 1918 as an effort to prevent another war, plunged back into the inferno of twentieth-century history. He made two moves which express the extremity of his outrage: he abandoned his native language to write two cantos in Italian, LXXII and LXXIII. (Their empty place is still held for them in *The Cantos*.) And, heedless of the unquestioning loyalty which a nation demands of its citizens in wartime, he protested the actions his own country was taking in speeches broadcast over Rome Radio, invoking the American Constitution as his authority, still desperately hoping to steer history off what he saw as its deadly course. As the war went on, those speeches grew more and more frantic, more angry and vituperative, until, as he later acknowledged, he "lost his center."

In May 1945, this strident political activity was forcibly terminated. Pound was arrested by the United States Army when it occupied Rapallo, and taken to an Army prison camp near Pisa, the Disciplinary Training Center (D.T.C.). Having tried, in his own mind, to save the world, he now found himself accused of treason. He was placed in solitary confinement in a wire cage on which the sun blazed by day and floodlights by night. No one was allowed to speak to him. Neither family nor friends knew his whereabouts. After some weeks, he had a nervous collapse, and thereafter received better treatment. He was given some notebooks and stationery pads to write on, and at night was allowed to use the typewriters in the medical compound. Here, in the prison camp, between May and November 1945, he composed *The Pisan Cantos*.

In Pisa, Pound's lyric voice returned, sounding with elegiac pathos from his isolated cage in a prison camp in the midst of a Europe torn apart by war. Reading this poetry, one feels that if the events in Pound's life which brought it into being had not occurred, he would have needed somehow to invent them, so fully, if unexpectedly, do they fulfill his intent to write a "poem including history." His *paradiso terrestre* was fated to turn elegiac as the dream of a new civilization crumbled in his mind's eye. For it was an earthly paradise which he had envisioned, rooted in time and place. Twentieth-century culture offered no coherent world view, no "Aquinas-map" such as Dante had to build his poem upon, and in blind strength of desire Pound turned to Mussolini's Fascism in the hope that the economic reforms it advertised would provide the basis from which a new common culture might develop. Many people made the same mistake, but Pound's seems, in retrospect, peculiarly a poet's error, the liability of a mind which moves by metaphor—"Jefferson and/or Mussolini."

*The Pisan Cantos* are the crux, the trial and the touchstone, of Pound's lifework. In them, suddenly, the "poem including history" *becomes* history. The documentary poetics of the Malatesta Cantos, of the Sienese, Chinese, and American history cantos, trains itself upon the here-and-now as the sixty-year-old poet, caught by his own errors in the nets of history, with waves of worldwide catastrophe crashing over him, struggles to survive. In that struggle, the surviving and the witnessing become one inseparable act. And the documentary mode which had dominated the poem during the thirties now proves an instrument of unmatched sensitivity for recording an utterly lonely and endangered consciousness in the extremes of suffering, collapsing the lyric voice and the concrete historical world. The poem is the interface between a solitary mind and the common world. The landscape of *The Pisans*, though it is literally seen through the poet's eyes, is not merely a personal view. It is the landscape of prisoners and guards, of camions and dusty roads, of skies and insects minutely observed. And even the memories and fantasies which animate it are not solipsistic visions, but emerge from a mind which, through fifty years' devoted study, through its entanglements with historical reality, and most of all through its unsurpassed linguistic resourcefulness, has ceased to be that of one human being and become representative of an epoch. In its broken visions, we read the limits of our culture. The Western literary tradition is the ship Pound goes down with, after forty years of striving for a renaissance, a revival by means of an infusion of medieval, Renaissance, Revolutionary American, and Eastern philosophic energies. His losses in Pisa are simultaneously personal losses and cultural losses. He writes "As a lone ant from a broken ant-hill / from the wreckage of Europe, ego scriptor" (Canto LXXVI). When, Odysseuslike, he remembers his lost companions, they are "Fordie [Madox Ford] who wrote of giants / and William [Butler Yeats] who dreamed of nobility / and Jim [Joyce] the comedian singing" (Canto LXXIV). In the Pisans, fragments of Whitman, Shakespeare, Chaucer, Jonson, Ovid, the Roman Catholic liturgy, Homer, and Confucius float disconnectedly. The heritage they jaggedly mark is what Pound saw at stake in the two world wars of his time, and the historical drama of our failing culture, our "humanism," is recorded in *The Pisan Cantos.* For the failures of that heritage, Pound suffers with his time: "I don't know how humanity stands it / with a painted paradise at the end of it / without a painted paradise at the end of it." (Canto LXXIV) Yet poetry, language, philosophy, are also literally a saving power in the poems: "that from the gates of death: Whitman or Lovelace . . ." (Canto LXXX) Whatever its value, that cultural heritage has not sufficed to prevent the cataclysms of twentieth-century history, nor even to keep Pound from well-intentioned but disastrously wrong judgments, political and linguistic. The floating fragments symbolize its wreckage on the rocks of history.

Even as Pound paints this shattered paradise, however, he demonstrates its consolations:

> . . . the clouds over the Pisan meadows
>> are indubitably as fine as any to be seen
> from the peninsula
>> οἱ βάρβαροι [hoi barbaroi] have not destroyed them
>> as they have Sigismundo's temple.
>>> (Canto LXXVI)

There is something very moving in the poet's survival and the triumph of the poem as the literal means and agent of that survival. The poem embodies the love he survives by—"Amo ergo sum [I love, therefore I am], and in just that proportion" (C, 493)—as an almost painfully tender responsiveness to his immediate surroundings:

> "the pride of all our D.T.C. was pistol-packin' Burnes"

> It comes over me that Mr. Walls must be a ten-strike
> with the signorinas
> > (Canto LXXXIII)

> dark sheep on the drill field and on wet days were clouds
> in the mountain as if under the guard roosts
> > (Canto LXXIV)

as well as in sharp, vivid fragments of memory, moments of the past that now return:

> Beloved the hours βροδοδάκτυλος [brododaktylos]
> > as against the half-light of the window
> > with the sea beyond making horizon
> the contre-jour the line of the cameo
> profile "to carve Achaia"
> > a dream passing over the face in the half-light
> > > (Canto LXXIV)

The vision of a better world which he has loved also remains to be uttered with firmness of heart:

> I surrender neither the empire nor the temples
> > > > plural
> nor the constitution, nor yet the city of Dioce
> each one in his god's name
> > (Canto LXXIV)

The poem makes manifest that "What thou lovest well remains," that love is the only redemption from time:

> > nothing matters but the quality
> of the affection—
> in the end—that has carved the trace in the mind
> dove sta memoria.
> > (Canto LXXVI)

The poet reaps the harvest of the beloved hours of past times, and in his extremity redeems even the agonized hours in the prison camp as, against the threat of death, the miracle of even the simplest life is felt: "When the mind swings by a grass-blade / an ant's forefoot shall save you." (Canto LXXXIII) Pound suffered greatly for his errors, and that such small saving blessings could come to the suffering being is not something we can regret. At the same time, given the still-unrecognized errors, we cannot avoid sensing that there is something dangerous, as well as noble, in the imagination's power to transform the prison camp inferno into the paradise of the poem. The very structure of *The Pisan Cantos*, which return, after elegy, pathos, and the tender transcription of the living landscape to a celebration of Fascist heroes, brings home the fact that the human imagination, despite all good intentions, is at least untrustworthy. It is a lesson we ignore at our peril.

In November 1945, Pound was taken to America, where, judged mentally unfit to stand trial, he was placed in a mental hospital in Washington, where he remained for the next thirteen years. His *Pisan Cantos* were published in 1948. The volume was awarded the Bollingen Prize for the most distinguished poetic work published that year, setting off a bitter controversy which even now has not been forgotten. How, people asked, could the United States government, which sponsored the prize, conceivably honor a Fascist sympathizer simultaneously under indictment for treason? The judges, who included Conrad Aiken, W. H. Auden, Louise Bogan, T. S. Eliot, Robert Lowell, Katherine Anne Porter, Allen Tate, and Robert Penn Warren, defended their decision by saying that "To permit other considerations than that of poetic achievement to sway the decision would destroy the significance of the award and would in principle deny the validity of that objective perception of value on which civilized society must rest." One judge, Allen Tate, wrote that even had Pound been a convicted traitor, which he was not, "in his concern for language he had performed an indispensable duty to society" (Stock, 551). There is no question that Pound went wrong in placing his hopes for a *paradiso terrestre* in Mussolini and Italian Fascism, and there is no question that that fatal error issued from a faculty of judgment driven off course by an intensity of vision and desire. There are lines in the poem that we can understand only by remembering that Pound's views were formed largely on the basis of publications controlled by the Italian government, and there are others that we cannot even wish to forgive. But, given Pound's lifelong claims for the social value and necessity of art, it is surely mistaken to argue that the greatness of his poem rests on merely aesthetic criteria, or to imagine that so profoundly historical a poem could conceivably be divorced from its historical and political context. What makes Pound's poem important, rather, is that its errors are not idiosyncratic and personal. They are the same errors which whole nations committed; they are the errors of twentieth-century history. And they are profoundly tied to the problematics of language in the modern world, which is why there is so much to be learned from their documentation in the poetry of so great a master—or perhaps one should say conductor—of language as Pound. The poetry of *The Pisans* entangles error with the most humane motives. Pound's long poem, because of its errors, not despite them, is a site where we can see represented, and perhaps learn to understand, the history of our time.


*from* CANTO LXXIV                                    [SP, 153]


These eleven passages from Canto LXXIV excerpt less than a third of its long meditation. We notice in them two striking changes of mode. First, we hear the voice of the poet more distinctly and continuously than ever before in *The Cantos*. For the first time, there is no epic "subject"—no Homeric or Ovidian episode, no Italian, Chinese, or American history, no usura theme or mystical vision. Now it is the inner speech of the human voice that we hear, or more properly, overhear, speaking a language supple and alive, a language wrought of forty years' devotion to the tones, sounds, and weights of words. It is a speech at once stylized and perfectly at ease, an agile, conversational voice that is also a poetic language of powerful beauty and resonance. The second change is that the "ideogrammic method" of the earlier cantos modulates within this voice to a kind of stream-of-consciousness in which the mind moves by associative processes from immediate perceptions to memories, from one idea or image to another, by a logic which is latent in the images rather than spelled out in the words. Understanding the poem involves following the thread of these connections through a given passage. This task is sometimes more, sometimes less difficult. But the strange music of *The Pisans* is so much its own reward as to guarantee and encourage the time it takes to begin to grasp their train of thought, and the persevering reader will be rewarded by a richer music still.

Canto LXXIV, and *The Pisan Cantos*, open with lines recording the assassination of Benito Mussolini, the Italian Fascist leader who, with his mistress, Clara Petacci, was executed on April 28, 1945, and ignominiously hung by the heels in a public square in Milan. Pound's relation to Italian Fascism is too complex to treat adequately here, but a few remarks may delineate it. The lines make immediately clear that Pound had projected his dream of a just society—an earthly "city of Dioce"—onto Mussolini (as did, in fact, many other American liberals for a time); and his downfall represented the death of all those hopes, read in the image of the peasant's bent shoulders. That Mussolini had long ago betrayed the ideals which Pound and his other early sympathizers thought he stood for, Pound, living in Italy, reading government-controlled newspapers, did not comprehend. He continued to believe that Mussolini would implement the radical economic reforms which he thought fundamental to a just society: as he later wrote, "As I see it, Mussolini followed Andrew Jackson in his opposition to the tyranny of state debts." (Heymann, 266) Thus, Pound compares the fallen leader to Manes and to Confucius, the former because he believed that Mussolini set out to vanquish an evil which might otherwise overcome good; and the latter because, as he wrote in *Guide to Kulchur*, "The Duce and Kung fu Tseu equally perceive that their people need poetry; that prose is NOT education but the outer courts of the same." (144) There is no question of renunciation, for Pound does not yet perceive the errors of his perceptions, and nothing else—no mere desire to save his skin, for example—could induce him to abandon his beliefs. It is this patently unself-serving character of Pound's political errors which mitigates our response to them, and draws our attention to the social vision of which Mussolini's regime was a tragic deformation.

Manes: third-century Persian founder of the Manicheans, crucified for his heretical belief that good and evil constitute equal and opposite forces in the universe.

DIGENES: i.e., *digonos* (Greek), twice-born, an epithet of Dionysos.

Possum: Pound's nickname for T. S. Eliot, whose "The Hollow Men" ends *"This is the way the world ends / Not with a bang but a whimper."*

Dioce: Deioces, a king who founded Ecbatana in the sixth century b.c. According to Herodotus, the city was encircled by seven concentric walls, each higher than the last, painted white, black, purple, blue, orange, silver, and gold.

the process: the Confucian way, the philosophy of life described in *The Unwobbling Pivot,* which begins, "What heaven has disposed and sealed is called the inborn nature. The realization of this nature is called the process. The clarification of this process . . . is called education." (Conf, 99) Cf. *"from* Canto LXXXIII" (SP, 177).

What you . . . the way: Cf. *The Unwobbling Pivot:* "You do not depart from the process even for an instant; what you depart from is not the process." (Conf, 101)

washed . . . candor: from Tsang's elegy for Confucius: *"Washed in the Keang and Han* [rivers], *bleached in the autumn sun's slope, what whiteness can one add to that whiteness, what candour?"* (Conf, 194). Cf. Canto LXXX (C, 495).

candor: This word, meaning frankness and sincerity, stems from the Latin word *candidus,* meaning shining whiteness, which Pound recalls here.

smell of mint: Cf. Canto LXXIV (C, 438): "Le Paradis n'est pas artificiel / but spezzato, apparently / it exists only in fragments      unexpected excellent sausage, / the smell of mint, for example . . ."

a white ox: Cf. Canto LXXVIII (C, 483): "and as for the solidity of the white oxen in all this / perhaps only Dr Williams (Bill Carlos) / will understand its importance."

the road toward Pisa: the Via Aurelia, near the prison camp.

the tower: the leaning tower of Pisa, visible from the camp.

a lizard: Cf. Canto LXXXIII (SP, 178): "When the mind swings by a grass-blade/an ant's forefoot shall save you / the clover smells and tastes as its flower"; and Canto CXVI (C, 796): "To be saved by squirrels and bluejays?"

white bread: The quality of its bread was for Pound an index to a society's values. Cf. Canto LV (SP, 136): "With usura, sin against nature / is thy bread ever more of stale rags / is thy bread dry as paper, / with no mountain wheat, no strong flour."

Mt Taishan: Pound renames the mountain visible from the prison camp after the sacred Mt. Taishan near the birthplace of Confucius in China.

Carrara: a city in Tuscany, famous for its marble.

Kuanon: the Chinese goddess of mercy, often invoked in *The Pisans*.

Linus, Cletus, Clement: three martyrs invoked in the liturgy of the Roman Catholic Mass.

scarab: a beetle or beetle-shaped gem, a sacred image in Egyptian art, to which Pound compares the appearance of the Catholic priest, clad in his vestments, bending at the altar.

plowed . . . Scotus: The images of silk, light, virtue, and the sacred come together in the closing passage of *The Unwobbling Pivot:*
> *As silky light, King Wen's virtue*
> *Coming down with the sunlight,*
> > > *what purity!*
> . . .
> This unmixed is the tensile light, the
> Immaculata. There is no end
> > to its action. (Conf, 187)

virtù: Italian: the realized and expressed nature of something, its potency. Cf. Canto XXXVI and *The Great Digest* (Conf, 73): "The *virtu*, i.e., this self-knowledge [looking straight into the heart and acting thence] is the root."

sunt . . . Scotus: The quoted phrase comes from a sentence in *De Divisione Naturae* by the medieval philosopher Johannes Scotus Erigena: "omnia quae sunt lumina sunt," "all things that are are lights," to which Pound alludes throughout the canto.

As of Shun . . . waters: Cf. notes on the three ideal emperors of Canto LIII (SP, 146)

paraclete: In Catholic theology, the Holy Spirit as advocate or intercessor; cf. "paraclete or the verbum perfectum: sinceritas" (C, 427).

Tempus . . . loquendi: Latin: "A time to be silent, a time to speak." *Tempus loquendi, tempus tacendi* was the motto of Sigismondo Malatesta, inscribed on Isotta's tomb in the Tempio, and comes from Ecclesiastes 3:7. Pound quotes it at the opening of Canto XXXI.

Never . . . dixit [Latin: said] Lenin: In "What Is Money For?" Pound quotes from Lenin's 1917 article, "Imperialism, the Highest Stage of Capitalism," concerning the damaging effects of the exportation of capital: "The exportation of capital, one of the most essential economic bases of imperialism, still further isolates this *rentier* stratum from production, and sets the seal of parasitism on the whole country living on the exploitation of labour of several overseas countries and colonies." Lenin is himself quoting the English economist S. G. Hobson. (SPr, 299)

and gun . . . sales: Cf. Canto XXXVIII.

23rd year: The Fascist government reckoned time from the March on Rome in 1922.

Till: St. Louis Till, an American soldier executed at Pisa.

Cholkis: the land of the Golden Fleece.

Snag: another prisoner at Pisa.

hamadryas: hamadryads, tree-nymphs.

Vai soli: probably "Vae soli," a Latin phrase meaning "Woe to one that is alone," quoted in Jules Laforgue's "Pierrots," which Pound translated in 1917: "Your eyes! Since I lost their incandescence / Flat calm engulfs my jibs, / The shudder of *vae soli* gurgles beneath my ribs."

(Tr, 438) The source of the phrase is Ecclesiastes 4:10: "For if they fall, the one will lift up the other: but woe to they who are alone when they fall; for they have not another to help them up."

'HΛION ΠΕΡΙ'HΛION (HELION PERIHELION): Greek: "sun around sun."

Lucina: light-goddess, an epithet of Diana, the moon-goddess, and of Juno; also the name of the Roman goddess of childbirth.

a hard man: Cf. Canto LXXX (C, 513): "I have been hard as youth sixty years."

leopard: an image of himself.

chrysalid: butterfly. color di luce: Italian: "color of light."

as the sun . . . fingers: Cf. William Morris's "Defence of Guenevere," lines 120–25.

Lordly . . . o'ergiven: Cf. Pound's "The Seafarer": "Grey-haired he groaneth, knows gone companions,/Lordly men are to earth o'ergiven" (SP, 21); HSM, Part I, IV and V (SP, 63, 64); and Canto I, where Tiresias prophesies that Odysseus will "lose all companions" (SP, 96).

Fordie: Ford Madox Ford, originally Ford Madox Hueffer (1873–1939), English poet, novelist, critic, and editor, and an important early influence on Pound. He "wrote of giants" in *The March of Literature* (1939).

William: the Irish poet William Butler Yeats (1865–1939); Pound served as his secretary and companion from 1911–14. Cf. Cantos LXXXII (C, 525) and LXXXIII (C, 533–34).

Jim: the Irish novelist James Joyce (1881–1941). Pound campaigned for the publication of his *Ulysses* (1922), at first banned by the censors.

Plarr: Victor Plarr (1863–1929), English poet and librarian of the Royal College of Surgeons, memorialized in *Mauberley's* "'Siena mi fè" as M. Verog. In "The Wisdom of Poetry" (1912), Pound writes that Plarr and a collaborator "developed the functions of a certain obscure sort of equation, for no cause save their own pleasure in the work. The applied science of their day had no use for the deductions, a few sheets of paper covered with arbitrary symbols—without which we should have had no wireless telegraph." (SPr, 361–62)

Jepson: Edgar Jepson (1863–1938), English novelist who, Iris Barry recalls, used to bring jade pieces to show to the writers who gathered each week at the Tour Eiffel Restaurant in London during 1917–18. ("The Ezra Pound Period," *Bookman*, October 1931, 167)

Maurie: Maurice Hewlett (1861–1923), English novelist with whom Pound spent Christmas in 1911. Cf. Canto LXXX (SP, 171).

Newbolt: Sir Henry John Newbolt (1862–1938), English poet whom Pound visited with Hewlett on Christmas Day, 1911. In his 1939 obituary on Ford, Pound referred to Newbolt as a member of "the arthritic milieu that held control of the respected British critical circles." (SPr, 462)

Kokka: Urquell Kokka, cited by Pound as a source of notes on "custom indicating high culture" in *Guide to Kulchur:* "Comfortably at the Regence he remarked that if you are covered with brass chains, a sword, etc.; if your sartorial sheath is rigid and every time you move something jangles you naturally do not loll." (83)

Mr Edwards: a fellow prisoner. jacent: recumbent.

Baluba: African tribe studied by Leo Frobenius. Cf. Canto XXXVIII (SP, 132).

"doan . . . table": someone in the prison camp, perhaps the "Mr. Edwards" above, made Pound a table from a packing crate against regulations. Cf. Cantos LXXIX and LXXXI (C, 485, 519).

nient' altro: Italian: "nothing else."

who putteth . . . measure: Leviticus 19:35 reads, "Ye shall do no unrighteousness in judgment, in meteyard, in weight, or in measure." Cf. Cantos LXXIV and LXXVI (C, 440, 454).

First . . . 11: The verse reads, "And that ye study to be quiet, and to do your own business, and to work with your own hands, as we commanded you."

300 years culture . . . : Pound was against America's entry into World War II. (SP, 179)

constitution: the American constitution. Cf. Canto LXXIX: "God bless the Constitution / and *save* it." (C, 486)

Dioce: See above, page 207.

each . . . name: Cf. Canto LXXVIII (C, 478–79), where Pound describes his journey from Rome to Gais during World War II as an analogue of Aeneas' journey from Troy to Latium to found Rome, "bringing his gods into Latium."

as by Terracina . . . Anchises: In his 1930 "Credo," Pound wrote, "Given the material means I would replace the statue of Venus on the cliffs of Terracina [a town in central Italy]." (SPr, 53) The imagery in this passage associates the statue with Botticelli's painting "The Birth of Venus" in Florence, and perhaps with Olga Rudge; cf. Canto LXXIV (C, 435): "she did her hair in small ringlets, à la 1880 it might have been, / red, and the dress she wore Drecol or Lanvin / a great goddess, Aeneas knew her forthwith." Cf. also Cantos I, LXXIV, and LXXVI (SP, 98, 158, 160).

Zephyr: the west wind, personified in Botticelli's "The Birth of Venus."

Anchises: Venus' mortal lover; from their union came Aeneas.

the process. See above, page 207. Cf. Canto LXXIV (C, 443): "By no means an orderly Dantescan rising / but as the winds veer . . . as the winds veer in periplum."

Pleiades: group of seven stars in the constellation Taurus which rises in spring and sets in autumn. her mirror: the sea.

Kuanon: See above, p. 208.

this stone . . . sleep: Cf. Canto LXXIV (C, 426): "of sapphire, for this stone giveth sleep"; and Canto LXXVI (SP, 162): "Her bed-posts are of sapphire / for this stone giveth sleep."

a painted paradise: The image comes from Villon's "Paradis peint où sont harpes et luths" in the *Testament*. Cf. Canto XLV: "with usura / hath no man a painted paradise on his church wall / *harpes et luthes*." (SP, 136)

magna NUX animae: Latin: the great; Greek: night; Latin: of the soul, alluding to St. John of the Cross's "Dark Night of the Soul." Cf. the subsequent excerpt (SP, 158).

Barabbas: Offered the choice of freeing Christ or freeing the criminal Barabbas, the crowd in Jerusalem chose to free Barabbas. Pound's analogy is immodest, though he had not, like the other prisoners, committed the usual crimes, such as "rape and murder with trimmings."

nox animae magna: Latin: great night of the soul.

Taishan: See above, p. 208.

As it were . . . amorous: Cf. the reference to the funeral director's daughters whose "conduct caused comment" in Canto XXIX. (C, 142)

To study . . . harvest: Cf. Book I of the Confucian *Analects*, which Pound translates,

1. He said, Study with the seasons winging past, is not this pleasant?
2. To have friends coming in from far quarters, not a delight?
3. Unruffled by men's ignoring him, also indicative of high breed.
(Conf, 195)

the process: See note, p. 207.

E al . . . Luna: Italian: And in the corner, Cunizza / and the other: "I am the moon." Cf. Canto LXXVI (C, 452–53). Cunizza da Romano, lover of Sordello, freed her slaves by a deed of manumission in 1265. Dante places her in the third heaven of Venus (*Paradiso*, IX). Here she is a persona for a woman in Pound's life, perhaps Dorothy Pound.

Νύξ (nux) animae: Greek: night; Latin: of the soul.

San Juan: St. John of the Cross (1542–91), the Spanish mystic.

ad posteros: Latin: for posterity.

Time . . . evil: Cf. Canto XXX: "Time is the evil. Evil." (SP, 126)

βροδοδάκτυλος (brododaktylos): Sappho's dialect version of the Homeric *"rhododaktylos,"* "rosy-fingered," epithet for the dawn in the *Iliad* and the *Odyssey*, which she applies to the moon. The word occurs in a fragment on which Pound bases "Imerro" (SP, 37) and lines in Canto V (C, 17–18). Cf. Canto LXXX (SP, 169).

as against . . . half-light: Cf. the "cameo" photograph of Olga Rudge with her violin by a window in Mary de Rachewiltz's *Discretions*.

le contre-jour: French: against the light.

"to carve Achaia": Cf. HSM, Part II, I: "Pisanello lacking the skill / To forge Achaia." Pisanello, a fifteenth-century Italian medalist who worked on the Tempio Malatestiano, "forged Achaia" by creating an image of his own time to stand with those of the ancient Greek medalists.

Venere, Cytherea "aut Rhodon": Italian: Venus; Latin: Cythera "or Rhodes."

vento . . . veni: Italian: wind of Liguria; Latin: come. Liguria is the region of Italy which includes Rapallo, where Pound lived, and San Ambrogio, home of Olga Rudge.

Mr Beardsley: Aubrey Beardsley (1872–98), English illustrator and art editor of *The Yellow Book*, 1894–96. Cf. Canto LXXX (SP, 169).

*formato locho:* The image comes from Cavalcanti's "Canzone d'Amore." Pound translates the phrase as "in a sacred place" in his earlier version and as "the formèd trace" in the Canto XXXVI version. See also Canto LXXVI (SP, 160). Pound discusses the phrase at some length in his "Cavalcanti" essay (LE, 187–88), concluding, "To keep all the distinctions the 'formato *locho*' would have . . . to be the 'fantasia' itself, already pervaded by the *accidente*, which *comes from* the seen form. As to 'form'; you may here add the whole of medieval philosophy by way of footnote."

Arachne . . . fortuna: Italian: Arachne brings me good fortune. Cf. Canto LXXVI (C, 461). Arachne, a mortal, was so fine a weaver that Athena, the goddess of weaving, grew jealous and had her turned into a spider. Pound is probably reminded of the story by an actual spider in his tent.

eikons: Greek: images.

Trastevere: (Italian: across-the-Tevere, or Tibur) a district in Rome located on the opposite bank of the Tibur from the central city. Pound is thinking of the mosaics in the Church of Santa Maria in Trastevere, and the passage seems to allude to his hopes for a new civilization to match "Achaia." See above, p. 214.

crystal jet: The image of crystal, signifying invisible forces in nature, recurs throughout *The Cantos* (see, for example, Cantos IV, LXXIV, XCI).

Serenely . . . clearness: Pound remembers Verlaine's "Clair de Lune": "Et sangloter d'extase les jets d'eau, / les grands jets d'eau sveltes parmi les marbres" ("And sobbing with ecstacy the fountains,/the tall, slender fountains among the statues").

out of hell . . . : Cf. the exit from hell in Cantos XV and XVI (C, 66–69).

Zephyrus / Apeliota: the west and east winds.

liquid: Cf. Canto IV: "Thus the light rains, thus pours, *e lo soleills plovil* / The liquid and rushing crystal" (C, 15).

nec . . . est: Latin: It is not an accidental attribute; that is, it is essential.

est agens: Latin: It is an agent.

dust to a fountain pan otherwise: that is, without the animating light, the mind would be only dead matter, like the fountain without the water.

Hast 'ou . . . ever?: Pound echoes Ben Jonson's "Her Triumph," included in the Speare anthology which he found in the prison latrine (see p. 228) and given in *Confucius to Cummings*, 173–74:
> Have you seen but a bright lily grow
>    Before rude hands have touched it?
> Ha' you marked but the fall o' the snow
>    Before the soil hath smutched it?
> Have you felt the wool of beaver,
>    Or swan's down ever?
> Or have smelt o' the bud o' the briar?
>    Or the nard in the fire?
> Or have tasted the bag of the bee?
> O so white! O so soft! O so sweet is she!
Cf. Cantos LXXXI and CX (C, 520, 777).

the rose in the steel dust: that is, the rose pattern into which a magnetic field arranges steel filings held on a flat surface. Pound uses it in the Cavalcanti essay as an image of the forces in the universe which the modern mind no longer "sees" imagistically, and in *Guide to Kulchur*, he elaborates the connection between imagistic thinking and the medieval mind:

> The *forma*, the immortal *concetto*, the concept, the dynamic form which is like the rose pattern driven into the dead iron-filings by the magnet, not by material contact with the magnet itself but separate from the magnet. Cut off by the layer of glass, the dust and filings rise and spring into order. Thus the *forma*, the concept rises from death. (152)

Cf. also Dante's *Paradiso*, XXX.

Lethe: the river in Hades over which the dead must pass, losing all memory of this life. Cf. Canto LXXVII (C, 472).

## *from* CANTO LXXVI                                   [SP, 160]

Pound writes the famous lines which situate *The Pisan Cantos*— "As a lone ant from a broken ant-hill / from the wreckage of Europe, ego scriptor"—in the midst of Canto LXXVI. The inscription is particularly appropriate there, for the canto's jagged juxtapositions reflect the shattering of Europe and of Pound's dream of Europe. The canto is a field of fragments which refer obscurely to a past in which the whole of their meaning resides, or express desire for a wholeness to be found only, if ever, in the future. In a sense, then, the incoherence of these broken fragments is superficial, for they form a mindscape of allegorical ruins suggesting the irrecoverable coherences both of the dreams before their shattering and of the vision perfected and fulfilled. But while the poem can only be understood by grasping something of those visions, its immediate significance rests not in past or future but in the shattered present of 1945 to which its shards belong.

The canto thus comes into being between past and future, memory and desire, and contemplates these absent paradises from the hell of the present. The war, the prison camp, the failure of the Fascist and the American dreams as Pound had dreamed them, form a dark backdrop to the poet's meditation, continually breaking through the paradisal imagery and preventing the *atasal* or hypostatic union with the divine. There is honesty in this drama of the insubstantiality of paradisal moments. Even as the poet struggles to affirm and lament the lost dreams, and to solace himself with their memory, the images fade in the air and leave him in tears, with only the empty wind as "comforter." If the canto effects a redemption of the poet from his hell, and of his vision from its disastrous history, it is only by virtue of the elegiac truth which its fragments express, as he struggles to understand the terms of a *paradiso terrestre*. The redemption is not, finally, by vision but by elegiac pathos, a suffering that is not only for the loss of dreams but also for their unattainability.

There are two main themes in the selections here. The first is the fate of the Fascist dream, for Pound "the altar on the rostrum," which he had hoped would reform government so as to bring human society and nature into a concord at once political and religious. The second is the lost personal paradise inhabited by the poet's loved ones, from whom he was completely cut off after his arrest. The "nothing matters but the quality of the affection" lines, the San Ambrogio landscapes, the message sent to "La Cara," all allude to this world, which, as he represents it, also originated in a vision (the Anchises/Cythera motif) and led to great suffering, "polla pathein." But the paradises of memory and desire do not finally dominate the poem. There is nothing to counter the broken dreams but the ambiguous and insubstantial, yet enduring, grace of nature—the clouds, the wind, the morning-glory twined around a grassblade. No paradisal moment occurs; "Le Paradis n'est pas artificiel," but a state of mind that comes and goes with the wind. The extreme cost of this admission on Pound's part might easily be overlooked. It is, in effect, an anguished relinquishing of the faith and hope he had lodged in political action, in the belief that a *paradiso terrestre could* be "artificial," constructed in the world by human minds and hands.

l'ara sul rostro: Italian: the altar on the rostrum.

20 years of the dream: i.e., of the Fascist era.

Mozart: Wolfgang Amadeus Mozart (1756–91), the Austrian composer.

Ponce . . . de Leon: Juan Ponce de Leon (*ca.* 1460–1521), the explorer who sought the fountain of youth and discovered Florida instead.

alla fuente florida: Italian: to the; Spanish: flowery fountain.

Anchises: Cf. note, p. 212. her: Venus / Aphrodite's.

Cythera potens: Latin: powerful Cythera (Venus / Aphrodite). Κύθηρα δεινά (Kythera deina): Greek: dread Cythera. Cf. Cantos LXXIX and LXXX (SP, 167, 169).

the crystal body: See note, p. 215.

Κόρη Δῆλια δεινά (Kore, Delia deina): Greek: Kore ("daughter," that is, Persephone, Demeter's daughter); dread Delia (i.e. Artemis/Diana, goddess of the hunt and of Delos). et libidinis expers: Latin: And untouched by passion. πολλὰ παθεῖν (polla pathein): Greek: to suffer much. Kore may be a figure for the poet's daughter, and the passage may reflect the difficult family situation to which she alludes in her memoir *Discretions*, 186–88.

nothing matters . . . memoria: See note on "formato locho," p. 214.
dove sta memoria: Italian: where memory rests, from Cavalcanti's "Donna mi prega"; cf. Canto XXXVI.

and if . . . sugar: Cf. "from Canto LXXIV," SP, 156.

Adams: John Adams (1735–1826), second President of the United States and subject of Cantos LXII-LXXI. His "remark" is given first in Canto LXXI, (C, 416):

> Every bank of discount is downright corruption
> taxing the public for private individuals' gain.
>        and if I say this in my will
> the American people wd/pronounce I died crazy.

and repeated in Canto LXXIV (C, 437). See headnote to Canto XLV, the Usura Canto.

camions: trucks.

Sergeant XL: a sergeant McD. at the prison camp.

Lay in soft grass . . . : This scene describes the cliffs over the sea above the mountain hamlet of Sant' Ambrogio, where Olga Rudge lived.

ac ferae familiares: Latin: and tamed wild animals.

*a destra:* Italian: to the right.

*atasal* . . . hypostasis: from the eleventh-century Persian philosopher Avicenna, meaning "conjunction or contiguity with God," a lower state than "hypostasis," the mystical union.

nec personae: Latin: nor masks.

Dione: earth- or sky-goddess, mother of Aphrodite, second consort of Zeus; perhaps a figure for Dorothy Pound.

Helia: Pound's coinage, from "Heliad" or sun-goddess; perhaps a figure for the poet's daughter (cf. "Delia").

Κύπρις (Kypris): a name for Aphrodite, from the island sacred to her.

here rested: i.e., the poet, from writing.

squeak-doll: Pound possibly alludes to himself with respect to his radio broadcasts.

Bracken: Brendan Bracken (1901–58), British publisher and politician, Minister of Information, 1941–45.

B.B.C.: British Broadcasting Company.

ego scriptor: Latin: I, the writer.

spiriti questi? personae?: Italian: spirits these?; Latin: masks?

tangibility . . . sphere: Cf. Canto LXXIV (SP, 159).

Thetis: a sea-nymph, mother of Achilles.

Maya: Maia, mother of Hermes.

'Αφροδίτη (Aphrodite): goddess of love.

Zoagli: seaside town south of Rapallo, visible from the cliffs above Sant' Ambrogio.

οἱ βάρβαροι (hoi barbaroi): Greek: the barbarians, i.e., the American Army, which had invaded Italy.

Sigismundo's Temple: the Tempio Malatestiano; see Canto IX.

Divae Ixottae: Latin: divine Isotta, an inscription in the Tempio, which was dedicated to Sigismondo's wife Isotta degli Atti.

La Cara: Italian: the dear one, probably Olga Rudge. amo: Latin: I love.

her bed-posts: Cf. Canto LXXIV (SP, 157).

pervenche: French: periwinkle.

et sequelae: Latin: and following.

Le Paradis n'est pas artificiel: French: Paradise is not artificial, a negative echo of Baudelaire's book on hallucinogens, *Le Paradis artificiel* (1860).

states of mind: Cf. Pound's 1918 formulation: "A god is an eternal state of mind." (SPr, 47)

δακρύων (dakryon): Greek: tears.

L.    P.: Pierre Laval and Henri Philippe Pétain, officers of the Vichy government in France during World War II, afterward tried and convicted of treason. Pound's honoring of them follows in part from his drastic misapprehension of the aims of National Socialism. gli honesti: Italian: the honest ones.

J'ai . . . assez: French: I have had pity for others / probably not enough.

l'enfer non plus: French: neither is hell.

Eurus: the east wind.

la pastorella . . . dea: Italian: The little girl swineherd . . . the fair-haired goddess. Pound is thinking of his daughter Mary and her companion Margherita in the South Tyrolean hamlet of Gais.

woe . . . power: Cf. the end of Canto LXXVIII (C, 483): "there / are / no / righteous / wars."

This excerpt records the poet waking at dawn in the prison camp, with the red sunlight coming over the mountain he has renamed after the sacred Mt. Taishan. The first words that come to him represent the natural world as alive: the moon is a face, the spirits Eos and Hesperus preside over the cycle of dawn and dusk, the clouds in the west are "battalions." Such descriptive figures have been common in poetry since Homer's "rosy-fingered dawn." But for Pound these are more than quaint conceits. Indeed it would not be much of an exaggeration to say that the spirit that infuses the natural scene is as real to him as the moon and clouds themselves. He writes himself into the scene in the image of "Old Ez" folding his blankets so as not to "wrong" the sacred light by slumbering through its advent. In another moment, these first waking thoughts give way to an improvised morning chant in celebration of the dawning day, because, as he says at the end, "aram nemus vult"—"the grove demands an altar."

This is not the first moment in *The Cantos* when we are suddenly confronted with the fact of how profoundly religious a poet Pound is, but it is perhaps the most startling. Pound's eclectic morning chant takes off from his idea of the rites of Eleusis, working memories and particulars of the prison camp into a litany of Dionysos and the Kore myth, with their accouterments of lynxes, grapevines, and pomegranates. It is all gorgeously exotic, yet at the same time it is *sui generis*, and curiously genuine. Pound is not alluding to any particular source here, but singing his own chant in the vestiges of a mythic language which, however fragmentary and opaque its remnants, can still serve him to express something not thought but felt and desired. He consecrates the day, composing an impromptu homage out of rumors of the old rituals of time, wine, and love which once bound people to each other and to nature.

This exoticism is the crux, for what strikes us most forcibly in this incantation, after its strange beauty, is how unsharable it is. The poet's morning rites allude to an ancient past when the mysteries of life and death were celebrated collectively in rituals that once served to "hold the whole human race together" (see Canto XLVII), yet their performance there in the prison camp is irremediably solitary. Pound's litany is eminently, and humorously, sociable, reaching out to include his fellow inmates and the prison camp guards as well as backward to populist presidents—"O lynx, wake Silenus and Casey"—yet not even the ease and gaiety of his language can make "Casey" entirely at home in the poem, or disguise the essential weirdness of the situation. For nothing about this morning service is as peculiar as the simple fact of its existence. Despite Pound's gestures of inclusion, Casey and Sweetland, Polk and Calhoun, seem caught like brambles in the exotic fabric of the poem, and we can only watch while the poet pays his lonely homage to the lost gods he has invoked in his work as in his life. We are reminded of the personal rituals Pound has enacted earlier in *The Cantos* (II, XVII, XLVII), and of his speculation in *Guide to Kulchur* that "a modern Eleusis" may be "possible in the wilds of a man's mind only."

Yet we also come to see that this exoticism is not so much a cause of the poet's solipsism as a symbolic mitigation of it. Every utterance is a social act, and in improvising his hymn from a ghostly memory of a lost past, Pound is doing something quite different from engaging in obscurantism, antiquarianism, or exoticism for its own sake. He takes us into the wilds of his mind only to remind us of a time when such a celebration did "hold the whole human race together," even as his modern Eleusis gives uncompromising expression to the spiritual loneliness of modern life.

Eos: Greek goddess of the dawn.

Hesperus: Greek name for the evening star (the planet Venus).

Lynx: Lynxes and panthers are sacred to Dionysos. Cf. Canto II.

Silenus: a satyr associated with Dionysos the wine-god, and possessed of Dionysiac wisdom.

Casey: Corporal Casey, one of the officers at the prison camp. Cf. Canto LXXIV (C, 438).

castagnettes: castanets, the Spanish rattles.

bassarids: Dionysian tree-nymphs.

Maelids: fruit-tree nymphs.

cossak: Earlier in Canto LXXIX (C, 488), Pound writes, "So they said to Lidya: no, your body-guard is not the / town executioner / the executioner is not here for the moment / the fellow who rides beside your coachman / is just a cossak who executes. . . ."; the manuscript version continues "because he likes to execute." (Yale MSS)

Salazar, Scott, Dawley: Pound's fellows at the prison camp.

Polk . . . Calhoun: Pound includes in his "field of lynxes" sacred to Dionysos (cf. Canto II) a roster of American Presidents who shared his, and John Adams', views on the economic system of the United States. John Tyler was President, 1841–45; James Knox Polk, from 1845–49. John Caldwell Calhoun was Vice-President, 1825–32. Cf. Cantos XXXVII and LXXIV (C, 436).

"retaliate . . . North": Calhoun viewed the Civil War as an economic war waged by the North on the South. Pound notes in "Economic Nature of the United States": "1814—Calhoun opposed the process in which the government was forced to get its own credit on loan." (SPr, 183)

the close garden of Venus: Cf. "from Canto LXXVI" (SP, 161).

Priapus: Greek fertility-god.

Ἴακχος (Iakkhos): the name by which Dionysos was invoked in the rites of Eleusis.

Io: Greek: Hail, a cry used to invoke the gods.

Κύθηρα (Kythera): a name for Aphrodite, goddess of love, from her sacred island Kythera (or Cythera).

having . . . equities: i.e., the Confucian equities (see, e.g., Conf, 65f, 83f, 91).

Sweetland: an associate at the prison camp.

ἐλέησον (eleison) Kyrie eleison: Greek: have mercy, Lord have mercy, from the Roman Catholic liturgy.

Astafieva: Serafima Astafieva (1876–1934), Russian dancer with Diaghilev's Ballet Russe who later ran a ballet school in London. Pound introduced her to T. S. Eliot, and Eliot caricatured her in "Whispers of Immortality" as "Grishkin." In Canto LXXVII, Pound remembers "Grishkin's photo refound years after / with the feeling that Mr. Eliot may have / missed something, after all, in composing his vignette" (C, 466), and cf. Canto LXXIX (C, 484). For "conserved the tradition," see HSM, Part I, XI.

Byzance: Byzantium.

Manitou: Among some American Indians, a spirit which is regarded with awe and reverence.

phylloxera: a disease of grapevines that destroyed many of the great European vinestocks in the late 1800s.

Ἴακχε Ἴακχε, Χαῖρε (Iakkhe . . . Khaire): Greek: Hail, Iakkhos.

AOI: an exclamation occurring often in the *Chanson de Roland*, an eleventh-century French epic.

"Eat . . . under world": Because Kore/Persephone ate the pomegranate seeds which her abductor Hades gave her, Zeus did not permit her to go back to earth for good; she had to return to the underworld for four months every year. Cf. Canto XLVII.

Κόρη, Κόρη (Kore): Persephone, Demeter's daughter, on whom the Eleusinian mysteries center. Cf. Canto XLVII.

six seeds: Variant versions of the Kore myth hold that she ate one, six, or eight pomegranate seeds.

Demeter: Greek goddess of fertility and the harvest.

Pomona: Roman goddess of apple and other fruit trees.

Melagrana: Italian: pomegranate.

Heliads: In Greek mythology, daughters of Helios the sun-god; they were changed into poplar trees as they wept at the grave of their brother Phaethon, their tears turning to clear amber.

crotale: Italian: rattlesnakes. Pound may also be thinking of the Greek *krotalon*, "castanet."

There is . . . thru it: Cf. "from Canto LXXX" (SP, 171), where Pound writes of the English rose.

γλαυκῶπις (glaukopis): Greek: "glare-eyed," "owl-eyed," or "grey-eyed," an epithet of Athena. See Davie, EP, 71f.

Kuthera: Cythera, or Aphrodite.

Will you . . . acorns: Roses are sacred to Aphrodite; Circe fed acorns to Odysseus' crewmen whom she had turned into swine.

ἰχώρ (ikhor): Greek: the fluid in the veins of the immortals.

kalicanthus: prickly saltwort.

Faunus: Roman god of nature, protector of farmers and herdsmen, identified with Pan.

Graces: In Greek mythology, three daughters of Zeus, personifications of beauty and charm.

Ἀφροδίτην (Aphroditen): Greek goddess of love (accusative form).

Ἥλιος (Helios): the Greek sun-god.

there is a red glow: Cf. Canto II: "There is a wine-red glow in the shallows." (SP, 99)

δεινὰ εἶ, Κύθηρα (deina ei, Kythera): Greek: You are awesome, Cythera.

Κόρη καὶ Δήλια καὶ Μαῖα (Kore kai Delia kai Maia): Kore [i.e., Persephone] and Delia [i.e., Artemis] and Maia [Hermes' mother]. Cf. "from Canto LXXVI" (SP, 160, 162).

trine . . . praeludio: Latin: threefold . . . prelude.

Κύπρις Ἀφρόδιτη (Kypris Aphrodite): Greek goddess of love, associated with island of Cyprus.

aram nemus vult: Latin: "the grove demands an altar."

# *from* CANTO LXXX   [SP, 168]

The full text of Canto LXXX is an eight hundred-line act of remembrance. Its themes are more varied and more loosely organized than in Canto LXXIX, yet one thread runs through it all:

> Quand vous serez bien vieille [When you are very old],
> 　　remember that I have remembered
> mia pargoletta [my little one, i.e., the poet's daughter]
> 　and pass on the tradition.
>
> 　　　　　　　　　　　　　　　　　　　　(C, 506)

The words themselves are elegiac, foreshadowing many endings: of the year, of the poet's life, of the "tradition" itself. The war is over, and Pound will soon be leaving Italy and Europe, where he has spent the past forty years:

> 　so that leaving America I brought with me $80
> 　　and England a letter of Thomas Hardy's
> 　　and Italy one eucalyptus pip
> from the salita that goes up from Rapallo
> 　　　　　　(if I go)
>
> 　　　　　　　　　　　　　　　　　　　　(C, 500)

Nearness to endings opens the gates of memory again. Pound has, in *The Pisan Cantos*, shored fragments against his ruin in order to survive; now the act of remembering takes on another dimension, that of preserving and handing down the tradition to which he has devoted his life. To an extraordinary degree, Pound's personal memories are cultural memories. Many of the things he has "loved well"—the old friends, the "sacred" places, memorable happenings, words and music—belong to Western culture, not only his personal experience. In writing these memories into the poem, Pound recreates and passes on the tradition even as he partakes of it. Yet even the recreation is elegiac: there is no final forgetting, in *The Pisans*, that the tradition woven into the poet's past is no longer strong and vital. As Pound writes Canto LXXX, the war has ended; Auschwitz and Hiroshima have shown to what ends the idea of "culture" can be abused. The canto is as much a memorial, a historical marker to cultural traditions which did not keep us from enormous barbarisms, as it is a testimony to their living value.

Pound's meditation registers the problematics of his lifelong devotion to culture and "beauty." The first passage selected here is about the passing away, as well as the passing down, of the tradition. Pound first invokes his old friend Nancy Cunard, whose

Hours Press had published the deluxe edition of *A Draft of XXX Cantos*, and who had later become estranged from Pound because of their political differences. The cluster of details which follows at once recalls the European cultural tradition and marks its fragmentation in the modern period: the few words of Provençal, the wave pattern carved in the stone of an old French castle, another old friend and his painting. "Out of my solitudes let them come," writes the poet, and these ghosts appear. With the next image of FitzGerald's unnoticed *Rubáiyát* being salvaged by Rossetti, the theme changes key, moving from Pound's particular memories to thoughts on the impoverishment of modern culture. Pound clings to his belief in the power of great art to direct the mind and will to the right path, yet his expression of this belief in the absurd speculation that the Axis powers' defeat has to do with their inferior musical taste leaves nothing to be said for it. If the world of Auschwitz and Hiroshima is "beyond good and evil," it has darker connections with the power of art and beauty than Pound is considering here. He speaks more truly when he writes, in Canto LXXVIII, "There are no righteous wars." (C, 483)

Thinking about the decline of art in modern culture, Pound first remembers the opera singer's theory: "People have I don't know what strange fear of beauty." Then he recalls Beardsley's riposte to Yeats's inquiry as to "why he drew horrors": "Beauty is difficult," which Pound emphasizes: "So very difficult, Yeats, beauty so difficult." Next, he alludes to "Modern Beauty" (1899), a poem by Arthur Symons which begins: "I am the torch, she saith, and what to me / If the moth die of me? I am the flame / Of beauty," and ends:

> I live, and am immortal; in mine eyes
> The sorrow of the world, and on my lips
> The joy of life, mingle to make me wise;
> Yet now the day is darkened with eclipse:
> Who is there lives for beauty. Still am I
> The torch, but where's the moth that still dares die?

Finally, a fourth idea, the conception of beauty as a *knowledge* now lost: "All that Sandro [Botticelli] knew, and Jacopo [del Sellaio] / . . . / lost in the brown meat of Rembrandt." (Cf.

Canto XLV, "With usura the line grows thick.") The passage
ends with an allusion to a commentator on Confucius who urges
the necessity of guiding the "leather and bones," the "raw meat"
of physical matter, into a harmonious illumination of "the process,
a fountain of clear water descending from heaven immutable."
(Conf, 99)

There is little comfort in any of this, and the full text continues
with a plunge into near despair: "Je suis au bout de mes forces [I
am at the end of my strength]," Pound writes as he thinks of his
errors, disappearing into French to accuse himself: "Les larmes
que j'ai créees m'inondent / Tard, très tard, je t'ai connue, la
Tristesse [The tears I have caused engulf me / Late, too late, I
have known you, Sadness]" (C, 513). From the edge of hopeless-
ness, it is poetry—specifically, M. E. Speare's 1940 *Pocket Book
of English and American Verse*, found by accident in the latrine—
which rescues him:

> That from the gates of death,
>     that from the gates of death: Whitman or Lovelace
>         found on the jo-house seat at that
> in a cheap edition! [and thanks to Professor Speare]
> hast'ou swum in a sea of air strip
>     through an aeon of nothingness,
> when the raft broke and the waters went over me.
>
> (C, 513)

The poems hold him back from madness and despair. Words are,
in the most literal sense, his salvation—"Leucothea's bikini," the
magic veil the sea-nymph tossed Odysseus when his raft broke and
the waters went over him. But there is also a melancholy self-
scrutiny in this poem written in extremity about the saving grace
of poetry. Does Pound in his despair silently compare his poem
to Beardsley and Velásquez? One might surmise he does, since he
goes on to end the canto in a manner he has never before used in
his long poem: regular strophes, complete with what he calls in
*Mauberley* "the sculpture of rhyme." His theme is London—"our
London, my London, your London." First, a jangling jingle bids
a sardonic farewell to the England of the war years, and remarks
the possibility of economic reforms. Thinking of England takes
Pound back to specific memories of his own years there (1908–

20). He recalls a visit to the Talbot estate in Salisbury Plain, which belonged to a relative of his wife Dorothy Shakespear, where a copy of Henry III's 1225 revision of the Magna Carta was kept in a glass case in a tower. (Ironically, about the time Pound in Pisa was writing about this England of "rust, ruin, death duties, and mortgages / . . . / and more pictures gone to pay taxes," the heir to the Talbot house, according to Dorothy Pound, was selling that very charter to the British Museum—to pay taxes. See Terrell's *"Magna Carta* . . . and Pound's Associative Technique. . . .") Then his mind moves to "Chesterton's England," the England Pound grew to loathe during World War I and abandoned for Paris in 1920. The passage concludes with another jingle about the Talbot family seal, on which a slender dog appears, and a few strokes sketching the antique air of the place.

After a momentary cut to the prison camp and the present, Pound returns to his England, remembering a Christmas spent at the Salisbury estate of Maurice Hewlett, author of a historical novel about Mary Queen of Scots, whose Italian secretary, David Rizzio, was murdered by jealous nobles. The theme of political violence and bloodshed in English history next issues in three quatrains which allude to the English Wars of the Roses, modeled on the *Rubáiyát* stanza. In its way, this is surely one of the oddest moments of *The Cantos*. To find something like it, we would have to go all the way back to the "Envoi" of *Mauberley*. Pound here seems to be imagining a road not taken in his own poetic career. He treats the war theme that has preoccupied him since 1915 in uncharacteristic quatrains, as though to try whether "the sculpture of rhyme" might speak more forcefully against war and bloodshed. The question is tacitly answered by Pound's return to the finely sculpted asymmetries of the Pisan line at the end of the canto, which, in their own way, resemble the stone fragment from Excideuil, the old French castle, with the wave pattern on it. The anachronistic quatrains stand embedded in his modern form like a painted fan in a cubist collage, a sign of the unmendable break between the old idea of beauty and the modern world upon which the poem revolves.

Nancy: Nancy Cunard (1896–1965), poet and publisher of *A Draft of XXX Cantos* (1930). Pound stood up for her when her mother disowned her because of her alliance with the black singer Henry Crowder (see Canto XXXVIII). During the thirties, she and Pound came to serious disagreement over politics.

vair . . . cisclatons: Provençal: "of varied color . . . gowns [ciclatons]."

wave . . . stone: See the photograph in Kenner's *The Pound Era*, (337); and cf. Canto XXIX (C, 145).

Excideuil: a town in Dordogne, France, which Pound visited with T. S. Eliot in 1919.

Mt. Segur: Montségur, in southern France, site of a ruined sun temple designed to mark the summer solstice by the angle of light through its apertures. Cf. Canto LXXIX (C, 452).

city of Dioce: Ecbatana, built by King Deioces of the Medes. See Canto LXXIV, note to SP, 153 on p. 207.

Que . . . lune: French: That every month we have a new moon.

Herbiet: Georges Herbiet, who, under the name "Christian," translated Pound's "Moeurs Contemporaines" into French in 1921 for the Dada periodical *391*.

Fritz: Fritz-René Vanderpyl (1876–19??), Dutch art critic whom Pound visited at 13 rue Gay-Lussac in Paris, where he kept a life mask of himself on the balcony. He and Pound considered that the statue in the Luxembourg Gardens visible from the balcony resembled a " 'Beer-bottle on the statue's pediment! / 'That, Fritz, is the era, to-day against the past, / Contemporary.' " (Canto VII, C, 25)

Orage: A. R. Orage (1875–1934), Social Credit theorist and editor of *The New Age* and *New English Weekly*, to which Pound regularly contributed writings on economics and culture. See Pound's "Obituary: A. R. Orage" and "In the Wounds" (SPr, 407–21).

Fordie: Ford Madox Ford; see Canto LXXIV, note to SP, 156, on p. 210.

Crevel: René Crevel (1900–35), French author whose novel, *Les Pieds dans le plat*, Pound considered a sign of an "awakening in Paris." (SL, 249)

de . . . vengan: Spanish: Out of my solitudes let them come, a paraphrase of a line of Lope de Vega. See SR, 208.

lay there . . . remaindered: A remaindered copy of Edward Fitz-
Gerald's *Rubáiyát of Omar Khayyam* was salvaged by Dante Gabriel
Rossetti (1828–82), the Pre-Raphaelite poet and painter. Cf. HSM,
"Yeux Glauques."

Cythera: Aphrodite, goddess of love and beauty.

or did they fall: i.e., the Axis powers.

Münch: Gerhardt Münch, a pianist and composer who participated in
the Rapallo concert series which began in 1933, and whose transcription
of one voice of Clement Janequin's "Chant des Oiseaux" for violin
appears as Canto LXXV. The violin was Olga Rudge's instrument.

Bach: Johann Sebastian Bach (1685–1750), German composer, of whom
Pound wrote in *Guide to Kulchur*, "Bach builds up from the bottom, as
distinctly as Wren did. In Bach's case the result is magnificent. . . .
There is no doubt that Bach's spirit is in great part that of a robust ma-
terial world." (153)

Spewcini: Giacomo Puccini (1858–1924), Italian composer, of whom
Pound wrote in *Guide to Kulchur*, "I suspect . . . that the infant Mozart
did not enflame all Italy, because THEN Italy knew so much more
. . . about that kind of beauty in music than it does today in the back
slosh of Mascagni and Puccini." (154)

man seht: German: *man sieht* (one sees).

Les hommes . . . beauté: French: People have I don't know what
strange fear of beauty. Monsieur Whoosis: Mr. What's-his-name.

La beauté . . . quickly: The poet is William Butler Yeats (1865–1939);
the artist, Aubrey Beardsley (1872–98), who died of tuberculosis. See
Canto LXXIV, note to SP, 159, on p. 214. Sir Edward Burne-Jones
(1833–98) was a Pre-Raphaelite painter who influenced Beardsley's
early work. Cf. HSM, "Yeux Glauques."

Arthur: Arthur Symons (1865–1945), English poet and critic whose
study of the Symbolist poets influenced Yeats, Pound, and Eliot.

βροδοδάκτυλος Ἠώς (brododaktylos Eos): Greek: rosy-fingered dawn,
a recurring phrase in Homer's *Iliad* and *Odyssey*. Here Pound uses
Sappho's dialect word instead of Homer's *rhododaktylos*.

Κύθηρα δεινά (Kythera deina): Greek: awesome Cythera.

pale eyes . . . fire: Cf. HSM, "Yeux Glauques."

all that Sandro . . . Jordaens: See Hugh Kenner's illustration of this passage in *The Pound Era*, 364. Sandro Botticelli (1444–1510) and Jacopo del Sellaio (1422–93) were Florentine painters; Velásquez (1599–1660) was a Spanish painter; Rembrandt van Rijn (1601–69) was a Dutch painter; Peter Paul Rubens (1557–1640) and Jacob Jordaens (1593–1678) were Flemish painters.

"This alone" . . . comment: Pound translates Chu Hsi's comment in *The Unwobbling Pivot* (Conf, 99): "The main thing is to illuminate the root of the process, a fountain of clear water descending from heaven immutable. The components, the bones of things, the materials are implicit and prepared in us, abundant and inseparable from us."

Oh to be . . . out: Pound borrows from Browning's "Home Thoughts from Abroad": "Oh to be in England / Now that April's there."

Winston: Winston Churchill (1874–1965), Conservative Prime Minister of England from 1940 until the 1945 Labor Party victory. Pound denounces him as a warmonger, and criticizes him for returning England to the gold standard and for allowing control of credit to remain with private banks instead of with the government. (See Canto XLV headnote.)

To watch a while . . . taxes: See headnote.

John's first one: The first Magna Carta, drafted by the nobles and signed under duress by King John of England (ca. 1167–1216), was issued in 1215.

Chesterton: G. K. Chesterton (1874–1936), English writer and critic whom Pound considered an active perpetrator of second-rate culture.

When a dog . . . small butt: See headnote. A butt is a barrel of wine or ale.

Let backe . . . go bare: from a sixteenth-century drinking song, titled "Jolly Good Ale and Old," by John Still, which Pound read in Speare's anthology.

boneen: piglets.

Claridge's: a fashionable London hotel.

Maurie Hewlett: Maurice Hewlett (1861–1923), English novelist with whom Pound spent Christmas in 1911 (cf. Canto LXXIV, SP, 156). See headnote.

Lady Anne: probably Lady Anne Low, a relative of the Scottish noble who instigated the assassination of Mary Queen of Scots' secretary.

Le Portel: Cf. the reference to Swinburne in Canto LXXVII (C, 523):
> When the french fishermen hauled him out he
> recited 'em
>            might have been Aeschylus
>         till they got into Le Portel, or wherever
> in the original.

The anecdote concerns the English poet Algernon Swinburne, who once encountered trouble while swimming off the coast of Étretat in France, and had to be rescued by some French fishermen, who sailed to Yport while he entertained them by reciting poetry. Pound misremembers Yport as Le Portel. Swinburne comes to mind because he dramatized the story of Rizzio's murder in his Mary Stuart trilogy.

How tiny . . . him: i.e., where the Scottish nobles stabbed David Rizzio in 1566. See headnote.

La Stuarda: Mary Stuart (1542–87), Queen of Scots 1561–68.

Si tuit . . . marimen: Provençal: If all the grief and tears and misery, the opening line of Bertran de Born's "Planh for the Young English King" (SP, 12). Cf. Canto LXXXIV (C, 537).

leopards and broom plants: Brooker notes that these are the heraldic devices, respectively, of Richard the Lionhearted, King of England 1189–99, and Henry II, King of England 1154–89, father of the Henry whom Bertran's poem mourns. (334)

Tudor . . . rose: Pound adapts FitzGerald's "Iram indeed is gone with all his rose" to this lyric recalling the English Wars of the Roses (1455–85), the struggle over the British throne by the houses of Lancaster (whose emblem was a red rose) and of York (whose emblem was a white rose).

Howard . . . Boleyn: Catherine Howard (ca. 1521–42), fifth wife, and

Anne Boleyn (ca. 1505–36), second wife, of King Henry VIII of England, who had them both beheaded.

Or . . . FRANCE: Pound seems to be referring to the fact that France surrendered to the Axis powers on June 22, 1940, while England, under Churchill, fought on alone.

Serpentine: a lake in London's Hyde Park.

the pond . . . the sunken garden: Round Pond and the sunken garden in Kensington Gardens, London.

her green elegance: i.e., the "green midge" that the lizard is stalking near Pound's tent in the prison camp, and that Pound has protectively removed from danger. Cf. Canto LXXXI (SP, 174): "Paquin, pull down! The green casque has outdone your elegance."

rain ditch: Cf. Canto LXXIV: "and they digged a ditch round about me / lest the damp gnaw thru my bones." (C, 429)

## *from* CANTO LXXXI                    [SP, 172]

Canto LXXXI opens with a meander of memories, which lead eventually to three lines of reticent pathos:

> AOI!
> a leaf in the current
>                 at my grates no Althea
>
>                                   (C, 519)

This cry of distress and loneliness as Pound returns from the comforting refuge of the past to his appalling present directly precedes the passage excerpted here. The lines that follow partly assuage this misery and loneliness by a series of imaginary communions. Unlike the seventeenth-century poet Richard Lovelace, who wrote a poem called "To Althea from Prison" (included in Speare's anthology), Pound has no one at his barbed-wire grates. In Canto LXXXI he finds in the "live tradition" of poetry and song as much of companionship and comfort as he knows in the prison camp.

These communions begin with unheard melodies. The opening passage—marked "libretto," words for music, in *The Cantos*—is a lyric, a song with a refrain both heard and sung by the poet, who is borne up by its power from his depths into "the aureate sky." "There," he wrote in the manuscript version, "I heard such minstrelsy / as mocketh man's mortality." (Yale MSS) The wind that lifts him is the song, the "air," that he hears, and that inspires—or "breathes into" him—his own song. The song pays homage to the spirits of the great seventeenth-century English lyric tradition. It names the composers Lawes, Jenkins, and Dowland, and alludes intrinsically to Ben Jonson by a pattern of speech derived from his "Have you seen but a bright lily grow" (see Canto LXXIV, SP, 159). Intertwined with the motive of homage, however, is that of community. Indeed, one significance of Pound's return to seventeenth-century song rather than, say, to a lyricist such as Yeats or Keats is the central role of music in the celebration of concord and conviviality. (It is no casual fact that Dionysos, the presiding deity of *The Cantos*, is a god of music as well as of wine.) We see this motive clearly in Pound's modulation from Jonson's "Have you" to the more intimate "Hast' ou." This tender archaism occurs in lines whose sense might be heard by the poet as well as spoken by him, and it stresses the love of community which prompts the songs not only of all the poets, composers, and instrument-makers, the singers and instrumentalists, who participate in this tradition, but of listeners and readers too. At the same time, its archaic note (as well as the literal absence of music, singers, and players) registers this community as a figment of desire, an imaginary scene. The "Hast' ou" makes the loss of the tradition sharply felt even as Pound recovers the memory of the lyric tradition in a brief interlude between the main acts of his long poem.

At the close of the song, Pound quotes two lines from Chaucer's "Merciles Beaute." He is still thinking of the music of poetry, as the line "And for 180 years almost nothing" shows, but in a moment a shift occurs which makes manifest the power of poetry's music to redeem loneliness and isolation. For as he "listens to the light murmur" of Chaucer's words, their "eyes of love" bring into his tent, that is, somehow initiate, a vision which is a strange elaboration of those two lines. It is a "hypostasis" of Chaucer's image of a beauty conveyed by eyes which pierces and slays, drawn in its specifics upon Pound's own need of an "Althea," of the comfort of people, words, communication. The eyes which enter the tent are mysterious presences, a "new subtlety" which neither Chaucer's words nor his own words name. He describes what he sees: several pairs of eyes, in "half mask's space," inter-passing, penetrating, shining with the colors of sky, pool, and sea. These eyes, like Chaucer's or Jonson's words, carry a message to the poet in the cage who has lost everyone and everything: "What thou lovest well remains." It is the same message Chaucer and Jonson bequeathed, a paradisal message. The eyes, the "seen," bring "the palpable / Elysium, though it were in the halls of hell"—the mind's paradise that bears the "formèd trace" of all it has loved well. But with the assurance of that heritage, the eyes also bring an exhortation, the famous "Pull down thy vanity" passage which deflates the writer's romantic pretensions and ranks his creations in the larger-than-literary, larger-than-aesthetic context of "the green world." The self-accusations Pound has made before ("Les larmes que j'ai créees m'inondent") now take external shape as the vision becomes an oblique confession of wrongness and error—a confession which would have cost too much, there in the prison camp, had it not been simultaneously an affirmation of love and memory, and of a place in the green world.

At the end of the canto, the vision has vanished, and the shaken poet salvages from his self-accusations of vanity that part of his life which he had devoted to carrying on "a live tradition," gathering it from the "fine old eye" of a Blunt, a Yeats, a Hardy ("Swinburne my only miss," C, 523). This last passage precipitates the significance of the shift from the music to the eyes of Chaucer's lines: for the poet's eye, like the eyes in the tent, "speaks" with a flame, a breath, a spirit, not of physical life but of spiritual life. This is the life that poetry has always affirmed, and that Pound has devoted himself to saving in a world increasingly bereft of spirit; and it is the breath of the particular tradition which Pound extends in Canto LXXXI.

This is the reason why Pound, who learned from greater living poets than Wilfred Scawen Blunt, makes this minor poet (rather than, say, Yeats) his example, for Canto LXXXI is, finally, an anti-Romantic poem. Speaking against vanity, it bypasses the great Romantics to affirm a minor lyric tradition. Moreover, it is quite literally Blunt from whom Pound gathered the tradition which Canto LXXXI extends, for the enfolding of memories and images with historical particulars continues to constellate a rose from the dust of the past. In a 1913 *Poetry* article, Pound had praised Blunt as "the last of the great Victorians, by reason of his double sonnet," "With Esther." In 1914, with Yeats, Aldington, Flint, and others, Pound had arranged a "Peacock Dinner" in his honor:

> Because you have gone your individual gait,
> Written fine verses, made mock of the world,
> Swung the grand style, not made a trade of art,
> Upheld Mazzini and detested institutions.

> (Norman, 137)

And in 1945, among the poems in the Speare anthology Pound found Blunt's "With Esther," gathered by another hand and eye. Might Speare, compiling his anthology, perhaps have noticed Pound's earlier praise? Is there a "live tradition" even in that choice? In any case, as George Kearns has pointed out (167), the poem which Blunt composed, Pound praised, and Speare chose appears a startlingly exact "inspiration" for Canto LXXXI:

> He who has once been happy is for aye
>   Out of destruction's reach. His fortune then
> Holds nothing secret; and Eternity
>   Which is a mystery to other men,
> Has . . . given him its joy.
>   Time is his conquest . . .
>        . . . When I set
>
> The world before me, and survey its range,
>   Its mean ambitions, its scant fantasies,
> The shreds of pleasure which for lack of change
>   Men wrap around them and call happiness,
> The poor delights which are the tale and sum
>   Of the world's courage in its martyrdom;
>
>   . . .
> When cities deck their streets for barren wars
>   Which have laid waste their youth, and when I keep
> Calmly the count of my own life and see

On what poor stuff my manhood's dreams were fed
Till I too learn'd what dole of vanity
Will serve a human soul for daily bread,
—Then I remember that I once was young
And lived with Esther the world's gods among.

(Speare, 295–96)

"With Esther" seems almost a blueprint for the themes of Canto LXXXI. But the differences between the two poems tell us as much as the likenesses. Blunt's style and form reflect the coherence and serenity of a world not yet torn apart by the "barren wars" he decries, whereas the formal center of the canto, written two world wars later, shifts and turns unexpectedly, "a leaf in the current" of history. Finally, however, it is how much shared ground there is between these two vastly different paradises of love and memory that underwrites the communion and the hope for community in Canto LXXXI, and that most deeply connects the leaf Pound has fashioned to the roots of human life and of the lyric tradition.

zephyr: the west wind. Cf. Canto LXXIV (SP, 157). Pound is probably thinking of the image of the wind in Botticelli's "Birth of Venus," but he speaks of himself being borne up by the wind. See headnote.

aureate: golden.

*Lawes:* Henry Lawes (1596–1662), English composer who set Waller's "Go, Lovely Rose" to music (see HSM, "Envoi"), and whom Pound placed with Dowland, Young, and Jenkins in *ABC of Reading* to exemplify "the period of England's musicianship." (151)

*Jenkyns:* John Jenkins (1592–1678), English composer whom Pound included in a musical program he arranged for a Rapallo concert.

*Dolmetsch:* Arnold Dolmetsch (1858–1940), French musician who made copies of early instruments; Pound owned one of his clavichords. Dolmetsch wrote a book, titled *Pathways of Song* (1938), in which he included Dowland's setting of Jonson's "Have you seen but a bright lily grow."

viol: stringed instrument.

grave . . . acute: musical notation; grave indicates slowness and solemnity, and acute indicates a hard, shrill tone.

Waller: Edmund Waller (1606–87), English poet whose "Go, Lovely Rose" inspired the "Envoi" of *Hugh Selwyn Mauberley*.

Dowland: John Dowland (1563–1626), English composer and lute-player; see Dolmetsch.

Your eyen . . . susteyne: from the poem "Merciles Beaute," attributed to Chaucer.

180 years: Pound may be thinking of the years between Jenkins' death and Dolmetsch's birth.

Ed . . . mormorio: Italian: And listening to the light murmur. In the manuscript, Pound follows this line with, "As I was listening to the enchanted song." His use of Italian here sets a Dantesque tone for the apparition of the eyes.

hypostasis: substance, essence, essential principle, as distinguished from accidental characteristics.

carneval: Italian: carnevale, or carnival, when masks are worn.

diastasis: the separation between the eyes (their "stance").

the full image: The text of *The Cantos* reads "the full Eidos," a Greek word with the sense of knowing, vision, apparition.

Whose world . . . none?: Cf. Canto LXXX (C, 172): "our London / my London, your London."

Elysium: the Elysian Fields of Greek mythology, where the blest have their home after death.

Paquin: a Paris couturier.

casque: French: helmet.

"Master . . . beare": an adaptation of Chaucer's "Reule wel thyself, that other folk canst rede" in "Ballade of Good Counsel," which Speare prints as "Subdue thyself, and others shall thee hear."

Blunt: Wilfred Scawen Blunt (1840–1922), English poet who, because he opposed his country's imperialism, campaigning for home rule for

Ireland, India, and Egypt, was censured by officials of the Empire. He was jailed for activities on behalf of Irish nationalism in 1888. See headnote, and see Pound's account of the dinner in his honor in *Poetry*, March 1914.

## *from* CANTO LXXXIII                    [SP, 175]

Canto LXXXIII, written in September, 1945, is the next to last of the Pisan series. All the fighting had finally ended; Japan had officially surrendered on September 2. The poet, looking out from his cage, records what he can see: time and weather, the rainy September dawn. The mood is of weariness ("There is fatigue deep as the grave") and apparent tranquility ("Dryad, thy peace is like water"); but underlying this peace is a deep anxiety as Pound awaits the end of his imprisonment at Pisa and his transfer to the United States for indictment and trial. This is a canto full of tears: "DAKRUŌN, ΔΑΚΡΥΩΝ" ("Weeping, weeping"), he writes as he thinks of his beloved Venice and wonders, "Will I ever see the Giudecca again? / or the lights against it, Ca' Foscari, Ca' Giustinian / or the Ca', as they say, of Desdemona?" (C, 532). He waits out the time in his cage.

The rainy dawn landscape in the prison camp finds many likenesses in Pound's thoughts. In composing its reflection in the poem, he brings together the outer world of rain and light and the inner one of tears and mind. Eyes—his own, the dryad's, the sun's— mediate between the *plura diafana*, the many manifestations of light, and intelligence. As always, the physical beauty of the Pisan vista presses toward the religious and ethical in Pound's perception. In the first passage selected, the rain has conjured spirits to whom the "caged panther" offers his tears. A voice speaks to him: "Nothing, nothing that you can do." It once belonged, perhaps, to his daughter ("Dryad"), for it has been a full year since he traveled from Rome to Gais to tell her about his two families; but now, disembodied, it also speaks the frustration of the prisoner: a caged panther, powerless to act. There is a deep dissatisfaction, a distance, in the beautiful images of the mountain in the mist and the eyes like clouds. The names he gives them—"Taishan," "Chocorua," "Dryad"—dislocate them from their bodies and their histories. "The hidden city moves upward," writes the poet, invoking his dream of a *paradiso terrestre*, but the statement seems curiously detached not only from reality but from what we have learned to regard as its true referent, that is, Pound's faith in it. Pound's faith has been shaken. The weariness of Canto LXXXIII, "deep as the grave," follows on this failure of words—the only power the poet has—to "do." "Nothing, nothing that you can do." The distance between the poet's words and the world seems suddenly as boundless, as unimaginable, as that between the mountain of Pisa and the "phantom mountain" that Pound calls "Taishan," "Chocorua." The names float above it; they cannot move it. Their ground has disappeared. "Only the stockade posts stand."

In this unease, Pound turns to Mencius, the Chinese philosopher whom he has been translating in the D. T. C. Mencius supplies the concept and imagery by which Pound moves from the landscape to ethics. As Wendy Stallard Flory notes, Pound draws here on Mencius' discussion of the "passion-nature," a natural power which nourishes the individual in harmony with "the process":

> It is exceedingly great and exceedingly strong. Being nourished by rectitude, and sustaining no injury, it fills up all between heaven and earth. . . . It is the mate and assistant of righteousness and reason. Without it, *humanity* is in a state of starvation. . . . It is produced by the accumulation of righteous deeds; it is not to be attained by incidental acts of righteousness.
>
> (Legge, II, 190, quoted in Flory, 223)

But what is perhaps most interesting about Pound's use of this imagery is how obscure this force remains, despite the twelve lines which define it in a structure reminiscent of the definition of love in Canto XXXVI (the Cavalcanti translation). The mist full of light becomes "this breath," qualified in six subsequent clauses. It is crucial, yet also mysterious. The definitions have sharp edges, assured clarities, but the "breath," whatever it is, floats free of them; detached from its historical context, it is rootless and insubstantial. The fragments of Mencius strive to make something of—

to possess and interpret—"the brightness of *"hudor* [water]" that suffuses the landscape. They express the poet's desire to be one with a natural world which seems irrevocably estranged ("that he eat of the barley corn / and move with the seed's breath"); but in the end, they too are impotent to move the mountain. The ideograms Pound is translating, analyzed, give only an image perilously near the picturesque: "the sun as a golden eye / between dark cloud and the mountain."

In the next excerpt, Pound turns again to nature, observing it without the mediation of ideas. The move is instinctive; as often before in Pisa, Pound finds "When the mind swings by a grassblade / an ant's forefoot shall save you." As to the saving power of nature, a passage from Pound's essay on Mencius is illuminating:

> It is OF the permanence of nature that honest men . . . come repeatedly to the same answers in ethics. . . .
>
> Shin and Wan had a thousand years between them and when their wills were compared they were as two halves of a tally stick.
>
> From Kung to Mencius a century, and to St. Ambrose another six or so hundred years, and a thousand years to St. Antonino, and they are as parts of one pattern, as wood of a single tree.
>
> (SPr, 89–90)

Again, it is faith in a shared world and in a shared human mind which underlies Pound's close observation of the wasp, with the increasingly precise names he derives from watching it: "Brother Wasp," a misnomer corrected to "La Vespa" as Pound remembers that it is the female who builds the nest, and finally to "Madame La Vespa" when he observes the infant emerging from the nest. The mint leaves, which crop up in the poem as they do in the earth at Pisa, and the clover symbolize the natural patterns of recurrence which Pound conceives as the guarantee of ethical harmony. But the pathos of this beginning again at the ground, so to speak, this attempt to "call things by their right names," resides in its inadequacy to a modern world so far removed from the natural world. And Pound's awareness of this inadequacy comes through at the end of the canto where, reflecting on American politics, he recognizes that not "right names" but slippery and inexact figures of speech govern political thought and the expression of power. He cannot quite accept the implications of this insight. In his mother's time, he remembers, "it was respectable, / it was social, apparently, / to sit in the Senate gallery / . . . / to hear the fire-works of the senators." (C, 535–36) If this custom of the body politic were still observed, Pound wonders, and "if Senator Edwards cd/ speak / and have his tropes stay in the memory 40 years, 60 years," might then "the hidden city move upward"? Exhaustion pervades the canto's last lines, which are as painfully inadequate to Pound's own situation as they are to history. The poet, who has grown old with some illusions that history has devastated, seeks his rest. He will end the Pisan sequence, one canto later, with the simplest of verities:

> If the hoar-frost grip thy tent
> thou wilt give thanks when night is spent.

Δρύας (Dryas): Greek: dryad, a tree-nymph.

Taishan . . . Chocorua: Pound calls the mountain visible from the Pisan camp after the sacred Chinese mountain near Confucius' birthplace, and after Mount Chocorua in New Hampshire.

the hidden city: Cf. the "city of Dioce" in Canto LXXIV (SP, 153).

Plura diafana: a phrase from Bishop Grosseteste's medieval light metaphysics, meaning "many manifestations of the divine light." Cf. "diafan" in Canto XXXVI (SP, 127).

Heliads: daughters of Helios, the sun-god. Cf. Canto LXXIX (SP, 165).

'udor    ὕδωρ (hudor): Greek: water.

the process: See note to Canto LXXIV (SP, 153).

Clower: perhaps William Clowes, printer of two of Pound's early works, *Gaudier-Brzeska* and *Lustra*.

La vespa: Italian: the wasp.

Bracelonde: perhaps the forest of the Arthurian legends, Brocéliande.

Perugia: town in central Italy.

Piazza: perhaps the Piazza Quatre Novembre in Perugia, with its Fontana Maggiore.

old Bulagaio: Bulagaio is an old quarter of Perugia.

Mr. Walls: a fellow prisoner in the D. T. C. Cf. Canto LXXXII (C, 523).

Jones: an officer at the D. T. C.

Senator Edwards: Ninian Edwards (1775–1833), United States Senator from Illinois, 1818–24.

Down, Derry-down: a phrase from the refrain of an English folksong, "The Keeper": "Hey down, ho down, / Derry derry down / Among the leaves so green O."

## *from* CANTO XCI (1955) [SP, 179]

If Pound's Pisan experience had seemed an inferno, worse was to come. In November 1945, he was taken from the D. T. C. to Washington, D.C., and indicted for treason for his Rome Radio broadcasts. Judged incompetent to stand trial, he was held at St. Elizabeths Mental Hospital until 1958, when, by the concerted efforts of many friends and fellow writers, including figures as diverse as Robert Frost, T. S. Eliot, and Dag Hammarskjold, the United States Department of Justice was finally persuaded to drop the charges and release him. He then returned to Italy to live out the rest of his years.

While in St. Elizabeths, Pound composed two installments of *The Cantos: Section: Rock-Drill* (1955), from which these passages of Cantos XCI and XCIII are taken, and *Thrones de los cantares* (1959). Again the canto form takes a new direction: its space becomes the mind's own place, curiously indifferent to quotidian circumstances. The motives we've encountered before— modernist memory, personal anguish, didactic fury, improvisational mythmaking, Greek, American, and Chinese history, nature, light, and so on—recur in these cantos. But the poet's voice has changed. It is familiar—indeed, many lines quote verbatim lines of earlier cantos (e.g., "J'ai eu pitié des autres pas assez")—but also strange. Nothing in its speech strikes us so forcibly as the sheer music of its words. It is as though the substance of the old themes has now become immaterial, and the poem itself attenuated into language as a pure body of sound, abstracted from its old signifying intentions. The poem's long dream of finding a common language has failed, and what is left is the sensual body of the words.

This passage from Canto XCI, brief as it is, exemplifies this quality. A love poem, it celebrates a redeeming affection that has come to the old poet in the hospital for the insane and "stirred my mind out of dust." (C, 632) Love is inspiration, the breath of life and song, and brings with it the joy of poetic creation. For Pound, this act is holy: "qui laborat, orat" ("who works, prays"). Love, for him, sublimely expands to embrace its likenesses in memory and nature, which he arranges into the faceted crystal of the poem.

ab . . . vai: Provençal: "with the joy that comes into my heart," a line Pound adapts from *"Per la doussor c'al cor li vai"* ("by the sweetness that enters his heart") from Bernart de Ventadorn's *"Quan vei la lauzeta mover"* ["When I see the lark on the wing"] and from William of Aquitaine's *"Ab la dolchor del temps novel"* ("With the joy of the new season"). The musical notation in medieval neumes seems to be Pound's remembered version of the melody to which Bernart's line was set (see James J. Wilhelm). Pound's translation begins:

When I see the lark a-moving
For joy his wings against the sunlight,
Who forgets himself and lets himself fall
For the sweetness which goes into his heart;
Ai! what great envy comes into me for him whom I see so rejoicing!
(Tr, 427)

His Canto XCI version "makes it new" by signifying a love which brings his heart the joy of the lark—that is, the joy of the lyric poet.

Reina: Italian: Queen. 300 years: Perhaps Pound is thinking of the last three hundred years, during which the finely drawn clarity of medieval and Renaissance art has been "sunken."

qui . . . orat: Latin: who works, prays.

Undine: Pound's name for the artist Sheri Martinelli, who visited him at St. Elizabeths; he loved her, she said, "because I symbolize the spirit of love to him."

Circeo: a promontory on the sea near Rome. Cf. Canto XXXIX (C, 195): "with the Goddess' eyes to seaward / By Circeo, by Terracina, with the stone eyes / white toward the sea," in which Pound echoes his "Credo": "Given the material means I would replace the statue of Venus on the cliffs of Terracina. I would erect a temple to Artemis in Park Lane. I believe that a light from Eleusis persisted throughout the middle ages and set beauty in the song of Provence and Italy." (SPr, 53)

Apollonius: Apollonius of Tyana, first-century Pythagorean philosopher whose *Life* was written by Philostratus. He becomes an important alter ego in the *Rock-Drill* cantos, for he too was a visionary who was regarded as a threat by the political powers of his time. He was arrested and tried for treason by the emperor Domitian and defended himself impressively, vanishing at the end of his speech with the words, "For thou shalt not slay me, since I tell thee I am not mortal." When Pound writes "Thus Apollonius," he alludes to this escape, and to the lark's wings of love and poetry, by which he escapes the horrors of his own imprisonment.

Helen of Tyre: In *The Spirit of Romance*, Pound wrote, "There would seem to be in the legend of Simon Magus and Helen of Tyre a clearer prototype of 'chivalric love' than in anything hereinafter discussed." (91n) This weird legend, invented by Simon Magus, concerns his rescue of a woman he thought a reincarnation of Helen of Troy from a brothel in the Phoenician city Tyre. The image thus alludes to another escape from imprisonment by one "not mortal."

Pithagoras: the early Greek philosopher Pythagoras (ca. 580–497 B.C.) who believed that human beings have divine powers which link them to the gods, and taught a way of life in accord with those powers. Pound cites Pythagoras' thought as the power by which Apollonius made his escape.

Ocellus . . . Tyre: a Pythagorean philosopher. Pound implies that Ocellus was the "pilot-fish" which guided Simon to Tyre. et libidinis expers: Latin: and untouched by passion; cf. Canto LXXVI (SP, 160).

Justinian, Theodora: Justinian was the Byzantine emperor, 527–65; Theodora was his wife.

pensar . . . ripaus: Provençal: "To think of her is my repose," from Arnaut Daniel's "*En breu brisaral temps braus*" (see Tr, 171).

Miss Tudor: Queen Elizabeth I of England (1558–1603). galleons: Spanish warships.

he: Sir Francis Drake; see below.

Crystal . . . healing: Pound may be thinking of Dante's culminating vision in *Paradiso*, Canto XXXIII:
> O abounding grace, by which I dared to fix my gaze on the Eternal Light so long that I spent all my sight upon it! In its depth I saw that it contained, bound by love in one volume, that which is scattered in leaves throughout the universe, substances and accidents and their relations as it were fused together in such a way that what I tell of is a simple light.

*compenetrans:* Latin: interpenetrating.

Princess Ra-Set: Pound's fusion of two Egyptian deities, Ra, the sun-god, and Set, the water-god, who in one papyrus enters the sun-god's chariot. Pound may have been thinking of his daughter, Mary, and her marriage to the Egyptologist Boris de Rachewiltz.

convien . . . amando: Pound quotes from Dante's *Paradiso*, Canto XXVI: "the mind must be moved by love."

Drake: Sir Francis Drake (1540?–1603), English admiral who helped defeat the Spanish Armada in 1588 and captured many Spanish treasures for Queen Elizabeth, who eventually knighted him.

ichor, amor: Ichor is the Greek word for the liquid in the veins of the gods; amor is Latin, love.

J. Heydon: John Heydon, seventeenth-century mystic whose *Holy Guide* Pound recommended for its illumination of "the joys of pure form . . . inorganic geometrical form" (GB, 127). Heydon appears in the discarded *Poetry* Cantos of 1917. He called himself "Secretary of Nature" and "read" natural objects as "signatures" of a great cosmic design.

This elegiac passage from Canto XCIII is a quiet prayer by the aged poet for his daughter, asking "that the child / walk in peace in her basilica, / The light there almost solid." The autumn leaves that blow from his hand are an image of his own life, moving toward its close. Thoughts of his past years bring remorse—"J'ai eu pitié des autres. / Pas assez!"—and he asks "For me nothing." But his prayer for his daughter is a way of attempting to redeem past errors. By means of it, his eyes can look toward the future, beyond his own death; his hopes are for those who come after him. Judging himself as having had too little pity, he prays for "compassion" as his child's peace. (One is reminded of Henry James urging his nieces and nephews to "Be kind, be kind, and be kind!") As he feels his long struggle nearing its end, he expresses a wish to assure its worth and meaning in the image of the child walking in the light he has invoked, and tried to capture, in his poetry.

This passage, with its litany of beseeching, recalls a very early poem, "The Alchemist: Chant for the Transmutation of Metals" (1912), in which the alchemist calls upon feminine spirits to "Bring the burnished nature of fire . . . Give light to the metal." In Canto XCIII, time's alchemy has transmuted the alchemist's lead and gold, and the process itself, into an allegory of cultural tradition, the transfer of creative energies and values from one generation to the next. "Ysolt, Ydone," the Provençal ladies, merge with new deities, and it is the lead of the poet's own time-bound struggle which he seeks to transform into the gold, the light, of the daughter's more blessed life. He dreams that by his efforts, and by time's alchemies, the child will walk in the earthly paradise that he has tried all his life to create. What is perhaps most moving in this late rewriting of the earlier poem is its implicit acknowledgment that its vision belongs to a world of fantasy and magic which real time and real life can hardly approach. Pound's belated prayer, in all its sincerity and pathos, knows its own unanswerability.

agitante calescemus: from Ovid's *Fasti*, VI.15: "*est deus in nobis, agitante calescimus illo*" ("there is a god in us, who, *stirring, kindles us*"). Cf. Canto XCVIII (C, 685) and CIV (C, 739).

Lux in diafana: Latin: Light in its manifestations. Cf. Canto XXXVI (SP, 127).

Creatrix, oro: Latin: Creator, I beseech.

Ursula benedetta: Italian: Blessed Ursula, i.e., St. Ursula, guardian of virgins.

per dilettevole ore: Latin, translated in the preceding line.

Ysolt, Ydone: Isolde, of the legend of Tristan and Isolde, and Ydoine, of the legend of Amadis and Ydoine, both of which Pound discusses in *The Spirit of Romance* (80–84). Cf. "The Alchemist" (P, 76).

Picarda: Piccarda dei Donati appears in Dante's *Paradiso*, Canto III, in the first order of the blessed, for saints whose faith was marred by inconstancy. Piccarda's "failure" was to have been abducted from her convent by her brother Corso and forced into an odious marriage. See "The Alchemist" (P, 76).

wing'd head . . . caduceus: Boris de Rachewiltz suggests that Pound saw in "the serpent head-dress of the Ureus . . . the Egyptian origin of the caduceus." (179) The caduceus is Mercury's wand, topped with two entwined serpents.

Isis-Luna: Isis is the moon-goddess of ancient Egypt, a fertility goddess pictured as wearing a horned crown.

black panther: Cf. Pound's image of himself as "the caged panther" in Canto LXXXII (SP, 175).

J'ai . . . assez!: French: I've had pity for others. / Not enough! Not enough!

her basilica: In *Discretions*, Pound's daughter Mary de Rachewiltz describes how she and her husband Boris obtained a ruin of a castle in the South Tyrol and worked to restore it. When she visited her father in St. Elizabeths in 1953 to try to obtain his release, he told her "All you can do is to plant a little decency in Brunnenburg." (292)

# FROM *Women of Trachis* (1954)

[SP, 183]

This passage is the first chorus from Pound's translation of
Sophocles' tragedy *Women of Trachis*. As was usual with Pound's
translations, this one received mixed reviews from the classicists,
stirring up controversies about the nature and aims of translation
(see headnotes to "The Seafarer" and "Homage to Sextus Pro-
pertius"). Pound's main interest in this translation lay in bringing
to life an ancient classic for a modern American audience. At-
tempting this, he broke with the highly formal speech of earlier
English translations, and employed instead a deft, fast, street-
talking idiom, which he conceived as a stylized version of "the
common speech." Thus, where the Loeb translator renders an ex-
change between Deianira and the Chorus in this way:

Chorus:     If thou hast warranty thy charm will work,
            We think that thou hast counselled not amiss.
Deianira:   No warrant, for I have not tried it yet,
            But of its potency I am assured.
Chorus:     Without experiment, there cannot be
            Assurance, howsoever firm thy faith.
Deianira:   Well, we shall know ere long, for there I see
            Lichas just starting; he is at the gate.
            Only do you be secret; e'en dark deeds
            If they be done in secret bring no blame.

Pound cuts the ceremonious rhetoric, and suddenly we hear people
talking:

Chorus:    Don't seem a bad idea, if
                 you think it will work.
Daysair:   No absolute guarantee, of course,
                 but you'll never tell till you try.
Chorus:    Nope, no proof without data,
                 no proof without experiment.
Daysair:   There he is. Be gone soon,
                 keep quiet about this for a bit,
                     what they don't know won't hurt us.
                 You can get away with a good deal in the dark.

Pound sacrificed the stately and noble decorum of Sophocles' original for a colloquial style because he thought a formal rhetoric would alienate the modern audience from the substance, the drama, of the play. His attempt failed, of course; *Women of Trachis* has seldom been performed, and has never reached the large, middle-American audience for whom he envisioned it. It survives as a curious document of his lifelong dream of a common culture, here imagined as an American audience celebrating a three-thousand-year-old cultural history in the experience of the drama, as the ancient Greeks used to do every year in viewing the tragedies composed for the Festival of Dionysos. It was Schiller who said, "All peoples who possess a history possess a paradise." This intuition informs Pound's lifework also, in its beginnings and in its end, and is the key to its dreams, its failures, and its greatness. He could not say of his poem, as Herakles says of his own history when he sees its final shape, "WHAT SPLENDOR! IT ALL COHERES!" Yet Pound's work has a different kind of integrity, true to his own time, and expressed, "against the current," the memory and the vision of a community which continues, in a skeptical, fragmented, and dispirited age, to define us both by its absence and by its new possibilities. His *Women of Trachis*, then, is part of the larger drama of a modern poet's life, dedicated to values which belong not just to the past but to an imaginable future.

KHOROS: The chorus of a Greek tragedy consisted of several actors whose vantage point with respect to the action was that of townspeople (here, the women of Trachis, a city in ancient Greece); they sang or chanted lines to music while performing stately dance movements back and forth across the stage.

PHOEBUS: Phoebus Apollo, the sun-god.

Alkmene's son: Herakles, the hero of the tragedy and Daysair's husband, at this point off adventuring in parts unknown. me: i.e., Daysair, with whose interests the chorus partly identifies.

Daysair: Deianeira, Herakles' wife, who tries to win him back with a love potion after he has fallen in love with Iole. Unbeknownst to her, it seems, the potion is a poison which brings Herakles to his death.

Cretan of Cadmus' blood: Herakles was a descendent of Cadmus, who founded the city of Thebes.

Orcus: Roman god of death.

Lady: i.e., Daysair, whom the chorus reproves for succumbing to despair.

Zeus: in Greek mythology, the high god who determines the fate of mortals.

# WORKS CITED

## BIOGRAPHY, SCHOLARSHIP, AND CRITICISM
## ON POUND AND HIS WORK

Alexander, Michael. *The Poetic Achievement of Ezra Pound.* Berkeley: University of California Press, 1979.

Berryman, Jo Brantley. " 'Medallion': Pound's Poem." *Paideuma,* 2 (1973), 391–98.

Brooker, Peter. *A Student's Guide to the Selected Poems of Ezra Pound.* London: Faber and Faber, 1979.

Bush, Ronald. *The Genesis of Ezra Pound's Cantos.* Princeton: Princeton University Press, 1976.

Connolly, Thomas E. "Further Notes on Mauberley." *Accent,* 16 (Winter 1956), 59.

Cowley, Malcolm. *Exile's Return: A Literary Odyssey of the 1920's.* New York: Viking, 1951.

Davie, Donald. *Ezra Pound.* New York: Viking and Penguin, 1976.

——. *Ezra Pound: Poet as Sculptor.* New York: Oxford University Press, 1964.

Dekker, George. *Sailing after Knowledge.* London: Routledge & Kegan Paul, 1963.

de Rachewiltz, Boris. "Pagan and Magic Elements in Ezra Pound's Works." *New Approaches to Ezra Pound,* edited by Eva Hesse. Berkeley and Los Angeles: University of California Press, 1969.

de Rachewiltz, Mary. *Discretions.* Boston: Atlantic-Little, Brown, 1971. Reissued as *Ezra Pound, Father and Teacher: Discretions.* New York: New Directions, 1975.

Edwards, John Hamilton, and William W. Vasse. *An Annotated Index to The Cantos [I–LXXXIV].* Berkeley and Los Angeles: University of California Press, 1959.

Espey, John. *Ezra Pound's Mauberley: A Study in Composition.* Berkeley and Los Angeles: University of California Press, 1955.

Flory, Wendy Stallard. *Ezra Pound and The Cantos: A Record of Struggle.* New Haven, Conn.: Yale University Press, 1980.

Goodwin, K. L. *The Influence of Ezra Pound.* London: Oxford University Press, 1966.

Harper, Michael F. "Truth and Calliope: Ezra Pound's Malatesta." *PMLA,* 96 (1981), 86–103.

Heymann, C. David. *Ezra Pound: The Last Rower.* New York: Viking, 1976.

Homberger, Eric, ed. *Ezra Pound: The Critical Heritage.* London: Routledge & Kegan Paul, 1972.

Hutchins, Patricia. "Ezra Pound and Thomas Hardy." *Southern Review,* 4 (Winter 1968), 90–104.

Kearns, George. *A Guide to Ezra Pound's Selected Cantos.* New Brunswick, N.J.: Rutgers University Press, 1980.

Kenner, Hugh. "More on the Seven Lakes Canto." *Paideuma,* 2 (1973), 43–46.

——. *The Poetry of Ezra Pound.* New York: New Directions, 1951.

——. *The Pound Era.* Berkeley and Los Angeles: University of California Press, 1971.

Norman, Charles. *Ezra Pound: A Biography.* New York: Macmillan, 1960, 1969.

Olson, Charles. *Charles Olson and Ezra Pound: An Encounter at St. Elizabeths,* edited by Catherine Seelye. New York: Grossman, 1975.

Palandri, Angela Jung. "Homage to a Confucian Poet." *Paideuma,* 3 (1974), 301–11.

Peacock, Alan. "Pound, Horace, and Canto IV." *English Language Notes,* 17 (1980), 288–92.

Pearlman, Daniel D. *The Barb of Time: On the Unity of Ezra Pound's Cantos.* New York: Oxford University Press, 1969.

Reck, Michael. "A Conversation between Ezra Pound and Allen Ginsberg." *Evergreen Review,* June 1968.

Richardson, Lawrence. "Ezra Pound's Homage to Propertius." *Yale Review,* 6 (1947), 21–29.

Robinson, Fred C. " 'The Might of the North': Pound's Anglo-Saxon Studies and 'The Seafarer.' " *Yale Review,* 71 (Winter 1982), 199–224.

Ruthven, K. K. *A Guide to Ezra Pound's Personae (1926).* Berkeley and Los Angeles: University of California Press, 1969.

Sanders, Frederick K. *John Adams Speaking: Pound's Sources for the Adams Cantos.* Orono, Maine: University of Maine Press, 1975.

Stock, Noel. *The Life of Ezra Pound.* New York: Pantheon, 1970.

Sullivan, J. P. *Ezra Pound and Sextus Propertius: A Study in Creative Translation.* Austin: University of Texas Press, 1964.

Surette, Leon. *A Light from Eleusis: A Study of Pound's Cantos.* New York: Oxford University Press, 1979.

Tanselle, G. T. "Two Early Letters of Ezra Pound." *American Literature,* 34 (1962), 114–19.

Terrell, Carroll F. *A Companion to The Cantos of Ezra Pound.* Berkeley and Los Angeles: University of California Press, 1980.

——. *"Magna Carta,* Talbots, the Lady Anne, and Pound's Associative Technique in Canto 80." *Paideuma,* 5 (1976), 69–76.

Thomas, Ronald E. "Catullus, Flaminius, and Pound in 'Blandula, Tenella, Vagula.' " *Paideuma,* 5 (1976), 407–12.

Wilhelm, James J. "Notes and Queries." *Paideuma,* 2 (1973), 333–35.

Yip, Wai-lim. *Ezra Pound's Cathay.* Princeton, N.J.: Princeton University Press, 1969.

Zimmermann, Hans-Joachim. "Ezra Pound, 'A Song of the Degrees': Chinese Clarity versus Alchemical Confusion." *Paideuma,* 10 (1981), 225–41.

## SOURCES, BACKGROUND, AND RELATED WORKS

Adams, Charles Francis. *The Works of John Adams.* 10 vols. Boston: Little, Brown, 1850–56.

Alexander, Michael J., trans. *The Earliest English Poems: A Bilingual Edition.* Berkeley and Los Angeles: University of California Press, 1970.

Cecil, David. *Visionary and Dreamer: Two Poetic Painters: Samuel Palmer and Edward Burne-Jones*. Princeton, N.J.: Princeton University Press, 1970.

Cournos, John. *Autobiography*. New York: G. P. Putnam's Sons, 1935.

De Sanctis, Francesco. *History of Italian Literature*, trans. Joan Redfern. New York: Basic Books, 1935.

Gautier, Théophile. *Emaux et Camées*. Edition Definitive avec une Eauforte par J. Jacquemart. Paris, 1881.

Giles, H. A. *A History of Chinese Literature*. London: Heinemann, 1901.

Gombrich, E. H. *Art and Illusion: A Study in the Psychology of Pictorial Representation*. Princeton, N.J.: Princeton University Press, 1960.

Jones, Philip J. *The Malatesta of Rimini and the Papal State*. Cambridge: Cambridge University Press, 1974.

Legge, James. *The Chinese Classics: Translated into English with Preliminary Essays and Explanatory Notes*. 2 vols. London: 1867.

McCulloch, J. P., trans. *The Poems of Sextus Propertius*. Berkeley and Los Angeles: University of California Press, 1972.

Mackail, J. W. *Latin Literature*. New York: Charles Scribner's Sons, 1895.

Marsh, Edward. *A Number of People*. New York: Harper, 1939.

Nelson, Benjamin N. *The Idea of Usury: From Tribal Brotherhood to Universal Otherhood*. Princeton, N.J.: Princeton University Press, 1949.

Shaw, J. E. *Cavalcanti's Theory of Love*. Toronto: University of Toronto Press, 1949.

Speare, M. E., ed. *The Pocket Book of English and American Verse*. New York, 1940.

Whistler, James Abbott MacNeill. *The Gentle Art of Making Enemies*. London: Heinemann, 1890.

Yeats, William Butler. *Essays and Introductions*. New York: Macmillan, 1961.

# INDEX